IN THE TRENCHES
Installing and Administering Linux

LINDA MCKINNON
and AL MCKINNON

Gearhead Press
Delivering technical information to IT professionals

PUBLISHED BY
Gearhead Press
a unit of Gearhead Corporation
2760 East W.T. Harris Boulevard
Charlotte, North Carolina 28213

© 2000 Gearhead Press

All rights reserved. No part of this book may be reproduced or transmitted in any form or by any means, electronic or mechanical, including photocopying, recording, or by any information storage and retrieval system, without written permission from the publisher.

Library of Congress Control No. 00-134952
ISBN 1-930713-00-2

Printed in Canada
1 2 3 4 5 6 7 8 9 10
First printing, October 2000

Gearhead Press books are distributed in the United States and Canada by Publishers Group West. For ordering information, call 510-528-1444 or visit PGW's Web site *(http://www.pgw.com)*. For information about corporate sales or international editions, contact Gearhead Press at 704-598-6262 (phone), 704-598-6207 (fax), or by visiting its Web site, *www.gearheadpress.com*.

"Red Hat" is a registered trademark of Red Hat, Inc. Used with permission. All other brand names and product names mentioned herein are trademarks, registered trademarks, or trade names of their respective holders.

The authors and publisher have taken care in the preparation of this book, but make no express or implied representations or warranties of any kind, and assume no responsibility for errors or omissions. In no event shall the authors or publisher be liable for incidental or consequential damages in connection with or arising out of the use of the information or programs contained herein.

Acknowledgments

First and foremost, thanks to Linda for the inspiration to write this book. It was your observations about the demands of Linux/UNIX professionals that led to the development of this reference. Thanks also to National Public Radio in the U.S. and the Canadian Broadcasting Corporation in Canada for keeping us company while we wrote: may your flow of ideas never be stemmed. Finally, I dedicate this book to the memory of Keeler, our beloved old dog and faithful companion who spent her last few months watching us pound out thousands of words and trace out miles of mouse lines. She is sorely missed.

—*Al McKinnon*

Thanks to all the folks that came to me and said, "Please write that down for us." Without you, I never would have embarked on this literary tour. A special thanks to my peers who shared their views, and my students who shared their ideas and needs. During the last five years, I have taught both basic and advanced Linux/UNIX curriculum to more than 1200 individuals. You know who you are; you guided my choice of topics. This book is dedicated to those who we have yet to convert from that other operating system.

—*Linda McKinnon*

Contents

INTRODUCTION .... **xv**

CHAPTER 1: LINUX ORIGINS **1**
A Brief History of UNIX 1
   UNIX Is Born 3
   UNIX Becomes Commercialized 4
   UNIX Moves toward Standardization 4
   Further Developments 7
   Multics Revisited 7
History of Linux 8
Linux Features 9
   Free Software 10
   Mix and Match 10
   Hardware and Software Compatibility 11

CHAPTER 2: GETTING STARTED USING THE LINUX SYSTEM **13**
Logging In and Out 13
   Logging In 14
   Logging Out 14
Creating User Accounts and Passwords 15
   Users Accounts 15
   Passwords 16
Command Syntax 17
Viewing the Date: date and cal Commands 18
Requesting Data on Logged-In Users 20
   who, who am i, and whoami Commands 20
   finger Command 21

Sending and Receiving Mail: mail Command 22
    Send Mail 22
    Receive Mail 23
Sending Messages to the Screen: write and wall Commands 25
    write Command 25
    wall Command 27
Conversing Online: talk Command 27
Blocking Messages and Conversations: mesg Command 28
Additional Tools: clear, echo, banner, and wc Commands 29
    clear Command 29
    echo Command 30
    banner Command 30
    wc Command 32
Exercises. 33
Quiz 36

CHAPTER 3: LINUX DOCUMENTATION AND SUPPORT 37

Distribution Package Documentation 38
    Official Linux Distributions. 38
    Downloaded Linux and Other Unofficial Distributions 39
Current Linux Distributors 40
Linux and UNIX Online Information. 41
    man Command 41
    info Pages 45
    locate and slocate Commands 47
    Usage Facility 49
The Linux Documentation Project 50
    LDP Guides. 50
    HOWTOs 51
    FAQs 52
    Projects 52
Linux Books and Magazines. 53
More Linux Information Sites on the Internet. 55
    Linux Online 55
    Linux Online in Canada 55
    Software Sources 55
    X Windows Sources 56
    Linux Newsgroups 56
    Linux mtools Sites 57

Exercises 58
Quiz 62

CHAPTER 4: FILES AND DIRECTORIES IN LINUX 63

File System Structure and Hierarchy 63
    File Types 63
    Directory Contents 64
    Hierarchical Structure 65
    Path Names 67
Navigating the File Structure 68
    Locate the Working Directory Path: pwd Command 68
    Change the Directory: cd Command 69
Managing Files 69
    Create a Directory: mkdir Command 69
    Remove a Directory: rmdir Command 70
    Create or Remove Multiple Directories Simultaneously 71
    List a Directory: ls Command 73
    Display Directory Information: ls and stat Commands 76
    Linux File Name Guidelines 77
Accessing Floppy Disks 79
    ext2 File Systems 79
    DOS File Systems 82
    The mtools Utilities 84
touch Command 86
Exercises 88
Quiz 90

CHAPTER 5: USING FILES IN LINUX 93

Copying and Moving Files 93
    Copy a Single File: cp Command 93
    Copy Multiple or Special Files: cp Command 94
    Move and Rename Files: mv Command 95
Linking Files: ln Command 97
Viewing File Contents 98
    List File Contents: cat Command 98
    Display a File a Page by Page: more and less Commands 99
Removing Files: rm Command 100
Printing Files: lpr, lpq, and lprm Commands 101

Exercises. 103
Quiz 106

CHAPTER 6: LINUX FILE PERMISSIONS 107
Review of the ls -l Command 107
All about Permissions 108
Changing Permissions: chmod Command 109
    Symbolic Notation 110
    Numeric Notation 112
Setting Permissions: umask Command 114
    Check Permission Modes. 115
    Change Permission Modes 116
Creating Personal Directories 117
Giving the Write Permission on Directories 118
Functions and Required Permissions. 120
Exercises. 121
Quiz 124

CHAPTER 7: THE VI EDITOR 127
An Introduction to vi 128
Starting vi. 129
Exiting vi 130
Adding Text in Insert Mode. 131
Manipulating Text in Command Mode. 132
    Delete Text. 133
    Search and Replace Text. 133
    Move Text. 135
    Undo Buffer 136
    Copy Text 136
Executing Linux/UNIX Commands in vi 138
Options for Changing How vi Operates 140
Command-Line Editing 141
    Invoke Features of Other Editors 142
    Related vi Editors 143
Exercises. 144
Quiz 151

Contents

Chapter 8: Shell Basics 153
The Linux Shells 153
Shell Types 154
Metacharacters and Wildcards 156
    Asterisk 156
    Question Mark 158
    Square Brackets for Lists 159
    Exclamation Point 159
    Square Brackets for Ranges 160
Standard Files: Redirection and Piping ... 160
    File Descriptors 161
    Input Redirection 162
    Output Redirection 162
    Error Redirection 165
    Combined Redirection 167
    Association 167
    Connecting Commands with Pipes 169
Command Grouping with the Semicolon 172
Line Continuation with the Backslash 172
Exercises 174
Quiz 178

Chapter 9: Using Shell Variables 179
Variables and the Terminal Environment .. 179
Shell Variable Types 181
Listing Variable Settings: set Command .. 182
Setting Shell Variables by Variable Substitution ... 183
    Equal Sign 183
    echo $ 184
    unset Command 185
    Variable Substitution Sample 185
Setting Shell Variables by Command Substitution ... 187
Quoting Metacharacters to Disable Shell Interpretation ... 188
Command Line Parsing 189
Exercises 191
Quiz 195

Chapter 10: Linux Processes 197
Process Environments 197

Log-in Process 199
Parent-Child Relationships. 199
Processes and Variables 202
Exporting Shell Variables 203
Shell Scripts 206
Invoking Shell Scripts 207
   Option 1: Subshell Executes Only One Command 207
   Option 2: Executable Shell Script Files 208
   Option 3: Dot (.) or source Commands 209
Return Codes from Commands 210
Quiz 211

CHAPTER 11: CONTROLLING LINUX PROCESSES 213

Process Monitoring: ps Command. 213
Invoking Foreground and Background Processes 215
Terminating Processes 215
   Termination Methods 216
   The kill Command. 216
   kill Command Signals 218
Running Long Processes: nohup Command. 220
Job Control in the bash and tcsh Shells. 222
   Creating a List of Background or Suspended Jobs 222
   Suspending and Resuming a Foreground Task. 222
   Suspending and Resuming a Background Task. 223
   More Job Control Examples 224
Daemons: Never-Ending System Processes 226
Exercises. 227
Quiz 233

CHAPTER 12: CUSTOMIZING THE USER ENVIRONMENT 235

Setting Default Shell Variables 235
   Sample /etc/profile File 238
   Sample /etc/bashrc File 241
   Sample $HOME/.bash_profile File 242
   Sample $HOME/.bashrc File 243
Linux/UNIX Shortcut: alias Command 244
Using and Removing Aliases. 246
Shell History Commands 248

history Command 248
fc Command 248
Bang Command 249
Exercises 251
Quiz 254

CHAPTER 13: BASIC LINUX UTILITIES 255
Searching Directories for Files: find Command 255
The find Command with a Noninteractive Single Action 258
The find Command with an Interactive Single Action 259
Using Additional Options with the find Command 260
Locating Commands: whatis, whereis, and which Commands .. 263
Locating Data in a File: grep Command 265
Regular Expressions with Metacharacters................... 268
grep Options.. 269
Regular Expressions with Metacharacters................... 271
Other grep Commands: egrep and fgrep 272
Sorting Output: sort Command 273
Displaying Parts of Files: head and tail Commands............ 276
The head Command 276
The tail Command 277
Exercises 279
Quiz 282

CHAPTER 14: ADVANCED LINUX UTILITIES 283
Maximizing Work per Command: xargs 283
Combining xargs, find, and grep Utilities 287
Comparing find Functions and Shell Functions 288
The find command with the -links option 290
Reducing Keystrokes: Using find with alias 291
Determining File Types: file Command...................... 292
Comparing Text Files: diff Command 294
Comparing All Types of Files: cmp Command 299
Compressing Files: gzip, gunzip, and zcat Commands 300
Displaying Nonprintable Characters: cat Command Options 303
Assigning Unique File Names: Appending Information........ 305
Exercises 307
Quiz 311

Chapter 15: The Linux X Window System 313

- A Brief History... 313
- X Window Networking 315
  - Different Client/Server Environment Concepts 316
  - X Client Features 317
  - X Server Features 318
- X Window Managers.. 319
- X Window Fundamentals 321
  - Start X Manually....................................... 321
  - Exit X 321
  - Start X Automatically................................... 322
- Basic Components.. 324
  - Display... 324
  - root Menu... 325
  - Mouse Pointers, Input Focus, and Location Cursors......... 326
  - Window Frame 327
  - Icons 328
- xterm Fundamentals.. 329
  - Create an xterm Window................................ 329
  - Copy Text 329
  - Create a Scrollbar...................................... 330
  - Close an xterm Window................................. 330
  - Customize xterm 331
- Additional Basic X Window Commands 333
  - Become the root User 333
  - Let Another User Run a Client on Your System 333
  - Run a Client on Someone Else's System................... 335
  - xhost Command.. 336
- Exercises.. 338
- Quiz 346

Chapter 16: Installing Linux 347

- Doing Your Homework..................................... 347
  - Where Are You Starting From?........................... 348
  - Discovering and Chronicling System Equipment 349
- Investigating and Preparing 351
  - Identify System Attributes 351
  - Create a Linux Install Boot Disk.......................... 352

Contents

    Swap Space Options 355
    Hard Disk Partitioning. 357
Installing Linux on an IDE System. 359
    Invoke the Linux Installation Program. 359
    Giving Information to the Installation Program 360

APPENDIX A: COMMAND SUMMARY 385

APPENDIX B: EXERCISE ANSWERS 403

APPENDIX C: QUIZ ANSWERS 413

INDEX 425

Introduction

THIS BOOK HAS BEEN DESIGNED for those wanting to become Linux system professionals. Readers are not required to have extensive knowledge of Linux or any other UNIX-based operating system (SCO UNIX, HP-UX, AIX, and so on) but should have a working knowledge of information technology and networking technologies. In brief, experience always helps but is not necessary.

Those who have experience with other UNIX-based systems are advised to pay attention to the differences between Linux and other UNIX systems. Differences exist, and failure to appreciate them can lead to inaccuracies and frustration. Furthermore, not all versions or distributions of Linux are the same, so we cannot guarantee that everything will apply to all distributions or will apply to all distributions forever.

We have attempted to organize the topics and exercises in this book in a logical fashion. Readers are first introduced to an overview of Linux's history and philosophy. The same philosophy has been adopted by all Linux distributors and has led to the rapid adoption of Linux. After this overview, readers are introduced to the following technical aspects of Linux:

- ▲ Major features of the operating system
- ▲ Logging in and out and basic administration operations
- ▲ The hierarchical tree structure, as well as the functions carried out on files and directories
- ▲ The most predominant text editor, `vi`
- ▲ Shell concepts and operations supported by the various shells

- ▲ Ownership and control of jobs and processes and their respective processing environments
- ▲ Useful tools to help users and administrators customize their environments and write scripts
- ▲ The X Window System and its window managers
- ▲ Installation of Linux on an IDE system

The best way to learn these concepts and procedures is by using them. That is why we have included lots of examples, exercises, and quizzes. It is also why we have included a CD-ROM with the Red Hat Linux Publishers' Edition, Version 6.2. If you don't have access to a Linux system, this book will help you install the software from the CD-ROM.

After you get Linux up and running, you will be able to follow along, trying the various commands, features, and utilities to see how they work. For additional information on Linux, visit our publisher's Web site at *http://www.gearheadpress.com*. Here you will find white papers, technical updates, and supplemental exercises, plus chat and Q&A sessions with folks who can answer your questions.

Audience

If you need basic Linux user skills, this book is for you. If you plan to obtain system administration skills in Linux or any other UNIX-related operating system, this book is for you as well.

This book is aimed at those wanting to become Linux system professionals, and vast experience is not necessary to understand it. Advanced system administration concepts are mentioned but are not covered in depth.

To take advantage of all aspects of Linux introduced in this book, you will need a graphics terminal.

Objectives

After reading this book and experimenting with the techniques and concepts in the exercises and quizzes, you should be able to accomplish the following tasks (among other things). The text is generally organized in the sequence presented here as well:

- Log in to a Linux system
- Create user accounts and passwords
- Use Linux online documentation and other information
- Work with Linux files and directories
- Execute common Linux commands
- Use the `vi` text editor
- Describe the purpose and features of Linux shells
- Manage Linux processes
- Customize the Linux work environment
- Use common Linux utilities
- Use and customize a Linux X Window System environment
- Install Linux on an IDE system

Typographical Conventions

A monospaced font in regular text is used to highlight command names, command options, and variable names. Following are some examples:

- You can then use the `chmod` command to specify symbolic modes.
- You can check the current settings of permissions by using the `ls -l` command.

A monospaced font is used also for syntax, examples of command statements, and user input. Bold monospace represents computer or operating system responses. Note that monospaced italics, such as *username* or *hostname*, represents user input that varies according to the user's situation and task. For example, when you see *username*, you should type your specific user name). Examples follow:

```
$ cp source target<Enter>
$ cp file1 file2 . . . target_dir<Enter>

$ pwd<Enter>
/home/flintsfr/doc
$ cp /home/slatemr/pgms/suba programa<Enter>

$ cp -R /home/flintsfr/mydir /home/flintsfr/newdir
   <Enter>

$ bash<Enter>
$ echo $$<Enter>
395
$ echo $x<Enter>
4
```

Italics in text are used to indicate file names, directory names, path names, and general emphasis. Examples follow:

▲ The */etc/profile* is the default initialization file for the bash, ksh, and sh shells.

▲ Barney discovers that group and others have write permission on Fred's home directory, so he creates a file called *sneaky*.

▲ Remember that users of this shell script file *must* have both read and execute permissions.

Angle brackets describe keyboard keys: <Enter>, <Tab>, <Spacebar>, <Backspace>, <Delete>. <Ctrl>, and so on. Do not type the angle brackets; instead, press the corresponding keyboard key.

Examples are concluded with the ▲ symbol.

NOTE: *Information on features or tasks that is not immediately obvious or intuitive appears in notes.*

WARNING: *The handful of warnings in this book help you avoid disaster or unanticipated results.*

Linux users and systems managers typically work with diverse hardware systems, so be aware of the following keyboard-related issues:

▲ On a graphics keyboard, you may have to rely on the <Enter> key rather than the <Ctrl> or <Alt> keys.

▲ On an ASCII keyboard, you may have to use the <Return> key and not the <Send> key.

▲ When correcting typographical errors on the command line, use the <Backspace> key and not the cursor or arrow keys.

Chapter 1

Linux Origins

THIS CHAPTER PRESENTS A BRIEF HISTORY of UNIX and Linux, followed by an introduction to the major features of Linux. Although the current incarnation of Linux and respective shells, programs, and other processes have been written from scratch, they have also evolved from previous versions of Linux and other UNIX flavors (HP-UX by Hewlett Packard and Solaris by Sun Microsystems, among others). Knowledge of the history of these operating systems can help you predict the usefulness of a command, program, or function or more easily troubleshoot unanticipated results.

A Brief History of UNIX

UNIX development was initiated in 1969 by several researchers working at Bell Laboratories in New Jersey. Bell Laboratories had previously (1964–68) worked with General Electric and the Massachusetts Institute of Technology (MIT) on the development of a multiuser, time-sharing operating system called Multics (Multiplexed Information and Computing System). The project involved a partnership between private industry and a respected academic institution. As the project progressed, Multics was proving more difficult and more expensive than the partners had anticipated, deadlines were slipping, and the partners found they had differing philosophies and goals. So, in early 1969, Bell Labs withdrew from the Multics project.

Bell Labs researchers who had worked on it (Ken Thompson, Dennis Ritchie, Douglas McIlroy, Joseph Ossanna, and others) still wanted to develop an operating system for their own and Bell Lab's programming, job control, and resource usage needs. So, in addition to the comparatively routine activities they returned to, they also informally searched for an in-house alternative to the Multics project. Bell's executive managers, still somewhat scorched by the Multics project and burdened by internal politicking, however, were not immediately receptive to subsequent proposals.

During this same year, Thompson (later helped by Ritchie) wrote a simple space travel program called, naturally enough, Space Travel, first for Multics and then for the inflexible and inadequate GECOS operating system on a GE 635 computer. Space Travel on the GE 635 was unsatisfactory—that is, jerky, hard to control, and expensive from a CPU-per-dollar standpoint. Thompson soon found another computer, an already obsolete DEC PDP-7, with acceptable display capabilities. From a programming standpoint, Space Travel was a challenge: it was written with macros for the assembler on the GE 635 computer and then sent through a postprocessor, which produced paper tapes that were in turn fed into the PDP-7.

Thompson and Ritchie soon developed a new kind of primitive kernel for the PDP-7, plus a text editor, an assembler, a command interpreter (which we refer to as a shell), some rudimentary utilities, and a structured file system (including directories, special files that described system devices, inodes to describe file attributes, and so on). Many of these features were influenced by their previous work on the Multics project. And the PDP-7 achieved standalone capability! Almost all development thus far had been in DEC assembly language, although they had begun to develop a high-level language, called B, based on the existing BCPL language. B had been used to write a PDP-7 compiler.

In 1970, the developers requested and received a new computer, a DEC PDP-11, which had a new type of 16-bit processor and thus required alterations to the kernel code (this was their Version 1). B was used to develop a PDP-7 to PDP-11 cross-compiler. Their colleague Brian Kernighan suggested that the new operating system be called UNIX, as a sort of pun on Multics and as a way to contrast the simplicity of the new OS with the complexity of Multics.

UNIX Is Born

In a supportive and collegial environment, the researchers continued the development of their portable (as defined in the preceding section), simple as possible, high-level language operating system, which they called the UNIX Time-Sharing System. The B language continued in development, and later was called C. C let them create not only applications, but also system programs that could be ported to new architectures as long as compilers existed for those architectures. By 1973, they were even able to rewrite the entire UNIX kernel in C, for what they called Version 4 (V4). They had now risen above the hardware-specific assembly language environment in which UNIX had been born in 1969. The UNIX operating system was different: The developers kept the kernel as close to the essential input/output multiplexer as possible but built a collection of add-on programming tools that carried out log in and log out, command interpretation, file naming, console activity, and more in a vast array of functions. No longer did an application, built in a hardware-specific language, have to do it all. Applications could now do solely what they were intended to do (for example, text processing) and could rely on a high-level-language operating system to carry out I/O, file manipulation, printing, handling of several users at once, networking, interprocess communication, and so forth.

In 1973, AT&T/Bell recognized that hardware (especially telephone system hardware) and applications were changing, and that UNIX would have to become a standard interface between the two realms. Then, as hardware changed (or as hardware vendors changed), applications could keep functioning because UNIX could be ported.

From 1974 to 1977, UNIX source code was licensed inexpensively or for free to universities. This is because AT&T, going back to a 1956 United States-AT&T antitrust consent decree, was forbidden to sell software commercially. Instead, they had to make such computer technology licensable to and by the public. UNIX V6, released in 1975, was especially popular. It was free, and it was great for teaching about operating systems because it was distributed with its source code and students could follow along after they became familiar with the C language. It was great for program developers, too. They could write new applications—in C, for example—and then take full advantage of the UNIX operating system. DEC had provided thousands of PDP-11s to universities across the United States at very little cost. The perfect match of UNIX and PDP-11 was thus (accidentally) repeated many times. This was fertile ground for further UNIX development.

UNIX Becomes Commercialized

In 1979, AT&T announced that it planned to commercialize UNIX, an announcement that came true in 1983 with the release of its UNIX System V. Meanwhile, the University of California at Berkeley, among others, began developing its own version of UNIX, based primarily on UNIX V7. Berkeley was also implementing the Transmission Control Protocol/Internet Protocol (TCP/IP) networking protocol suite, which had been based on its Berkeley Systems Distribution (BSD) UNIX. The Internet itself was being developed and expanded, sponsored by the U.S. Department of Defense Advanced Research Projects Agency (that's why the original Internet was called ARPAnet).

The upshot of all this was the first major proliferation of different versions of UNIX in the early 1980s. AT&T was developing its System V UNIX; Berkeley was actively developing BSD UNIX; Sun Microsystems (founded by Berkeley Ph.D. Bill Joy) produced its own BSD-based UNIX called SunOS; Microsoft and the Santa Cruz Operation (SCO) were already distributing XENIX; Hewlett-Packard developed HP-UX for its workstations; DEC released ULTRIX; and IBM developed versions of UNIX for its PCs, PS/2s, and System/370s. (Later, in 1986, IBM would develop AIX, first for the RT 6150 and then for the RS 6000.) A former strength of UNIX, AT&T's free source code, was now becoming a weakness because so many new UNIX versions were being developed based on the precommercial V7, depending on the needs of the respective developers, who weren't following any type of standard.

UNIX Moves toward Standardization

In 1984, in an effort to promote open architecture standards that emphasized UNIX as the OS, several European vendors (among them Siemens, Amdahl, and Philips) formed X/Open. The membership was later augmented by American companies (including AT&T, DEC, and Sun) and Japanese ones (such as Hitachi and Wang). The open aspects they promoted included the development of systems that allowed applications to be easily ported among them, were interoperable, and allowed users to work on the various systems without extensive retraining. X/Open was interested in using member consensus to adopt and integrate open standards to ensure that new products conformed to them—but not to actually write them. (In 1987, X/Open was incorporated as a limited company, the X/Open Company Limited, whose shareholders were several worldwide information technology suppliers.)

In 1988, AT&T bought a large portion of Sun Microsystems, and now AT&T and Sun could collaborate on future versions of UNIX. The purchase in effect merged AT&T's System V and Sun's OS. In response, nine other vendors (IBM, DEC, HP, Bull, Nixdorf, Siemens, Hitachi, Philips, and Apollo) formed a consortium called the Open Software Foundation (OSF); membership ballooned to over 200 by 1991.

The OSF's approach was to produce a UNIX operating system and other software and then license the use of its products to its members and others. In fact, in late 1990, they would produce what they claimed was the first open UNIX operating system, called OSF/1. OSF/1 was based on Carnegie Mellon University's Mach, a UNIX operating system with original ties to BSD UNIX, which was developed by Carnegie Mellon from 1985 to 1994. However, after the introduction of OSF/1, only DEC adopted it outright; other OSF members—such as, IBM and HP—adopted only parts of it.

OSF also developed the Motif graphical user interface guideline and toolkit for further development of the X Window System. The X Window System and the X networking protocol had been under development at MIT since 1984. (X is discussed again in Chapter 15.)

As a countermeasure to OSF, AT&T and Sun allied themselves with yet more and different vendors to create the UNIX International trade association (UI). Members of this association—from computer manufacturers and software developers to consultants and academics and even government agencies—would advise AT&T regarding future development of System V UNIX, although AT&T would retain its proprietary control. By 1991, UI's membership reached more than 200 from a dozen or so countries. Although some overlap existed between the lower-rank members of OSF and UI, no such overlap existed among principal members or sponsors.

Stepping back a bit, 1987 saw the birth of MINIX, a much smaller UNIX-like operating system written by Prof. Andrew S. Tanenbaum of Vrije Universiteit in Amsterdam, Holland. This OS was written from scratch (meaning that it contained no AT&T code) for university instruction. MINIX is mentioned again in the next section, because it was Linus Torvalds's springboard to Linux.

In 1993, Novell purchased AT&T et al.'s UNIX Systems Laboratories, which included the source code to System VR4 (System V, Release 4, which was the amalgamation of System V, BSD, and Xenix) as well as the UNIX trademark. Novell then negotiated with X/Open to give X/Open the UNIX trademark. This deal gave X/Open the power to bless any new operating system as a version of UNIX if it met X/Open standards. One of those standards is XPG4.2 (X/Open Portability Guide 4.2), which includes several Portable Operating System Interface for UNIX (POSIX) standards, developed by the Institute of Electrical and Electronic Engineers (IEEE) for operating system interfaces. (For example, POSIX.1 is the application program interface standard for the C language; POSIX.2 is the shell and utility interface standard.) Later, in 1995, Novell sold its UNIXWare, including the source code, to SCO, which continues to develop UNIX to the present.

In this brief history of UNIX, a great deal out has been left out: UNIX development has continued on many fronts in the 1980s and 1990s and into 2000. To cover it all and do it justice would require an entire book. But before proceeding, we should mention that X/Open and OSF eventually merged, forming the Open Group in 1996. The Open Group still strives to promote, develop, and license open standards software, especially UNIX.

Further Developments

Today there are more than 80 UNIXes, from AIX to Xenix. Many are undergoing continual development (such as Linux, SCO UNIX, FreeBSD, and AIX), while some have stagnated and are no longer supported (for example, Carnegie Mellon University's Mach, although they still maintain Mach's Web site).

According to a GartnerGroup–Dataquest survey conducted in the third quarter of 1998, UNIX workstations accounted for 67.4 percent of the worldwide workstation market with respect to revenues. Shipments of UNIX increased 14.6 percent between the third quarter of 1997 and the third quarter of 1998, also in terms of revenues. In terms of units sold, UNIX workstations accounted for approximately half, indicating that UNIX systems dominate the mid- to high-end markets. This is a much better position than one would believe based on impressions obtained from the mainstream media.

Multics Revisited

You may wonder what happened to Multics. It was, indeed, developed. The first Multics system was unveiled by MIT and the remaining partners in 1969, late and not without problems. GE had jurisdiction over future Multics development, which it sold—along with its entire computer business—to Honeywell Corporation in 1970. Nevertheless, Multics systems were installed in several locations. Development during the 1970s included a new storage system, using the new concepts of logical and physical volumes to give it better recovery capabilities. And in 1977, the first commercial relational database was installed on a Multics system at Honeywell in Phoenix. Multics was used by MIT, the U.S. Air Force, GM, Ford, and the University of Southwest Louisiana and was purchased by a large number of organizations in Europe in the 1980s.

In 1985, Honeywell canceled further development of Multics. Over the next three years, however, they made several attempts to revive it, as did a few other companies who wanted to buy Multics. In 1988, Honeywell transferred maintenance of Multics to the University of Calgary, Canada. That university set up a corporation called ACTC

Technologies, which was eventually renamed Perigon Systems. Perigon was acquired by the CGI Group in late 1998. That's the last we have heard of Multics.

History of Linux

Any history of Linux would be remiss if it didn't mention MINIX because it was on a MINIX Usenet newsgroup bulletin board, *comp.os.minix*, that Linus Torvalds posted his now-legendary notices, one of which we quote from later in this section. As mentioned, MINIX was a small UNIX-like operating system written by Prof. Tanenbaum. Like several other versions of UNIX, MINIX was written from scratch, with no AT&T code, for university instruction. It is useful for anyone who wants to learn the basics of UNIX operation. It is available free on the Internet at *http://www.cs.vu.nl/~ast/minix.html*.

We suggest that you visit the site. You'll find out how MINIX has evolved and about the two current versions (MINIX 2.0 for Intel CPUs from 8088 to Pentium and MINIX 1.5 for Intel, Mac, Amiga, Atari, and SPARC). You'll also find out about the special copyright on MINIX by publisher Prentice Hall. MINIX is basically a type of public domain property.

In 1991, Linus Torvalds, a student at the University of Helsinki in Finland, created Linux. He wanted to develop an operating system that would exceed MINIX's modest standards. In August 1991, shortly after creating his Linux version 0.01, he published the following message to the *comp.os.minix* newsgroup:

> *Hello everybody out there using MINIX—I'm doing a (free) operating system (just a hobby, won't be big and professional like gnu) for 386 (486) AT clones. This has been brewing since April, and is starting to get ready. I'd like any feedback on things like/dislike in minix, as my OS resembles it somewhat. Any suggestions are welcome, but I won't promise I'll implement them :-)*

According to Torvalds, "I'd guess the first version (of v. 0.01) went out in the middle of September '91." The first official working version, v. 0.02, was made available in October 1991. To read the recollections of

Mr. Torvalds, visit Web sites such as *http://www.li.org/linuxhistory.shtml*. To see an early Linux timeline, visit *http://www.cs.buffalo.edu/~thies/Alt/Time_Line.html.*

Many additions and revisions followed, but the first complete, bug-free version, 1.0, was released in March 1994. These version numbers correspond to the kernel version only, not to versions of Linux distributions as applied by the respective manufacturers. The latest kernel version, as of this writing, is 2.2.15. A reasonably current kernel version timeline, developed by Martin Baehr, is at *http://minnie.cs.adfu.edu.au/Unix_History/linux.*

One of the most remarkable aspects of Linux's history is that it is a true child of the Internet. Torvalds posted his original notice and request for help over the Internet, and most of the improvements to Linux have come from more than 100 programmers from all over the world, courtesy of the Internet. And you can download Linux versions from the Internet, anytime!

Linux Features

To quote from Linux Online!: "Linux is a free UNIX-type operating system." It is a POSIX implementation, which means it meets Open Group POSIX standards (described previously in this chapter). It allows multitasking, simultaneous multiple users, the sharing of system libraries for efficiency, TCP/IP networking, virtual memory and swap spaces, and other UNIX OS features. Users or administrators can use a graphical user interface (GUI) or the command line.

Linux allows you to set up Internet or intranet services and is used by many for setting up Internet firewalls. In fact, because Linux does not require steep licensing fees and can be used on relatively inexpensive (and used) equipment, it is becoming a favorite of Internet service providers.

In addition, Linux can accommodate existing Microsoft Windows applications and can be dual booted with Windows operating systems. It can also be integrated into existing multivendor networks, especially UNIX-based ones because of their similarities. Soon Linux will be incorporated into mobile, handheld computing devices.

Free Software

Linux is free software, meaning that it is distributed under the terms of the GNU General Public License, developed by Richard Stallman. (To read about this ex-MIT software developer and his "free software as in freedom of speech, not free beer" philosophy, we invite you to visit his Web site at *http://www.gnu.org/philosophy/free-software-for-freedom.html*.) This does *not* mean that the Linux kernel, other associated software, or entire distributions are the same kind of free as you associate with public domain. It's also not shareware. Basically, *free software* means that you can use the software for any purpose; study it to see how it is built and how it works; adapt and improve it; and redistribute it free or for a price. But you cannot restrict the software after you have redistributed it (that is, you must distribute it under the GNU GPL, too), and you must provide the source code, just as it was supplied to you.

Sometimes, you will see references to *open source software*. This might be equivalent to free software or it might mean free download with copyright restrictions. If you find yourself faced with this terminology, it is best to investigate further.

Mix and Match

At least 32 Linux distributions are available in English and approximately 20 are available in other languages. Here, we define a *distribution* as an amalgamation of the Linux kernel with other associated software. The 52 distributions are not all the same. Each has a different focus, slightly different features aimed at a specific user audience (besides the obvious fact that the French editions, for example, are for the French audience). Each distribution has different perceived strengths and weaknesses.

In addition, you don't have to use a shrink-wrapped distribution: you may download the kernel of your choice. For example, instead of using a stable, tested kernel, you might want to live on the edge with a less tested, potentially less stable kernel. Or you might want to combine a certain kernel with different applications or other special features (such as RAID support or integration with a specific

Chapter 1: Linux Origins

network) than would normally be found with a standard distribution. Linux allows you to mix and match, use an existing distribution, modify a distribution, or create your own distribution.

You can purchase copyrighted software for Linux from software developers, new or established. Or you can obtain software from the Free Software Foundation *(http://www.gnu.org/fsf)*, which follows the GNU General Public License. Remember, GNU GPL software may not always be free as in no cost, but it is always free as in source code and no restrictions on the user, as described previously.

Hardware and Software Compatibility

Linux runs on Intel-compatible PCs, Alpha computers from Digital Equipment Corp., and Sun's SPARC computers. Linux can also talk to proprietary databases from IBM, Oracle, Sybase, Informix, and Pick and to open source databases such as PostgresSQL and MySQL. A wide variety of office applications run on Linux (StarOffice and Corel WordPerfect, to name two). Several GUI interfaces are available in open source but restricted, such as KDE, or free, such as GNOME. As mentioned, an introductory tour of the X Window System and some X Windows manager applications appear in Chapter 15.

Although Linux presently lacks the development for large-scale, mission-critical systems, its development community is working on it. Likewise, development continues on high availability and on the creation of a logical volume manager.

Chapter 2

Getting Started Using the Linux System

THE BEGINNING POINT FOR USING ANY OPERATING SYSTEM is logging in and out, so that's where we begin here. The chapter continues with Linux/UNIX commands for adding users, adding and changing passwords, and communicating with all or selected users on a Linux system. We include information on Linux/UNIX syntax and end with a description of several tools that we find useful and hope you do too.

NOTE: *The term "Linux/UNIX" is used here to describe commands that work on Linux as well as any UNIX-based system.*

Logging In and Out

Because Linux, like other UNIX systems, is a multiuser system, a basic level of security is implemented to control access. *Although passwords may be optional on some UNIX systems, they are mandatory on Linux systems.* The system administrator sets the initial password for each user, but users can change their own passwords after the first log-in to the system.

Logging In

After you have booted your system and are ready to log in, the screen displays the *hostname* `login` prompt (*hostname* refers to the name given to the computer during the installation of Linux). At this point, you enter your user name:

`hostname login:` *username*

You are then presented with the following:

`Password:`

This is where you type your password. For security, the password is not echoed back to (displayed on) the screen. If the password matches your records and this is the first time you have logged in to the system, the system replies as follows:

`[username@hostname username]$`

If you have logged in and out of the system previously, the system instead displays the following:

`Last login:` *day date time log-in location*
`[username@hostname username]$`

In either case, the $ prompt indicates that the system is now ready for you to enter additional commands.

Logging Out

To log out, you have three choices: the `logout` and `exit` commands and the <Ctrl>-d keypress. The first command looks like this:

`[username@hostname username]$` `logout<Enter>`

The `logout` command works only when you are in your own log-in shell, which is where you generally conduct your business anyway. (For more on the log-in shell, see Chapter 8.) If you should discover that `logout` does not work, use the `exit` command:

`[username@hostname username]$` `exit<Enter>`

or press <Ctrl>-d (repeatedly if necessary). Eventually, you will reach your log-in shell, where you can issue the `logout` command, or you will be logged out of the system.

NOTE: *If $ is part of the prompt, you are in your log-in shell.*

For any of the three logout methods, Linux has the same response:

```
distributorname Linux releasenumber
kernelnumber on a CPUname
hostname login:
```

Creating User Accounts and Passwords

On any Linux system, the system's root user or the system administrator creates user accounts and initial passwords. Ordinary users cannot create user accounts and cannot change the passwords of other user accounts.

If you have Linux installed on a home system or in a smaller network environment, you might not have a designated system administrator. Therefore, note that when we refer to a *system administrator*, we mean someone with root privileges.

Users Accounts

The first task in creating a user account, or record, is to choose a user name. Linux imposes no restrictions on user names, although we recommend that you do not use blank spaces, unprintable characters, or even mixtures of uppercase and lowercase characters because such names can cause problems not only at log in but also when you perform certain system administration tasks.

In addition, system administrators are usually advised beforehand about the format of user names (such as an abbreviated form of the user's name and the company name), who will soon be joining the organization's system, what group membership(s) those new users will be given, and what their security clearances and file systems access will be.

The syntax for user account creation is simple:

`[root@hostname/root]#` `useradd` *newusername*

or

`[root@hostname/root]#` `adduser` *newusername*

Why two commands? Each comes from a different version of UNIX, and Linux developers didn't want to play favorites. You may use either command; both do the same thing.

(The `useradd` and `adduser` commands are examples of linking, in which two names are linked to one command. We discuss the linking function in Chapter 5.)

Passwords

The system administrator also sets the initial password for a user. The syntax is

`[root@hostname/root]#` *passwd username*

Passwords are the primary mechanism for ensuring system security. For users to log in the first time, the system administrator must have already set their password.

After their first log-in, users can set their own passwords, but they generally can't set their own user names. After a user changes his or her password, it is *encrypted,* which means the password can't be decoded by other users, including the root user. Organizational policy generally requires that users change their passwords periodically (for example, every day, week, or month). Example 2.1 shows how users can set new passwords for themselves.

Example 2.1 ▼   passwd

```
[username@hostname username]$ passwd<Enter>
UNIX password: xxxx<Enter>
New UNIX password: yyyy<Enter>
Retype new UNIX password: yyyy<Enter>
Passwd: all authentication tokens updated successfully
```
▲

To prevent a user from being inadvertently locked out of the system through a simple typing error, the new password has to be entered twice. The system accepts the new password only if the new password meets Linux's basic rules and the two typed versions match. The old password is invalid thereafter.

Although Linux does not set restrictions on user names, passwords are a different story. We've already mentioned that the root user must establish the first password for every user. In addition, passwords are case sensitive.

Following are some guidelines for the root user when establishing a password and for ordinary users who are changing their password:

- Make your password at least six characters long.
- Do not make the new password similar to the last one.
- Do not use a so-called dictionary word (one used by Linux itself).
- Try to make a password that is fairly easy to remember but not easy for others to guess. Some bad examples include the word *password*, the sequence *qwerty*, the user's first or last name, the sequence *123456*, a name or phrase that might be attributed to the user, such as cat_lover, and the user's phone number, birth date, or favorite sports team.
- Try to mix numbers with letters.
- Write your password down and keep it secure but also available at all times.

Command Syntax

Linux commands generally follow the syntax and format of UNIX commands. The order and correct separation of elements are important. The command or process always comes first; this may be followed by one or more options, or *flags*, which may be followed by one or more arguments. You must separate options from the command and from each other by single spaces and precede them by a hyphen (-) character. In the following, -f and -l are options:

```
[username@hostname username]$ mail -f newmail<Enter>
[username@hostname username]$ wc -l filename<Enter>
```

The first line reads, "Bring me the contents of my mailbox for processing (reading, replying, deleting, and the like). Then, when I am finished, return the undeleted messages to an alternate mailbox, called `newmail`." The second line reads, "Count the number of lines in the `filename` file."

You may bunch together multiple options and precede them by a single hyphen (for example, `ls -lf`). If you do not precede an option with a hyphen, the system might try to treat it as an argument, which could result in an error message.

An *argument* is a further refinement of the command, usually indicating an object to be retrieved and worked on or an object to be created as a result of the requested process. Arguments must be separated from the option and each other by a single space. (Unlike options, arguments cannot be bunched together.)

Viewing the Date: date and cal Commands

The system administrator sets the date globally for the system or network; the user can then display the date with the `date` command. (For more on setting the date, consult the `man` pages for the `date` command.)

When use the `date` command to display the date, you can customize it in several ways, but by default, it requires no options. The syntax is simply

```
date
```

The time indicated is based on a 24-hour clock (for example, 1 P.M. is indicated as 13:00:00), followed by the time zone (for example, CST, for Central Standard Time).

The syntax for the `cal` (calendar) command follows:

```
cal [month] year
```

Chapter 2: Getting Started Using the Linux System

When entering the month, use the number of the month (a value between 1 and 12; January is 1), and not the name of the month or any type of abbreviation. When entering the year, use the full four digits (for example, 2000) and *not* the two-digit abbreviation. Although you won't get an error message using two digits, you will likely get erroneous results.

In Example 2.2, we show several ways to use the date and cal commands.

Example 2.2 date and cal

To check the date:

```
$ date<Enter>
Wed   Nov   11   1:07:34   CST   2000
```

To view an entire month:

```
$ cal 11 2000<Enter>
      November 2000
Su   Mo   Tu   We   Th   Fr   Sa
                   1    2    3    4
 5    6    7    8    9   10   11
12   13   14   15   16   17   18
19   20   21   22   23   24   25
26   27   28   29   30
```

To view an entire year:

```
$ cal 2001<Enter>
```

The text continues to scroll until you see only the last months of the requested year.

To see the calendar for an entire year, screenful by screenful:

```
$ cal 2001 | more<Enter>
```

19

The screen automatically fills with calendar text from January 1 to whatever the screen can hold, and then stops. Press <Enter> to advance one line at a time.   ▲

The last command in the example contains |, which is called a *pipe*. The pipelining, or piping, of commands is discussed again in Chapter 8; the `more` command is discussed in Chapter 5.

Requesting Data on Logged-In Users

who, who am i, and whoami Commands

The basic purpose of the `who`, `who am i`, and `whoami` commands (as well as the `finger` command) is to obtain information about the users currently logged in to the system.

The output from the `who` command is simply a list of users currently logged in, along with their stations and the time they most recently logged in. Example 2.3 shows that the root user has been logged in to the system console since 9:02 A.M. on February 12 and that flintsfr is logged in to the tty1 terminal and has been logged in since 11:10 A.M. of the same day.

Example 2.3 ▼   who

```
$ who<Enter>
root    console  Feb 12 09:02
flintsfr tty1    Feb 12 11:10
```
▲

Note that in Example 2.3, the response mentions that the root user is logged in at the console. The *console* is generally defined as the device (typically a terminal as opposed to a full-fledged workstation) directly attached to the computer on which Linux is running. By default, the console is the device that receives system messages. Every computer on which a copy of Linux has been installed must have a console defined at all times, and there must be only one console for that computer.

CHAPTER 2: GETTING STARTED USING THE LINUX SYSTEM

The -u and -m options are often added to the who command. The response to who -u displays all user names, their respective real names, workstation names, and log-in times, and the identities of the processes they are running.

The response to who -m is identical to that of who am i, which is shown in Example 2.4. For both commands, the system responds with the user name of the person who entered the command, the name of the user's workstation, and the user's log-in time.

Example 2.4 ▼ who am i and whoami

```
$ who am i<Enter>
flintsfr tty1 Feb 12 11:10
```
or
```
$ whoami<Enter>
flintsfr
```
▲

finger Command

The finger command displays information about the users currently logged in to the system, as shown in Example 2.5. The default response format is the full user name, log-in time, user's home directory, and user's log-in shell. You can use the finger command to look up information about users logged into a remote system as well. However, you must know the correct name of the remote system.

Example 2.5 ▼ finger

```
$ finger rubbleba<Enter>
Login: rubbleba                    Name:
Directory: /home/rubbleba         Shell: /bin/bash
On since Fri Feb 12 10:32 (CST) on tty2
No mail.
No Plan.
```
▲

You can create files called *.project* and *.plan* to enhance the responses received when you enter the finger command. The detailed

21

procedure is beyond the scope of this book, but here is an outline of the process. Suppose you, as user *p2smith3*, create hidden files called *.plan* and *.project* in your home directory. When creating these files, you must remember to provide the `r` permission for others on the files, as well as the `x` permission for others on the *p2smith3* home directory. (File and directory permissions are discussed in detail in Chapter 6.) When users invoke the `finger` command with the `p2smith3` argument, they are provided with all the information you have written into those files.

Sending and Receiving Mail: mail Command

The `mail` command is interactive and is used to both send and receive mail messages.

Send Mail

To send a message to another user on the same system, the format is

```
mail username
```

To send a message to more than one user on the same system, enter all user names after the `mail` command, separating each by one space:

```
mail username username
```

To send a message to one or more users on another system, type the user name followed by @ and the name of the system:

```
mail username@hostname
```

To send a message to more than one user on another system, separate each *username@hostname* entry by one space.

Example 2.6 shows how to send mail to a user on the same system (that is, on the same host) and to one on a different system. Notice that, whenever the `mail` command is invoked, the system responds with a `Subject:` prompt. Type a description line, which will appear in the receiver's list of incoming mail, and press <Enter> again. Now you can type whatever you want to communicate to the receiver.

When you have finished your message, press <Enter> and then press <Ctrl>-d. The system responds with a `Cc:` prompt. If you want to send copies of the message to others, type their usernames. When you are finished, press <Ctrl>-d again. The system sends the message and responds with a shell prompt (usually $ and a cursor).

Example 2.6 ▼ mail for Sending Mail

To send a message to a user on the same system:

```
$ mail rubbleba<Enter>
Subject: Meeting
Hey, Barney! Don't forget the Water Buffalo meeting
    tonight at Mr. Slate's!
Fred
<Ctrl>-d
Cc: <Enter>
```

To send a message to a user on another system:

```
$ mail slatemr@hostname<Enter>
Subject: Meeting Still OK, sir?
Is it still OK for the Water Buffalos to meet tonight
    at your house?
I already told the guys!
Flintstone
<Ctrl>-d
Cc: <Enter>
```
▲

Receive Mail

Whenever you log in, the system lets you know whether you have mail messages waiting in the username file (where username refers to your user name) in the */var/spool/mail/* directory. In Example 2.7, the username file is *team01*.

To view messages, the format is simply

```
mail
```

The `mail` program responds with a listing of the messages in the file. Note the program-specific prompt (&), which tells you that the `mail` program is now running.

Example 2.7 ▼ mail for Receiving Mail

```
You have mail.
$ mail<Enter>
Mail version 8.1.6/6/93 Type ? for help
"/var/spool/mail/team01": 2 messages 1 new
 U 1 team05@hostname.local Mon Jul 10 10:50 10/267
   "Call Us, re:Meeting"
 N 2 team02@hostname.local Tue Jul 11 09:05 16/311
   "Meeting Postponed"
& <Enter>
Message 1:
From team05 Mon Jul 10 10:50:32 2000
Date: Mon, Jul 10 2000 10:50:32 -600
From: team05@hostname.localdomain
To: rubbleba@hostname.localdomain
Subject: Meeting
Please call us regarding the status of the meeting we
    called for Thursday morning.
Fred                                                                ▲
```

Note the U and N designations at the beginning of each listed message. U means unread (a holdover message from a previous time when the user viewed his or her mail but didn't read that particular message). The N designation means new.

The You have mail message appears whenever users log in and have messages, but it is not displayed every time a new message arrives. System administrators can customize the shell to check on all mailbox files once every *xxx* seconds (for example, every 600 seconds). If the shell detects a new message in a user's */var/spool/mail/*username file, it displays the You have mail message. System administrators can customize this mail notification, as well.

Here are few options for reading your mail:

CHAPTER 2: GETTING STARTED USING THE LINUX SYSTEM

- ▲ To read the first message in the listing, press <Enter> or type 1 and then press <Enter>.
- ▲ To skip the first message and read the second message, type 2 and press <Enter>.
- ▲ To read the first new message in any listing, type t and press <Enter>.
- ▲ To read the messages in sequence, simply press <Enter> after starting at your chosen first message and then press <Enter> after reading each message in turn.

You can also type the following letters (among others) at the & prompt while reviewing your messages:

- ▲ d deletes messages
- ▲ m forwards messages
- ▲ r sends a reply
- ▲ q exits mail and leaves unread messages in the queue
- ▲ s appends a message to a file

To obtain a full list of available subcommands, type ? at the & prompt.

The mail -f command displays a list of messages in your personal mailbox, which is a file called *mbox* in your home directory. Normally, when you quit the mail program, undeleted (but already read) messages are written back to that file. By starting the mail -f aspect of mail, you can review and deal with these messages in the same way you dealt with the new or unread messages in */var/spool/mail/*username.

Sending Messages to the Screen: write and wall Commands

write Command

The write command immediately displays a message on the specified user's screen. You can send messages to a user on the local system or on another system on the network (simply replace *username* with

25

username@hostname). If a user is logged in on more than one terminal, the message is displayed on all terminals unless the originating user specifies the terminals to which the message should be sent, as follows:

```
write username ttyno
```

Otherwise, to reach the user on any and all terminals, the syntax is

```
write username
```

For a specific user to receive the message, however, he or she must be logged in at the time and must not have refused permission for the message to appear on his or her terminal. By default, Linux does not turn off the write permission; that is accomplished by the user with the `mesg` command (covered later in this chapter). Note that you cannot turn off messages from root.

In a `write` session, each user alternately sends and receives messages. Long messages can be placed in a file and directed or redirected to the other user (or users). The syntax is

```
write username < filename.ext
```

Example 2.8 illustrates `write` being used by two users. The receiving user uses the same syntax to reply to the originating user.

Example 2.8 ▼   write

User flintsfr sends:

```
$ write rubbleba tty1<Enter>
Barney, meeting at Slate's at 6!<Enter>
Fred<Enter>
<Ctrl>-d
```

User rubbleba receives:

```
Message from flintsfr@hostname on tty3 at 13:13
Barney, meeting at Slate's at 6!
Fred
EOF
```
▲

wall Command

The `wall` command sends a common message to all users logged in to the system. The syntax is

```
wall textofmessage
```

By default, all users can use the `wall` command. Example 2.9 shows the use of the `wall` command by the root user.

Example 2.9 ▼

wall

The root user sends the following (remember, the root user has the # prompt instead of $):

```
# wall Warning!! System Going Down!<Enter>
```

Every logged-in user receives the following:

```
Broadcast message from root (tty1) Wed Jul 19
14:04:48 2000 . . .
Warning!! System Going Down!
```
▲

Conversing Online: talk Command

The `talk` command allows two users to hold a conversation. As shown in Example 2.10, one user invites the other to talk as follows:

```
talk username
```

You can use the `talk` command locally on one system or across a network. To talk across a network, the syntax for both the invitation and the response is

```
talk username@hostname
```

If the invitation is accepted, the screen on each terminal splits in two horizontally. The messages typed by the other user appear in the top window; replies are typed in the lower window. To close the connection, press <Ctrl>-c.

Example 2.10 ▼ talk

Suppose Barney and Fred are both logged in. To talk to Fred, Barney enters

```
$ talk flintsfr<Enter>
```

Fred receives the following message immediately:

```
Message from TalkDaemon@hostname at 09:05. . .
talk: connection requested by rubbleba
talk: respond with: talk rubbleba
```

To accept the invitation, Fred follows the instruction and enters

```
$ talk rubbleba<Enter>
```
▲

What about those times when you don't want to be interrupted by messages or invitations to converse or when you want to resume receiving messages and conversations after having denied them for a while? The next section explains how to block and unblock messages.

Blocking Messages and Conversations: mesg Command

You have seen how you can use the `write`, `wall`, and `talk` commands for communicating with users. But sometimes users should not be interrupted. For those times, they can use the `mesg` command, shown in Example 2.11. The syntax is

```
mesg [y/n]
```

Note that the system does not acknowledge the command.

With `mesg` turned off (with n), others will not receive feedback from the system, with one exception: Messages from the root user cannot be turned off. The `write` and `wall` command messages from the root users always reach all users on the system.

Example 2.11 ▼ mesg

To not be interrupted:

```
$ mesg n<Enter>
```

To be open to messages and conversations again:

```
$ mesg y<Enter>
```
▲

By default, the system's shell start-up process permits messaging. If a user has just entered mesg n during a log-in session and then logs out and logs in again, the system resets the *username* to mesg y. To prevent messages from coming through after exiting and logging in again, the user must set mesg n again.

Users can override the default mesg y by including mesg n in their *$HOME/.profile* file. In other words, they can set mesg n in the script that runs automatically when they log in.

Additional Tools: clear, echo, banner, and wc Commands

From time to time, users and administrators have a need for additional tools to help them with routine duties. Here we present four tools that aren't related, revolutionary in scope or power, or needed every day. But they do help prevent confusion. Have a look at them and, for each one, ask yourself: Has there ever been a time when I could have used this? Almost every time, you'll likely answer, yes.

clear Command

If your screen is full of confusing data, old data, and the like, you may want to use the `clear` command. This command appears to execute simply and easily. What could be simpler than erasing a bunch of now unnecessary characters and leaving you with only a prompt and a clear terminal screen?

There's more to `clear` than meets the eye, however. To determine how to clear the screen, the `clear` process first checks the `TERM` environment specifications in RAM and then the */usr/share/lib/terminfo* directory, which contains the terminal definition files. If the `TERM` variable is not set or is set incorrectly, the command results in no action.

echo Command

The `echo` command makes the terminal reiterate what you have just typed, as shown in Example 12.2. This seems trivial when simply entered interactively on the screen but is valuable when included in shell scripts or similar files (for example, batch files). For instance, the `echo` command is helpful when you are writing a script file and want to be notified when certain instructions are executing.

Example 2.12 ▼

echo

```
$ echo Installing modem drivers now. . .<Enter>
Installing modem drivers now. . .
```

A few of the argument-like conventions that you can use with the `echo` command are `\b` to display a backspace character, `\n` to display a newline character, and `\t` to display a tab character. See the online `man` pages or other information sources for an exhaustive list.

banner Command

The `banner` command displays ASCII character strings in large format on the screen or printed as hard copy. It constructs the characters out of # symbols and displays them from the top down (not from left to right). Like `echo`, this command may seem trivial when you play with it at your terminal, but it can prove invaluable in a large office or network environment when, for example, you want to identify individual print jobs from a shared printer. The syntax follows:

```
banner [-wn] ascii_text
```

The -w option adjusts the width of the output. The -n option is the specified character width of the output you want. (Your screen width is normally 80). You cannot specify a width without also using the w option. If you want to display more than one word, you must put quotation marks (") around the phrase. Otherwise, banner prints only the last word it was given, if anything at all. All these options are shown in Example 2.13.

Example 2.13 ▼ banner

Without options, banner prints extremely large. So, to display *Hello!* so that you can see it:

```
$ banner -w40 Hello!<Enter>
```

To print a phrase and give yourself the ability to scroll up and down through the output:

```
$ banner -w40 "Hello Friends!" | less<Enter>
```

To send the output to a file:

```
$ banner -w40 "Print Job 1" > pjob1<Enter>
```

If the file doesn't exist yet, it is created during this process.

Finally, to use banner to append a *Print Job 1* label to an existing file that you want to print:

```
$ banner -w40 "Print Job 1" >> report1<Enter>
```
▲

Now you may ask, but how do I print these documents so that I can see what banner did? Printing documents is discussed in Chapter 5. For now, remember that if the report file already exists, banner appends its output to the *end* of the file. If you want the banner output at the front of the file, the output must be inserted before the rest of the material.

NOTE: *For further information on commands, consult respective online* man *pages by typing* man commandname. *Other information sources are discussed in Chapter 3.*

wc Command

When you need to know the attributes of a certain file, you can use the wc (word count) command. The basic syntax and a few command options follow:

```
wc [-l] [-w] [-c] filename.ext
```

The -l option counts the number of lines, -w counts the number of words, and -c option counts the number of characters (that is, the number of bytes). If you type:

```
$ wc filename<Enter>
```

you get:

```
    17      126     1085            filename
```
   (lines) (words) (characters) (name of file)

If you don't specify any options, you always get lines, words, characters, and the file name. You can shorten or lengthen the output by specifying options.

Exercises

1. Log in to the system with a user name such as team*xx*, where *xx* is a double-digit number. The first time you log in with a new user name, you are prompted to change your password. Keep the password the same as your log-in name. The passwords you supply on the command line are not displayed.

   ```
   $ Login: teamxx
   Password:
   You are required to change your password. Please choose
   a new one.
   New password: teamxx
   Enter new password again: teamxx
   ```

2. Change the password.

   ```
   $ passwd<Enter>
   Changing password for "teamxx"
   teamxx's Old password:
   teamxx's New password:
   Enter the new password again:
   ```

3. Verify that the new password has been set by logging out and back in with it.

   ```
   $ exit
   login: teamxx
   Password:
   ```

4. Display the system's date.

   ```
   $ date<Enter>
   ```

5. Display a count of the number of lines in the */etc/passwd* file.

   ```
   $ wc -l /etc/passwd<Enter>
   ```

6. Display the entire calendar for the year 2000.

   ```
   $ cal 2000<Enter>
   ```

7. Display the month of September for the year 1752.

   `$ cal 9 1752<Enter>`

   Do you notice anything peculiar about September?

8. Display the month of August for the year 1999 and then the year 99.

   `$ cal 8 1999<Enter>`
   `$ cal 8 99<Enter>`

   Are 1999 and 99 the same?

9. Display who is currently logged in on your system. Check to see when they logged in.

   `$ who<Enter>`

   or

   `$ finger<Enter>`

   NOTE: *If you use the* `finger` *command and see* ??? *in the Name field, optional user information was not added to the user profile (that is, in the* /etc/passwd *file) when it was created.*

10. Display only your log-in name.

    `$ whoami<Enter>`

11. Use banner to display *Out to Lunch.*

    `$ banner Out to Lunch<Enter>`

12. Use the `echo` command to write the character string *Out to Lunch* to your display.

    `$ echo Out to Lunch<Enter>`

13. Use the `clear` command to clear your screen.

    `$ clear<Enter>`

    NOTE: *If you are using an ASCII terminal and the* `clear` *command does not work, check to see that the TERM variable is correctly set.*

14. Send a note to yourself using the `mail` command. Provide a subject but ignore the `Cc:` (carbon copy) prompt.

    ```
    $ mail username<Enter>
    Subject: A Reminder to Myself<Enter>
    The meeting starts at 6:00 at Slate's.<Enter>
    <Ctrl>-d
    Cc: <Enter>
    ```

15. Start the `mail` process and list the messages in your mailbox. Read your message, save it, and quit the `mail` program. To list a brief summary of `mail` subcommands, type ? at the `mail` prompt.

    ```
    $ mail<Enter>
    ? t<Enter>
    ? s<Enter>
    "/home/teamxx/mbox" [New file]
    ? q<Enter>
    ```

16. Access your mail and delete the message you saved in your personal mailbox. Exit the `mail` program. Practice sending mail to someone logged in on your system.

    ```
    $ mail -f<Enter>
    ? d<Enter>
    ? q<Enter>
    ```

17. Log off the system.

    ```
    $ <Ctrl>-d
    ```

See Appendix B for answers.

Quiz

1. Which of the following illustrates the correct Linux syntax for the `mail` command?

   ```
   $ mail newmail -f
   $ mail f newmail
   $ -f mail
   $ mail -f newmail
   ```

2. What command would you use to send a mail message to *username*?

3. List three commands that you can use to communicate with logged-in users.

4. What output would you expect from the following command:

   ```
   $ cal 8
   ```

5. Which of the following commands would you use to determine when a particular user logged in?

   ```
   $ who am I
   $ who
   $ finger everyone
   $ finger username
   ```

See Appendix C for answers.

Chapter 3

Linux Documentation and Support

THE LINUX OPERATING SYSTEM comprises many subsystems and processes working together simultaneously. Thus, to monitor, measure, modify, and control your Linux system, you need information about commands, utilities, configuration, applications, and more.

We introduced you to a few basic commands and concepts in Chapter 2, and with every subsequent chapter, we introduce others. To fully understand some of these concepts, however, you might have to refer to or have knowledge of things that are not discussed at length in this book. Because it is difficult to absorb, let alone commit to memory, all the concepts, commands, and related information you need to make your Linux system perform the way you want, now and in the future, it is critical to be aware of all the sources of information available to you.

In this chapter, we list and discuss some sources of information and support that you'll be able to call upon immediately and later, whether inside your own shop or elsewhere in the Linux world. Although we cannot possibly cover all available information sources, we do provide an introduction to some of the more popular and helpful ones.

NOTE: *Throughout the book, when we suggest that you check other information sources, we are referring to the sources mentioned in this chapter.*

Distribution Package Documentation

You can obtain a Linux distribution in two basic ways: officially and unofficially. This section covers the information you can expect to find with both types of distributions.

Official Linux Distributions

Every official Linux distribution ships with a large amount of documentation, and that's one reason why we recommend that you purchase an official distribution. Most distribution packages contain the following information, specific to the Linux software you've purchased:

- ▲ **Features of the enclosed Linux software and applications.** You will learn which version of the Linux kernel you have, the hardware it supports, the applications you can install and use immediately, and what else is available and from where.

- ▲ **Installation instruction and assistance.** You will be told how to install Linux on your system (for example, how to install a graphical versus a text-based interface, and options for basic and custom installations) and how to do basic fine tuning.

- ▲ **Basic system administration instructions.** These are important because you have to know how to create and administer the root and other users on your system, just to get going.

- ▲ **Sources for troubleshooting and support, after you register your software.** Troubleshooting and support can be invaluable, especially if you are loading Linux for the first time or are updating to a version that is different from your current version. *Don't forget to register your software as soon as you unwrap or install it!*

▲ **A simplified history of UNIX and Linux.** This may aid your comprehension of the attributes and behavior of certain parts of your software, especially the actions of the shell (which we discuss in later chapters).

▲ **Instructions for obtaining additional documentation.** Most distribution materials are geared to specific audiences (the majority are geared to novices and nonexperts, some are geared to business users, some to programmers, and so on). But most packages contain references to their own hardcopy documentation, their own online documentation, and to other sources of information (books, magazines, Internet sites, and the like).

Downloaded Linux and Other Unofficial Distributions

Purchasing an official Linux distribution is not the only way to go. Some people and organizations acquire their copies of the Linux kernel, with or without the simultaneous acquisition of applications, by downloading Linux from the Internet or through other means.

If you take this route, you can find documentation in many venues. For example, recent years have seen an avalanche of books on Linux. You can find them at local bookstores, university or college bookstores, computer bookstores, and on the Internet. You can often find related applications or utilities in the same places.

Many books and magazines also contain CD-ROMs of one of the Linux distributions, although it is usually one or two revisions behind the distribution or kernel package you can obtain directly from the manufacturer. The same book and CD-ROM combinations customarily contain some applications as well. Meanwhile, new Linux-related magazines appear almost monthly. Later in this chapter, we list a few of these books and magazines.

New Linux-oriented Internet sites crop up all the time. We list several of the more established sites later in the chapter as well. Often they're affiliated with educational institutions, Linux support or interest groups, or other organizations that have adopted Linux in their own shops or are otherwise promoting its use. The information and services offered by these sources are varied, but almost always include installation instructions, some basic system administration help, troubleshooting advice, device drivers, fine-tuning tricks, and other types of support.

Linux support and user groups have emerged in almost every major urban center or region. Joining one of these groups is an economical and sociable way to learn more about Linux, obtain free or inexpensive software, and do a good turn by helping others with their problems. To find these groups, check your local computer newspaper (usually free at software and hardware vendors, at major newsstands and even at some convenience stores), go surfing with a good Internet search engine, or go straight to *http://www.linux.tucows.com* and drill down through the links found there. Other Internet sites will link you to support groups, too.

Current Linux Distributors

The operative word in the title to this section is *current*. When we began to write this book, there were certainly fewer distributors of Linux than there were at the publication of this book. And by the time you read this, there will no doubt be even more. If you're interested in investigating the various flavors of Linux, keep track of the distributions listed and described at the Linux Online! Web site at *http://www.linux.org*.

At last count, 32 full-featured distributions and 19 mini or specialty distributions were available in the English language, and 20 non-English distributions were available in Spanish, Italian, French, Portuguese, German, Chinese, Japanese, Thai, Ukrainian, Russian, Swedish, and Finnish. The Linux Online! site provides descriptions of the distributions, as well as links to the respective download sites. The site is well worth checking out, even if only to see how Linux's popularity has spread throughout the world in a few short years.

At the Web sites for the distributions listed at Linux Online!, you'll find some variation of the following types of information and services:

▲ Company history and description

▲ Purchase information

- Names and addresses of resellers
- Patches, updates, or bug fixes for the products, including kernel updates
- Announcements regarding security issues pertinent to their products
- Press releases regarding their company or Linux in general
- FAQs (frequently asked questions) regarding their products or Linux in general
- Related or linked Internet sites (such as ftp sites or mirror sites)
- Support contact information (such as telephone and fax numbers and email and surface mail addresses)

Some of these sources do not provide ftp sites to download their products but do provide sources for inexpensive CD-ROM copies.

Linux and UNIX Online Information

Linux and UNIX have a time-honored tradition of providing various forms of online help. In this section, we introduce the most popular and helpful sources: man pages, info pages, the locate command, and the usage facility.

man Command

Almost every Linux command, system call, or special file has an online manual page (man page), authoritative online documentation that you can access instantly from your Linux system directories. The man page is used in most if not all Linux and UNIX environments. Many users and system administrators use man exclusively.

Types of Information Available

You usually access the man pages from the command line. Depending on the information's origin and author as well as the format the author chose to use (this is where the history of the selected command or function might have some influence, as you'll see), several of the following categories of information will appear immediately on the screen in ASCII format:

- ▲ NAME: The name of the command, subroutine, file, and so on, and a brief description of what it does.

- ▲ SYNOPSIS: Syntax to use when invoking the command, subroutine, or file. (*Synopsis* is the term that those in the Linux and UNIX world use for *syntax*.) Typically, the syntax follows the format we introduced in Chapter 2, but you might also see a complete listing of all the options and arguments for the command in the particular version of Linux you are using. In the next section, we include some extra synopsis comments when we illustrate the results of entering the man who command.

- ▲ INTRODUCTION or DESCRIPTION: A more in-depth definition or description of what the command does. This section may also list or discuss the options and arguments, or it may list step-by-step instructions to follow before, during, or after the command is executed.

- ▲ OPTIONS: The available options and arguments.

- ▲ FILES: A list of files and their relation to the command. (For instance, you might need to consult a certain file to find the parameters of the command.)

- ▲ ENVIRONMENT: A list of the configuration files that are checked for certain parameters before a command is executed.

- ▲ EXAMPLES: Although examples are often found in the Introduction or Description section, an author might list a number of common examples for using the command, subroutine, or file in this Examples section.

- ▲ SEE ALSO: This part contains names of related commands or files or names of commands that might produce the same effect.

- ▲ HISTORY: The version of Linux or UNIX in which this command first appeared, the original developers, and other historical information.

- ▲ BUGS: Additional tips or cautions regarding how, when, where, and why you should use this command, file, or subroutine. You might also find directions regarding how and when *not* to execute the command.

- ▲ SUMMARY: Another section for presenting options, descriptions, uses, and the like.

- ▲ AUTHOR: The name of the individual or organization who developed the command, subroutine, or file or the name of the person or organization providing this information page. You might also find an address for reaching the author directly. Often, this section indicates whether the command originated with a version of UNIX or was developed especially for Linux.

- ▲ DERIVATION: At the bottom of the man page, you may find additional information regarding the origin of the command (sources such as AT&T or Berkeley, or version numbers or dates).

- ▲ DATE: The date of the man page's last update. This date does *not* indicate when the last update of the command's utility, options, or arguments occurred. The man pages themselves are not always updated when someone modifies an element of the program.

To consult the man pages for a command, subroutine, special file, or other element, the syntax is simple:

```
man commandname
```

"info - man"

Navigating man pages

After a man page is open, use the following keys to move around in it:

- ▲ <Spacebar> navigates down the file one screen at a time
- ▲ b navigates up the file one screen at a time
- ▲ d navigates down the file one-half screen at a time
- ▲ u navigates up the file one-half screen at a time
- ▲ <Enter> or the down arrow key navigates down the file one line at a time

- ▲ h displays a help screen with a number of other navigation commands; q quits the help screen and returns you to the man page
- ▲ / followed by a string and <Enter> searches for the string
- ▲ n finds the next occurrence of the previous search
- ▲ q exits the man page

After you exit the man page, these keys are no longer active for navigation, until you invoke the command again.

If at any time you want to suspend or stop man operation, press <Ctrl>-z. Later, you can reenter the man page where you left it by simply entering fg. These commands are discussed in Chapter 11.

Printing man Information

If you want to print the man page for a particular command, type

```
$ man commandname | lpr<Enter>
```

Alternatively, if you're using a PostScript printer, type

```
$ man -t commandname | lpr<Enter>
```

In Example 3.1, you see only a portion of the man pages available when you print information on the who command. But the example provides a sample of the output format. The coding in Synopsis sections use these typographical conventions:

- ▲ Optional fields appear in square brackets, [and]. You need not enter the option or argument.
- ▲ Mandatory fields appear in curly brackets. { and }. You must enter an option or argument after the command name.
- ▲ A pipe, |, separates two options or arguments. You must choose one or the other.

Example 3.1 ▼

```
$ man who<Enter>
NAME
who - show who is logged on
```

```
SYNOPSIS
who [-imqsuwHT] [--count] [--idle] [--heading]
    [--help] [--message] [--mesg] [--version]
    [--writable] [file] [am i]
DESCRIPTION
This documentation is no longer being maintained and
    may be inaccurate or incomplete. The Texinfo docu-
    mentation is now the authoritative source.
This manual page documents the GNU version of who. If
    given no non-option arguments, who prints the fol-
    lowing information for each user currently logged
    on:
login name
terminal line
login time
remote hostname or X display
If given one non-option argument, who uses that
    instead of /etc/utmp as the name of the file con-
    taining the record of users logged on. /etc/wtmp is
    commonly given as an argument to who to look at who
    has previously logged on.                         ▲
```

info Pages

The info pages use the same database as man but presents the information in a different format. Some say info is more powerful because it allows you to examine information in more bite-sized chunks and shows the relationships between the information you have searched for and other related information.

Another important feature of info, especially for new users, is that it presents its own instructions on the first screen and also allows you to enter a primer immediately after you invoke info. This hand-holding greatly enhances the likelihood of a successful search.

The syntax couldn't be simpler:

```
info
```

After invoking the command, the first ASCII character-based info screen appears, which declares that you are at the top of the info directory tree. Basic instructions follow as well as the opportunity to start the primer.

If you don't require the primer, press the <Tab> key or the up and down arrow keys to move among the many available user commands, system calls, subroutines, devices, file formats, games, system administration functions, and more. Example 3.2 lists the basic categories, not all the functions you can access from this screen. When you have selected a category, press the <Enter> key. You are then presented with a screen containing information about your selection.

Example 3.2 ▼   info

To invoke the info command:

```
$ info<Enter>
```

Linux responds with the `info` directory tree:

File →
```
Fire:dir Node:top Top of Info tree
"Basic Instructions"
*Menu:

*Commands
*System Calls
*Subroutines
*Devices
*File Formats
*Games
*Misc
*Sys Admin
```

Move the cursor to *Commands* and select it by pressing <Enter>. The mv command is among the options Linux displays next. Move your cursor to *mv* and select it in the same way (by pressing <Enter>). Linux jumps, or hyperlinks, to the mv information:

```
'mv':Move(rename)files
= = = = = = = = = = = =
"Syntax"
"Explanation"
"Options"
(etc.)
```

Move up and down through the information. Then press n to move to the next related topic or function (if any), p to move to a previous related topic or function, d to return to the first screen (that is, back to the top of the info directory), or q to exit info. ▲

You can invoke info from xterm windows, and additional info or man-like programs can be invoked from the window desktop. The names and types of these programs vary with each window manager. From KDE, for example, you can invoke KDE Help, and from Fvwm95, you can invoke xman. Both are graphically oriented. KDE Help allows you to navigate through hyperlinks with a mouse, as opposed to keyboard navigation through the ASCII-oriented info pages. See Chapter 15 for more.

locate and slocate Commands

The locate and slocate commands enable you to search for files whose names match or partially match the name or character pattern you specify. Note that you do not search the file system as such; instead, you search *slocate.db,* which is a database of file names on your system.

You can use metacharacters with locate and slocate to refine the results of your search. (*Metacharacters* are characters that the shell interprets as having special meaning; see Chapter 8 for details.) A search without metacharacters likely results in many more matches on the specified file name or pattern. And if the pattern you specify is also the name of a directory, watch out—all the file names found in that directory are returned.

If you activate slocate (secure locate) and disable locate, you provide a measure of security. That's because slocate also reads file permissions and ownerships and returns only file name matches that the requesting user has a right to see. The syntax for slocate follows:

```
$ slocate pattern
```

Before you can use the locate or slocate command, the root user must create *slocate.db.* Otherwise, you will receive a *no such file or directory* error message. To create the database, enter

```
$ /etc/cron.daily/slocate.cron<Enter>
```

The *slocate.db* database is not automatically updated unless the system administrator has created a system of automated updates. If *slocate.db* hasn't been updated, a search might miss the particular file name you need. A root user can quickly update *slocate.db* by entering

    $ updatedb<Enter>

By default, this command creates *slocate.db* starting at the root directory as its reference point.

> **NOTE:** *Check the* man *pages and other information sources for the options and arguments for all the commands mentioned in this chapter.*

Example 3.3 ▼

slocate

To find and list all files whose names contain the string *kill* irrespective of the characters that precede or follow that string in the name (which means file names such as *skill* and *killall* would be located):

    $ slocate kill<Enter>

On our machine, more than thirty file names were returned. The results vary for every machine unless they are all part of a new and identical installation (for example, a new network installation or a classroom environment).

To locate all strings that contain *kill.* (including the period), again irrespective of what precedes or follows that string:

    $ slocate *kill.*<Enter>
    /usr/X11R6/man/man1/xkill.1x
    /usr/doc/vim-common-5.3/syntax/skill.vim
    usr/lib/perl5/5.00503/i386-linux/auto/POSIX/kill.al
    .
    .
    .
    /usr/share/afterstep/desktop/buttons/fuf-kill.xpm
    /usr/share/afterstep/desktop/buttons/os8-kill.xpm
    /user/share/vim/syntax/skill.vim

Our machine returned twelve entries.

Finally, in the next three examples, no entries are returned. Can you determine why?

```
$ slocate kil*<Enter>
$ slocate kill.*<Enter>
$ slocate kill*<Enter>
```

The answer: The database search is more precise when you use metacharacters. In this example, no file name begins with *k*, so no names are returned. Even if, say, the *killall* file existed in the / directory (thus giving the file its simplest name), its database name is */killall*. Only *kil* or a similar search would find it. ▲

Usage Facility

The usage facility can prove invaluable. It is based on the same database used by man and info. You invoke this facility by requesting command usage help. The syntax follows:

commandname --help

If you enter a command incorrectly, Linux responds with information on what is wrong and how to correct the command entry, as shown in Example 3.4.

Example 3.4 ▼ Usage

To request usage information for the mount command:

```
$ mount --help<Enter>
Usage:mount [-hV]
      mount -a [-nfFrsvw] [-t vfstypes]
      mount [-nfrsvw] [-o options] special | node
      mount [-nfrsvw] [-t vfstype] [-o options]
         special node
      A special device can be indicated by -L label or
         -U uuid.
```

If you enter command-line information incorrectly, Linux responds with information on the correct usage:

```
$ mount -d /dev/fd0<Enter>
mount:invalid option -d
Usage: mount [-hV]
       mount -a [-nfFrsvw] [-t vfstypes]
       mount [-nfrsvw] [-o options] special | node
       mount [-nfrsvw] [-t vfstype] [-o options]
        special node
       A special device can be indicated by -L label
       or -U uuid.
```

The Linux Documentation Project

The Linux Documentation Project (LDP) is made up of guides, HOWTOs, FAQs, and projects. Perhaps the best way to describe it is to quote from its manifesto, which you can read at *http: //www.metalab.unc.edu/LDP*, the Project's Web site. An excerpt follows:

> The Linux Documentation Project is working on developing free, high quality documentation for the GNU/Linux operating system. The overall goal of the LDP is to collaborate in all of the issues of Linux documentation. This includes the creation of "HOWTOs" and "Guides." We hope to establish asystem of documentation for Linux that will be easy to use and search. This includes the integration of the manual pages, info docs, HOWTOs, and other documentation.
>
> LDP's goal is to create the canonical set of free Linux documentation. While online (and downloadable) documentation can be frequently updated in order to stay on top of the many changes in the Linux world, we also like to see the same docs included on CDs and printed in books.
>
> The LDP is essentially a loose team of volunteers with minimal central organization. Anyone who would like to help is welcome to join in this effort. We feel that working together informally and discussing projects on our mailing lists is the best way to go. When we disagree on things, we try to reason with each other until we reach an informed consensus.

LDP Guides

The LDP's guides are book-length documents that cover many aspects of Linux operations. To access them, drill down through the LDP Web site at *http://www.linuxdoc.org* or go directly to them at *http://metalab.unc.edu/pub/Linux/docs/LDP/*.

The guides have been published also by O'Reilly & Associates and others. Currently available and maintained guides include the following:

▲ Securing and Optimizing Linux

▲ Rute Users Tutorial and Exposition

▲ Linux Administrator's Security Guide

▲ Linux System Administration Made Easy

▲ Linux System Administrator's Guide

▲ The Linux Kernel Module Programming Guide

▲ Installation and Getting Started Guide

▲ The Linux Kernel

▲ The Linux Kernel Hackers' Guide

Unmaintained documents are no longer updated by their original authors, nor by anyone else affiliated with the LDP, so they may have become invalid. The LDP keeps them in their present state because they believe that even an old document may be better than no document. That said, following are some older and unmaintained guides:

▲ The Linux Network Administrator's Guide

▲ The Linux Programmer's Guide

▲ The Linux User's Guide

HOWTOs

Linux *HOWTOs* are documents that explain specific topics rather than the broad subjects generally found in the guides. Following is a summary of available HOWTOs and their location:

▲ 184 HOWTOs at *http://metalab.unc.edu/pub/Linux/docs/HOWTO*

▲ 5 unmaintained HOWTOs at *http://metalab.unc.edu/pub/Linux/docs/HOWTO/unmaintained*

▲ 115 mini-HOWTOs at *http://metalab.unc.edu/pub/Linux/docs/HOWTO/mini*

Remember that unmaintained documents are not updated and might now be invalid.

If you want to create your own HOWTO or become the new custodian of an unmaintained HOWTO, contact the LDP through its Web site. Occasionally, HOWTOs are published in hardcopy format, such as in *Linux Undercover* (Red Hat, 1998).

Your distribution of Linux might include copies of HOWTOs. Look in directories named */usr/doc/HOWTO*, */usr/doc/HOWTO/mini*, or something similar. You will probably have to uncompress the HOWTO files before you can view them.

FAQs

As of this writing, the LDP has 15 sets of frequently asked questions (FAQs) on its Internet site at *http://www.linusdoc.org* and also at *http://metalab.unc.edu/pub/Linux/docs/faqs*.

At one time, the LDP suggested that any new HOWTO documents also include a set of FAQs, because readers of the documents often have questions about the documents themselves or about how the document instructions relate to their own systems. Although the LDP no longer states that explicitly, we think it's still a good idea.

Your Linux software distribution might have FAQs as well; look for them in the installation manual and in directories named */usr/doc/FAQ* or something similar. You will probably have to uncompress the FAQ files before you can view them.

Projects

The LDP always has documentation and other projects under development. The projects are organized into several categories, such as hardware ports; kernel, drivers, file systems; papers; networking;

organizations and groups; Linux and free or open software; research and science groups; distributions; benchmarks and standards; and miscellaneous.

To get involved, check out the advice in the "Current Projects and Getting Involved" section of the LDP manifesto at *http://www.linuxdoc.org*.

Linux Books and Magazines

In the process of preparing course materials and writing this book, we were exposed to several sources of expertise and information, and we're grateful to them all. Here are some suggestions to help you find the ones you need:

▲ Check out the references presented at the Linux Web site at *http://www.linux.org/books*. You'll find a description and short evaluation of several current and prominent Linux reference books.

▲ Use your favorite Internet search engine. Type an appropriate description, such as *Linux books*, click the Search button, and watch your screen fill with Web site references. You will probably want to refine your search description to find something closer to your requirements. (Our search for *Linux books* returned well over a thousand responses, far too many to be useful.)

▲ Check out the book reviews in Linux paper magazines or online magazines, such as *Linux Weekly News* at *http://lwn.net*, or *Linux Planet* at *http://www.linuxplanet.com*.

▲ Use the search features at the e-commerce sites operated by large booksellers. You can get descriptions and order them as well.

▲ Take the time to visit your local computer bookstore or "big-box" bookstore. This is the best way to determine which books are best suited to your needs. Many establishments now allow you to peruse your potential purchase leisurely, even over an in-house beverage.

Although we're reluctant to recommend any particular Linux book out of the many available, we do suggest reading the following:

▲ *Operating Systems: Design and Implementation*, 2nd ed., by Andrew S. Tanenbaum and Albert S. Woodhull (Prentice Hall). Tanenbaum also maintains a MINIX Web site at *http://www.cs.vu.nl/~ast/minix.html*.

▲ *The UNIX Programming Environment*, by Brian Kernighan and Rob Pike (Prentice Hall Computer Books). These two Bell Labs researchers were heavily involved with the development of UNIX. This book, which presents the unique features of the UNIX design philosophy, is a classic.

Several Linux journals are listed in the Table 3.1. All are available as online magazines, and the first three are available in hard copy, too. You may already have heard of some of them, such as the *Linux Journal*, which has been publishing for five years or so. The others are similar in approach.

Table 3.1 Linux Online Magazines

Title	Web site
Linux Journal	http://www2.linuxjournal.com
Linux Magazine	http://www.linux-mag.com
Maximum Linux Magazine	http://www.maximumlinuxmag.com
Linux Planet	http://www.linuxplanet.com
Linux Weekly News	http://lwn.net
Linux Today	http://linuxtoday.com
Linux Center	http://www.portalux.com
Linux Start	http://www.linuxstart.com
Linux Gazette	http://www.ssc.com/lg/
32BitsOnline.Com	http://www.32bitsonline.com
Linux Focus	http://www.linuxfocus.org
Penguin Magazine	http://www.penguinmagazine.com
ZDNet Linux Zone	http://linux.zdnet.com

As mentioned, almost every urban center or region has some type of free or inexpensive computer-oriented newspaper. They are a great source of up-to-date articles, contacts for support or user groups, and advertisements of all kinds. Support groups typically have email-type newsletters, chat groups or newsgroups, and mailing lists as well.

More Linux Information Sites on the Internet

So many valuable Linux-related sites are on the Internet that it is difficult to decide where to begin and just as difficult to determine where to stop! We have already mentioned several Internet sites, and this section describes a few more that we hope you will find interesting and beneficial.

Linux Online

The official Linux Web site, at *http://www.linux.org*, is one of the more obvious place to start. Everything you need to know about Linux in general is there, organized into the following categories: General Information, Distributions, Applications, Support, In the Media, Projects, Hardware, User Groups, Book Store, Vendors, Events, Services, and About Us. You link to most other the other significant sites through the categories. You can even link to *http://www.isc.tamu.edu/~lewing/linux*, which is the site of Larry Ewing, the creator of the official Linux penguin logo.

Linux Online in Canada

The *http://wwww.linuxanada.net* site is great. Its major attraction is that it has many direct links to other excellent Internet sites. Its categories are Linux Books, Linux User Groups, Linux Facts, Linux Discussions, Linux News, Biz Press, and Linux Software.

Software Sources

The following sites, which can be accessed from the two just-noted sites, bear special mention because they are reputable sources for Linux software and applications. All have a similar structure (articles, software, links to other sites, and so on):

- ▲ *http://news.freshmeat.net*
- ▲ *http://slashdot.org* (calls itself "News for Nerds. Stuff that Matters.")

- *http://metalab.unc.edu/linux-source* (the quintessential source for the latest Linux kernels)

X Windows Sources

The following three sites deal with X Window System (explained in detail in Chapter 15).

- *http://www.xfree86.org* is the master Web site for X Window System. It is organized in the following categories: Mirror Sites, Contents, News/Current Releases, Contributors, Download, FAQs, Resources, Sponsors, Feedback. You can find ftp download sites at *ftp://ftp.xfree86.org/pub/XFree86/3.3.3.6* and *ftp://ftp.xfree86.org/pub/XFree86/4.0*.

- *http://www.kde.org* is the Web site for K Desktop Environment (KDE), one of the more sophisticated X Window managers (mentioned in Chapter 15). The site is organized as follows: Hot Spot, General Information, User Information, Worldwide Sights, Developer Information, Events; Supporting KDE, Thanks; Family, FAQ; Download, News.

- *http://www.gnome.org* is the Web site for GNU Network Object Model Environment (GNOME), considered by many to be *the* modern X Window manager. Based entirely on free software, it has links to the GNOME software and Manifesto sites and is otherwise structured like the two previous sites.

Linux Newsgroups

Usenet newsgroups are a worldwide system of computers that store, update, and exchange collections of discussion text files, organized by category. A few Linux-oriented Usenet newsgroups follow:

- *alt.linux* presents alternative views of Linux

- *alt.os.linux.slakware* provides alternative views of the Slackware Linux distribution

- *comp.os.linux.advocacy* offers an ongoing (and at times heated) debate between those who favor Linux and those who don't

- *comp.linux.hardware* has questions, answers, and other discussions of Linux hardware of assorted types
- *comp.os.linux.misc* has more questions, answers, and discussions of Linux hardware and software
- *comp.os.linux.networking* offers discussions of Linux, networking, and communications
- *comp.os.linux.setup* presents questions, answers, and discussions related to Linux installation and configuration
- *linux.appletalk* is the place for discussions regarding the use of Linux and Apple's LocalTalk networking protocol

Linux mtools Sites

The following sites provide information, software, and services regarding `mtools` (see Chapter 4). The `mtools` utilities allow easier manipulation of DOS floppy diskettes using newer commands that are unlike the somewhat stilted, older-style UNIX commands:

- *http://mtools.linux.lu*
- *ftp://www.tux.org/pub/knaff/mtools*

Exercises

1. Access the man pages for the man command itself.

   `$ man man<Enter>`

   Read the text so that you can better understand the functionality of the man command. Which navigation key sequences would you use to do the following?

   - Move down one screen at a time: <Spacebar>
   - Move down one half screen at a time: d
   - Move up one half screen at a time: u
   - Move down one line at a time: down arrow key or <Enter>
   - Move up one line at a time: up arrow key
   - Search for occurrences of the text string *ormat:* /ormat
   - Search for the next occurrences of the same text string: n
   - Quit from the man page: q

2. Assume that you want to find the program that generates today's date. Use the slocate command to search on the keyword *date*.

   `slocate date`

   From the list produced, find the command that displays the date. What is the name of the command and what directory or directories is it in?

3. Having found the date command in Exercise 2, use man without options to obtain the correct syntax of the command.

   `man date`

   When you have finished with the man page, type q to exit from it.

4. Invoke info from the command line.

   `$ info<Enter>`

Navigate downward in the first screen until you find the `date` command and then select it. What is the name of the file from which the `date` information has been extracted? What is the name of this node? What is the name of the next node?

5. Using `info` navigation keys, go to the next node. Press the n key. Is this node's name the same as what you anticipated from reading the `date` page in Exercise 4?

6. Press the p key to go back as far as you can to the most-previous node in this file. What is the name of the most-previous node?

7. Exit from the `info` pages by using the q key.

NOTE: *Exercise 8 is specific to the X Window System. If you are running KDE, go to Exercises 9. If you want to skip exercises on X Window and KDE variants of Linux, continue with Exercise 10.*

8. Exercises for X Window System:

    a. At the command line, enter `startx` and then press <Enter> to invoke the X Window System. When X Window System starts, you'll probably be placed in a window titled xterm. If necessary, click to activate the window (that is, to turn the title bar to a bright color and to ready the window for input).

    b. Invoke the X Window version of `man` by typing the following in the window's command line:

    `xman &<Enter>`

    A small window titled Manual Browser appears with three buttons: Help, Quit, and Manual Page.

    c. Click the Manual Page button. The Manual Page window appears, containing `xman` information.

    d. Click the Sections menu and while holding down the mouse button, more the cursor to the System Commands entry. Release the mousc button. Another manual page appears with an alphabetical listing of system commands.

e. Scroll down, if necessary, and click the `date` command. Scroll up and down the new window to read about `date`. When you are finished, click Sections or Options and continue your investigation of `xman`.

f. When you are ready to return to the original `xterm` window, exit `xman` by clicking the X (the close button) in the upper-right corner of the window frame.

9. Exercises for KDE (the K Desktop Environment):

   ▲ Invoke KDE and, using its start button or equivalent, find and invoke `KDE Help`, which is the KDE online help browser. A Welcome window with three major categories appears.

   ▲ Under the KDE Help Contents category, click the System man page contents link. The Online Manuals window appears.

   ▲ Click Section 1 - User Commands. The Online Manuals - Section 1 window appears.

   ▲ Scroll up and down by clicking the mouse in the right scrollbar, until you see the `date` command. Click to select it. The `man` page for `date` appears.

   ▲ Practice navigating by clicking the various blue titles with underlines or by clicking the menus on the gray menu bar. For example, to go back to the original KDE Welcome window, click GoTo and then select Contents. When you are finished, click the File menu and select Close or Quit.

   ▲ To leave KDE altogether, use the KDE Start button and select Logout. You are returned to the Linux command-line prompt.

10. At the command line, invoke the help option for `mount`. How does Linux respond? Pay special attention to the options that Linux says can be used with `mount`.

11. Try to invoke `mount` but deliberately use an incorrect option. How does Linux respond?

Chapter 3: Linux Documentation and Support

12. Dial into the Internet or activate the Internet browser on your system. Go to the Linux Web site at *http://www.linux.org*. Navigate around and become familiar with this site. When did Linus Torvalds release Version 1.0 of the Linux kernel? What is the current featured version, and when was it released?

13. Go to the Linux Documentation Project site at *http://metalab.unc.edu/LDP/*. What is the date of this copy of the LDP Web site? What is the date of the master copy on *metalab.unc.edu*?

14. Go to the Web site of the *Linux Journal* at *http://www.linuxjournal.com* and navigate it until you have familiarized yourself. What is the journal's slogan?

15. Go to the *freshmeat.net* Web site at *http://news.freshmeat.net*. What is the name of the first software package listed at the top of their Web site, beneath the *freshmeat.net* banner? What is the title of the first editorial?

16. Go to *http://www.deja.com*. At the top of the site, click the Discussions link. In the box, type `comp.os.linux.setup`. On the next line, select "Search all discussions in: Complete" to make sure that you search through all relevant correspondence. Then click the Find button. What is the date of the most recent message and its title?

See Appendix B for answers.

Quiz

1. In how many ways can you invoke the usage facility? What are they?

2. Provide the Internet addresses for the basic Linux Web site and the basic X Window System Web site.

3. What is the name of the official Linux penguin?

4. Which of the following commands or options uses a different database than the other three?

    - ▲ `locate`
    - ▲ `info`
    - ▲ `man`
    - ▲ `Help/usage`

5. What combination of commands and options do you use from the command line when you want to print `man` information but you do not have a PostScript printer?

6. Match the environments with the appropriate information source command:

▲ K Desktop Environment	`xman`
▲ ASCII/command-line info	`info`
▲ Fvwm95 "Help"	`"Help"`

7. What are Usenet newsgroups?

See Appendix C for answers.

Chapter 4

Files and Directories in Linux

IN CHAPTER 3, WE DISCUSSED A FEW BASIC COMMANDS for finding information. In this chapter, we delve a little deeper into the everyday activities you will conduct on your Linux system. The topics include the structure and hierarchy of Linux file systems, navigating that file structure, managing files, using floppy disks (`ext2` and DOS formats), manipulating DOS files with the `mtools` utilities, and using the `touch` command. If you are a UNIX veteran, you might consider these topics elementary. However, try to take time to review these concepts and tasks because they are fundamental to creating and maintaining a proper Linux file and directory system.

File System Structure and Hierarchy

The Linux operating system does not impose any internal structure on the contents of a file, nor are any specific attributes required. Only the application or tool is concerned with a file's structure and contents.

File Types

In Linux, everything—including devices—is represented as a file. Linux can recognize the following file types:

▲ *Ordinary files* contain either text or code data. Text files are readable by users and can be displayed or printed. Code data, also known as *binary files,* are readable by the computer. Binary files may be executable.

▲ **Directories** contain information that the system needs to access all types of files, but they do not contain the actual data. Each directory entry represents either a file or a subdirectory. Directories and subdirectories constitute a method of storing files in some type of logical order (such as alphabetical or numerical).

▲ **Special files** usually represent devices used by the system. An application of special files appears in the "Path Names" section in this chapter.

Directory Contents

All information about a file, except its contents, is stored in the file's *inode* (index node). Although it's customary to refer to a directory as a type of envelope that contains entire subdirectories and files and their contents, in truth a directory is a unique type of file that contains only the information needed to access files or other directories. As a result, a directory occupies less space than other types of files.

A directory resembles a table of contents: It lists the names of files and subdirectories and their corresponding inode numbers. When users execute a command to access a file, they use the file name. The system consults the directory to match the file name with its corresponding inode number and then accesses the inode table, which holds information about the file's characteristics, including its location (see Figure 4.1). After the system knows the location of the file, the data can be located.

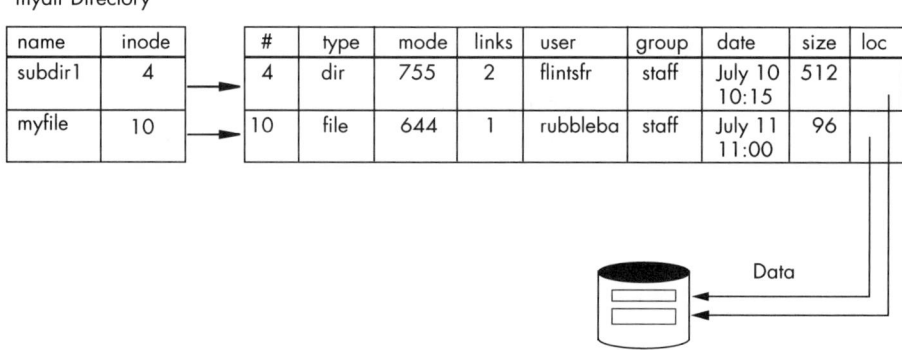

Figure 4.1: Directory contents.

The following categories of information are stored in the inode table:

▲ The file type (directory or file)

▲ The mode (directory or file permissions; see Chapter 6 for details)

▲ Links (which enable you to refer to a file by more than one name; see Chapter 5)

▲ The userid of the file's owner

▲ Group permissions

▲ The date the file was last accessed and modified

▲ The file size

▲ The file's location

Remember that the file name is stored in a directory, *not* in the inode table. Why not store the inode information in the directory and dispense with the inode table? Restricting information in the directory to file names and inode numbers simplifies directory management and allows for the efficient use of disk space.

Hierarchical Structure

The file structure depicted in Figure 4.2, called a *directory tree,* represents only part of a typical Linux file system. In this depiction, directory names appear in boxes, and file names are unboxed words.

The top of the structure is the root (/) directory. The root contains many directories that are critical in system operations. Root subdirectories depicted in Figure 4.2 are described in the Table 4.1.

You may also access files on other computers in the network. The details of this process are beyond the scope of this book. For now, just remember that from a user's perspective, the network is configured such that remote files appear to behave just like local files. The */home, /usr, /tmp,* and */var* directories are examples of directories whose files may be accessed by local and remote systems.

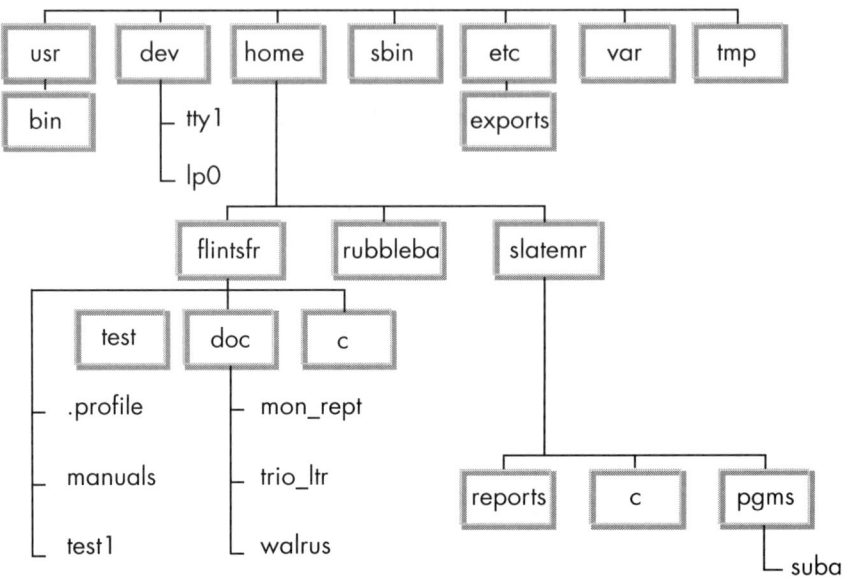

Figure 4.2: Linux directory tree.

Table 4.1 Root Subdirectories

Subdirectory	Description
/usr	System programs such as /usr/bin, which in turn contain user commands such as `ls`, `cat`, and `date`. Because the /usr directory generally contains system-related rather than user-related commands and utilities (despite its name), users do not have write access to this directory. In addition, because the files in this directory are system related, the directory is considered not very dynamic.
/dev	Special files that represent devices.
/home	User log-in directories and files. When a user is added to the system, he or she is allocated an individual subdirectory, the name of which is the same as the user's log-in name. When users log in, they are put in their own directory, and they may do whatever they want with it, such as create subdirectories within it and create, delete, move, copy, and rename files. Because users generally change their files regularly, the /home directory is considered quite dynamic.
/sbin	System utilities for system startup.

Continued

Table 4.1 Root Subdirectories (continued)

Subdirectory	Description
`/etc`	System configuration files used by system administrators.
`/var`	An abbreviation of variable, the *var* directory contains files that change with system activity. For example, this directory is typically used by or for many user-oriented programs, such as mail or printing.
`/tmp`	Holds files that are temporarily needed or created by applications and programs. For example, the `vi` editor (discussed in detail in Chapter 7) uses the */tmp* directory as a buffer space until the file being worked on is written to disk. Compiler programs use */tmp* to hold files written during compilation; when the compiler is finished, the files created there are eliminated.

Path Names

The purpose of a path name is to tell you the location of a file. You write a path name as a string of names separated by forward slashes (/). The rightmost name is a file name and can represent any type of file; the other names must be directories. A full path name, which is also referred to as an *absolute* path name, always begins with a forward slash (/). Path names that do not begin with a forward slash are relative.

The path names in Example 4.1 refer to files depicted in Figure 4.2. In the full path name, the first forward slash represents the root directory. In the relative path names, the current directory is presumed.

Example 4.1 ▼ Absolute and Relative Path Names

Full or absolute path name:

```
/home/flintsfr/doc/mon_rept
```

Relative path names (the current directory is */home/flintsfr*):

```
doc/mon_rept
./test1
../slatemr/pgms/suba
```
▲

NOTE: *Notice that the example contains two special files (those beginning with a single and a double dot), which were mentioned previously.*

In *./test1*, the dot (.) represents the current directory; in other words, it says "start in this directory and look for the file called *test1*." In the last example, *..//slatemr/pgms/suba*, the leading two dots represent the parent directory to the current directory, in effect saying, "go back up to the home directory, look in the *slatemr* directory for a directory called *pgms*, and then look there for a file called *suba*."

When you are trying to find a file, particularly in a complex structure, the single dot (.) and double dot (..) special files can save time by eliminating the need to describe the location of the file in relation to the root directory. They can be helpful also when programming an application if you do not know the absolute tree structure where the application may eventually be installed, but you do have a good idea where files are with respect to one another or to an executable.

Navigating the File Structure

Locate the Working Directory Path: pwd Command

The `pwd` (print working directory) command is a Linux/UNIX command for finding out which directory you are in—that is, where you are in the directory tree. This command always returns the full or absolute path name of the current working directory, as shown in Example 4.2. Without `pwd`, you would have no way of knowing which directory you are in. (Such information can be added to the command prompt, which we discuss later.)

Example 4.2 ▼ pwd

```
$ pwd<Enter>
/home/flintsfr
```

Change the Directory: cd Command

The `cd` (change directory) command allows you to navigate the directory structure. As with any commands that operate on directories, you can specify the relative or full path name. With relative path names, however, you *must* be certain of the directory you are working in. If you're not sure, use the `pwd` command. Here's the syntax:

```
cd [directoryname]
```

Using the `cd` command with no arguments automatically returns you to your home directory, the directory you were automatically placed in when you logged in to the system. This can be very handy or very confusing.

Example 4.3 ▼

cd

Suppose that you want to move from the current directory, */home/flintsfr*, to the */home/flintsfr/doc* directory. Here's how to do so using the relative path name:

```
$ cd doc<Enter>
```

To do so using the full path name:

```
$ cd /home/flintsfr/doc<Enter>
```

To go to your home directory:

```
$ cd<Enter>
```

To go to the parent directory of your current working directory:

```
$ cd ..<Enter>
```
▲

Managing Files

Create a Directory: mkdir Command

The `mkdir` (make directory) command creates new directories and names them according to the specified directory name. You may specify multiple directory names as long as you separate each by a space.

The syntax for the command follows:

```
mkdir [-m] directoryname(s)
```

Each new directory or subdirectory automatically contains the standard entries dot (.) and dot-dot (..). Use -m as an option before the chosen directory name to specify which permissions to set for the new directory when it is created. Ordinary users can create directories where they have write permission. (Permissions are discussed in Chapter 6.).

NOTE: *Unlike DOS, Linux does not allow you to abbreviate the* `mkdir` *command to* md.

Example 4.4 ▼

mkdir

Suppose you are in the root directory. Do the following to create a directory called *test* as a subdirectory of the */home/flintsfr* directory:

```
$ mkdir /home/flintsfr/test<Enter>
```
or
```
$ cd /home/flintsfr<Enter>
$ mkdir test<Enter>
```
▲

Remove a Directory: rmdir Command

Removing a directory involves two general steps. First, empty the directory of its contents; a directory is considered empty when it contains only the dot and double-dot entries. Second, remove the directory. The syntax is simple:

```
rmdir directoryname
```

Although you can be in the target directory to remove its contents, you can't be in the target directory when you intend to remove the directory itself. Two conditions must be met: The target directory

CHAPTER 4: FILES AND DIRECTORIES IN LINUX

must not be the working directory, and the target directory must be empty. Refer to Example 4.5.

Example 4.5 ▼

rmdir

To remove a directory that is not yet empty, do the following (and refer to Figure 4.2):

```
$ cd /home/flintsfr<Enter>
$ rm -r doc<Enter>
```

To remove an empty subdirectory while you're in */home/flintsfr*:

```
$ rmdir test<Enter>
```
▲

NOTE: *Linux does not display a screen message when the* `rmdir` *command is successful, so it is a good idea to make sure that the command worked as expected. To do so, execute the* `ls` *command on the parent directory. (See the "Listing Directories" section.)*

Create or Remove Multiple Directories Simultaneously

You can create two types of subdirectories. *Horizontal subdirectories* share the same parent directory. *Vertical* (or *recursive*) *subdirectories* are subdirectories of subdirectories of subdirectories. Figure 4.3 shows both types of subdirectories.

To create a horizontal subdirectory, you issue the `mkdir` command and list the desired subdirectories, with a space between each one. In Example 4.6, *dira, dirb,* and *dirc* become subdirectories of the *flintsfr subdirectory* (refer again to Figure 4.3).

Add the `-p` (path or parent) option to create vertical subdirectories. Thus, assuming that *dira, dirb,* and *dirc* were created as indicated in Example 4.6, you would type the following to create the vertical subdirectories *dird* and *dire* under *dira*:

```
mkdir -p dira/dird/dire
```

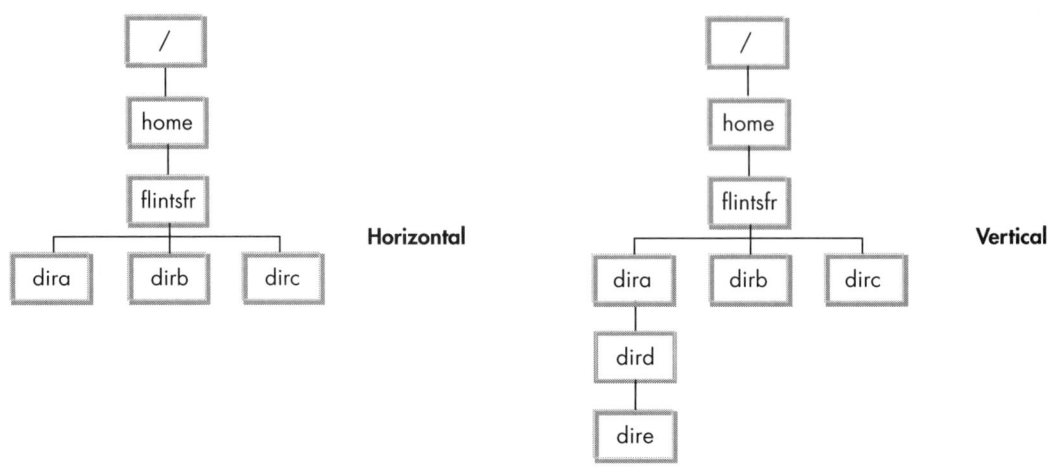

Figure 4.3: Creating multiple directories simultaneously.

Example 4.6 ▼   mkdir and rmdir

To create horizontal directories:

```
$ cd /home/flintsfr<Enter>
$ mkdir dira dirb dirc<Enter>
```

To create vertical directories:

```
$ mkdir -p dira/dird/dire<Enter>
```

To remove a directory and its subdirectories:

```
$ rmdir -p dira/dird/dire<Enter>                              ▲
```

In this example, the last specified directory, *dire*, is removed first, followed by *dird* and then *dira*. However, if you do not have write permission to one or more of the specified directories or if one or more of the directories are not empty, the command terminates at that point. For that reason, it is a good idea to check the status of your directories after the command has finished executing.

List a Directory: ls Command

The ls (list) command displays the contents of one or more directories. This command has several useful options, some of which are shown in action in Example 4.7. Here is the syntax:

ls [-a][-R][-l][*directoryname*]

If you do not specify a directory, the current working directory is examined. The -a option displays all hidden files. (For more information on hidden files, see the "Linux File Name Guidelines" section later in this chapter.) The -R option displays all subdirectories and their respective contents to the bottom of the directory tree, except the hidden files. Combining the -a and -R options results in a listing of subdirectories, files, and hidden files to the bottom of the directory tree.

By default, the information that the ls command returns is sorted in alphabetical order and no distinction is made between files and directories.

Example 4.7 ▼   ls

To list the contents of your home directory:

```
$ pwd<Enter>
/home/flintsfr
$ ls<Enter>
c doc manuals test test1
```

To list the contents of the same directory but this time list all files, including hidden files:

```
$ ls -a<Enter>
. .. .profile c doc manuals test test1
```

To list all files to the end of the directory tree:

```
$ ls -R<Enter>
c doc manuals test test1
c:
doc:
```

```
mon_rept  trio_ltr  walrus
test:
```
▲

The `ls` command with the `-l` (long listing) option displays file and directory information from the inode table, as shown in Example 4.8. It displays also the file or directory name from the files or directories themselves.

Example 4.8 ▼ Long Listings

```
$ ls -l<Enter>
total 5
drwxrwxr-x  2  flintsfr  staff  1024  Aug 26 10:18  c
drwxrwxr-x  2  flintsfr  staff   512  Sep 21 14:30  doc
-rwxrwxr-x  1  flintsfr  staff   320  Oct 14 09:15  manuals
drwxrwxr-x  2  flintsfr  staff   512  Sep 18 15:21  test
-rwxrwxr-x  2  flintsfr  staff   144  Oct 02 13:29  test1
```

The `total` amount refers to the number of 512-byte blocks allocated to the files in the directory. Using the `-li` options will also display the inode number:

```
$ ls -li test1<Enter>
29-rwxrwxr-x 2 flintsfr staff 144 Oct 02 13:29 test1
```
▲

Refer to to Table 4.2 for an explanation of the output from the `ls -l` command.

Table 4.2 Output from the ls -l Command

Field 1	Field 2	Field 3	Field 4	Field 5	Field 6	Field 7	Field 8
drwxrwxr-x	2	flintsfr	staff	1024	Aug 26	10:18	c
-rwxrwxr-x	2	flintsfr	staff	144	Oct 02	13:29	test1

▲ *Field 1* represents the file, directory, and permission bits. File and directory permissions are covered in Chapter 6. For now, we'll just point out that a *d* in the first position indicates a directory and a hyphen (-) in the first position indicates a file.

▲ *Field 2* is the link count. For directories, the link count indicates the number of subdirectories in that directory. Directories always have a link count of at least 2 (for . and ..). The link count for files indicates the number of names given to a single file. When you enter the command `rm filename`, for instance, you reduce the link count for a file by 1. A file is removed only when its link count reaches 0. For a discussion of linking and removing files, see Chapter 5.

▲ *Field 3* is the user name of the person who owns the entry (the file or directory). The owner is generally the person who created the entry, but ownership can be transferred.

▲ *Field 4* is the name of the group for which group protection privileges are in effect. Groups are generally created to organize users based on job description, organizational structure, project assignment, and so on, and their privileges determine the files and directories to which the group has access. Every user belongs to at least one group. The user in Example 4.8 is assigned to the group *staff*. We touch briefly on group concepts in Chapter 6, when we discuss file and directory permissions

▲ *Field 5* is the character count of the entry. Note that directory space is allocated in 512-byte increments. Thus, just looking at the output here will not necessarily give you a good idea of the number of files or subdirectories in the directory in question. Note that you don't make the directory allocation size smaller when you delete files. To decrease the size of a directory, you must move files to newer, smaller directories.

▲ *Fields 6 and 7* indicate the date and time that the contents of the file or directory were last modified. Other `ls` command options display other time attributes (for example, `-u` displays the last access time to the file and `-c` displays the time the inode was modified).

▲ *Field 8* is the name of the entry, whether file or directory.

Regarding the `ls -li` command, knowing the inode number is not important to a typical user. The functions of various file manipulation commands (such as `mv` and `cp`), however, are better understood if inode tables and the information in them are understood first.

Display Directory Information: ls and stat Commands

The `ls` (list) and `stat` (statistics) commands may be used to display information about files and directories because Linux treats directories as files for these purposes. In Example 4.9, the `ls` command displays inode table information. As shown in the example, the options `-l`, `-d`, and `-i` result in a long listing, with inode information and the inode number in the first displayed field.

Example 4.9 ▼ ls for Directories

To get a long listing with inode information and the inode number in the first displayed field:

```
$ ls -ldi mydirectory<Enter>
51 drwxr-xr-x  2  flintsfr  staff 512 May 18 15:22
   mydirectory                                         ▲
```

Linux systems maintain three timestamps for files and directories. Following are additional options you can use with `ls` to display each of these timestamps:

▲ `ls -lu` displays the access time

▲ `ls -l` displays the modification time

▲ `ls -lc` displays the updated time

The `stat` command displays inode information for a specified file or directory. The syntax is

    stat *directoryname*

In the `stat` results shown in Example 4.10, look at the `Access`, `Modify`, and `Change` lines. `Access` means the file has been read or written to and indicates the time and date when that last happened. When a file is read but no changes are made to it, the access time is changed, but not the modification or change times. `Modify` means the contents of the file or directory have been changed and indicates the time and date when that last happened. `Change` means the inode information has been changed and indicates the time and date when that last happened.

Example 4.10 ▼ stat

To get inode information for a specified directory:

```
$ stat mydirectory<Enter>
File: "mydirectory"
Size: 512              Filetype: Directory
Mode: (0775/drwxr-xr-x) Uid: ( 501/ flintsfr) Gid:
    ( 501/ staff)
Device: 10,8   Inode: 51    Links: 2
Access: Wed  Jul 12  18:13:21  2000 (00000.20:33:04)
Modify: Mon  Jul 10  13:22:17  2000 (00001.15:44:58)
Change: Mon  Jul 10  13:22:17  2000 (00001.15:44:58) ▲
```

Linux File Name Guidelines

Following are some guidelines and rules for creating file names in Linux:

- ▲ *Describe the file's content.* A file name should indicate what the file contains. However, make sure you do not create confusion when putting similar, but not identical, files in different directories.

- ▲ *Use only alphanumeric characters and selected symbols.* You may use all letters in the alphabet as well as numerals in file names. Letters may be uppercase, lowercase, or a combination. In addition, the following symbols can be used: number sign (#), at sign (@), underscore (_), plus sign (+), and hyphen (-).

- ▲ *Do not use embedded spaces.* Spaces should not be used within a file name because they might interfere with subsequent command execution, resulting in syntax errors. You *are* allowed to create a file with spaces if you enclose its name in single or double quotation marks (that is, *"filename"*, or *'filename'*). We strongly suggest that you not do this; think of the syntax you would have to use to execute commands on such file names.

▲ ***Do not use shell metacharacters.*** The following characters are not allowed because of their use in their use in command execution, system calls, and so forth: asterisk (*), question mark (?), greater than and less than signs (> or <), forward slash and backslash (/ and \), semicolon (;), ampersand (&), exclamation point (!), open and close brackets ([and]), vertical pipe (|), single and double quotation marks (' and "), and open or close parentheses, (and). If you inadvertently include one of these characters, the shell's interpretation will be unreliable and inconsistent.

▲ ***Do not begin with a plus sign or hyphen.*** You may use the plus sign (+) and hyphen (-) within a file name, but do not use them to begin the file name.

▲ ***Do not use command names.*** You should not name a file using a command name, unless you are creating an executable program file. The inadvertent use of a command might wreak havoc in a file system.

Other file name characteristics you should keep in mind follow:

▲ ***File names are case sensitive.*** Although potentially confusing, this requirement can result in increased flexibility.

▲ ***File names have a maximum length of 255 characters.*** Unlike some UNIX-based systems, Linux does not restrict file names to 14 characters. However, we recommend that you keep file names to a reasonable length, such as 16 characters. Bear in mind that some applications work with only 8-dot-3 file names (that is, *xxxxxxxx.xxx*, or 8-character file names and 3-character extensions), such as DOS file names. To ensure compatibility with other environments—if that is a concern—consider restricting file name length and format.

In addition, some applications append their own extensions or suffixes (such as *.tmp* or *.sam*) to denote a specific file type, so your file name conventions may have to accommodate this practice.

If the file name begins with a dot (.), the file name will be hidden from the standard ls *commands.* Linux/UNIX allows dots as legitimate file name characters as long as they are wholly contained within the file name; the system does not presuppose anything about the file based on the location of the dot. Some applications that run on Linux/UNIX, however, do not recognize the dot as part of the file name and therefore might react unpredictably when faced with such names.

Accessing Floppy Disks

Many users, especially new or ex-DOS and ex-Windows users, do not know that they may use floppy disks with Linux/UNIX. Although many of us work with UNIX-type systems in large networks and have abandoned *sneaker netting* (the fine old art of moving data by carrying it on floppy disks), some users still require it. In this section, we create Linux-like `ext2` and DOS file systems on floppies.

ext2 File Systems

You can create and manipulate files on floppies in as many ways as the half-dozen types of file systems that Linux provides. The `ext2` file system procedure described in this section should be used on floppies moving from one Linux-like system to another.

We will start at the beginning and format a floppy disk. Insert the floppy disk into your floppy disk drive. Then, as root or as an ordinary user, type

```
fdformat /dev/fd0H1440<Enter>
```

You must specify that the floppy disk is in device */dev/fd0*, that is, the first floppy disk drive. (For the second floppy drive, you would specify */dev/fd1*.) You enter H1440 (with no space between this specification and the */dev/fd0* device name) to tell the system that */dev/fd0* contains a 3.5-inch high-density floppy disk with a capacity of 1.44 MB. If your floppy disk is of another type, refer to the `fdformat` man page for the appropriate description.

When the system executes the command, it responds with

```
Double-sided, 80 tracks, 18 sec/track. Total capacity
   1440 kB.
Formatting ... (counts to 80) done
Verifying  ... (also counts to 80) done
```

Now that the floppy is formatted, the next step is to create a file system on it. Linux provides half a dozen or so types of file systems that you can create on a floppy. In the following, we create an `ext2` file system, to be compatible with the `ext2` file systems created on the hard disk during the Linux installation. As root user, type

```
# mkfs -t ext2 /dev/fd0<Enter>
```

Ordinary users should use `/sbin/mkfs` rather than the `mkfs` command alone, because `/sbin` is probably not in their `$PATH`.

The `-t` option indicates that the user is about to tell the system what kind of file system to install on the floppy disk. The option is followed by `ext2`, the default Linux file system type. After you enter the command, the system executes it and responds with

```
mke2fs 1.12, 9-Jul-98 for EXT2 FS 0.5b, 95/08/09
Linux ext2 filesystem format
Filesystem label=
360 inodes, 1440 blocks
72 blocks (5.00%) reserved for the super user
First data block=1
Block size=1024 (log=0)
1 block group

8192 blocks per group, 8192 fragments per group
360 inodes per group
Writing inode tables: done
Writing superblocks and filesystem accounting informa-
    tion: done
```

Simply put, the system has told you that it has finished formatting the floppy disk and is now awaiting further instruction. (For an explanation of the output, which is beyond the scope of this book, refer to one of the sources of information mentioned in Chapter 3.)

The next step is to *mount* the file system, which means that the system must be told to make the newly defined file system (the newly formatted floppy disk, in this case) part of its tree-like file hierarchy. Enter this command:

```
# mount -t ext2 /dev/fd0 /mnt/floppy<Enter>
```

NOTE: *It's best and easiest to do this as a root or superuser. For security reasons, an ordinary user is not allowed to mount or unmount a file system. An ordinary user can get around this, however, using* `mtools`, *which we discuss later.*

The `mount` command tells the system to make the `ext2` file system found on */dev/fd0* part of the total file system and to refer to the newly added file system as */mnt/floppy* (that is, a subdirectory called */floppy* in a subdirectory called */mnt*, all part of the root directory—you could call it other names, but this is the Linux convention). If you have entered everything correctly, the system will do as you command and respond with another root prompt.

To view what has occurred thus far, enter the following:

```
# ls -la /mnt/floppy<Enter>
```

The system responds with

```
total 14
drwxr-xr-x 3   root root    1024  Apr 28 16:36 .
drwxr-xr-x 4   root root    1024  Jan 31 11:31 ..
drwxr-xr-x 2   root root   12288  Apr 28 16:36 lost+found
```

The system has already named the largest subdirectory on the floppy *lost+found*. You can change its name if you want.

You are now ready to use the floppy disk as part of your file system, using Linux commands. Remember, though, that you can't just pop the floppy disk out when you are finished. First you have to unmount the file system on the floppy disk from the total file system. To do that, type

```
# umount /mnt/floppy<Enter>
```

or

```
# umount /dev/fd0<Enter>
```

Note that the command is `umount`, not unmount. Again, you have to be a root user to unmount a file system, just as you have to be a root user to mount it in the first place. In addition, you can't unmount from the floppy diskette's own file directories; you have to `cd` out of them. Otherwise, you will get a *device busy* error message.

Now you can remove the floppy. When you want to use it again, you must reenter the `mount` statement to get Linux to recognize it again, but you don't have to edit the */etc/fstab* file because those specifications remain.

DOS File Systems

To sneaker net between a Linux system and a DOS file system, you use commands similar to those discussed in the preceding section. We will start again with formatting a floppy disk.

As root or an ordinary user, type the following:

```
# fdformat /dev/fd0H1440<Enter>
```

You must specify that the floppy disk is in the */dev/fd0* device (that is, your first floppy disk drive). You told the system H1440 (with no space between this specification and the */dev/fd0* device name), which means that */dev/fd0* contains a 3.5-inch high-density diskette with a capacity of 1.44 MB. The system executes the command and responds with the following:

```
Double-sided, 80 tracks, 18 sec/track. Total capacity
   1440 kB.
Formatting ... (counts to 80) done
Verifying  ... (also counts to 80) done
```

Now that the floppy disk is formatted, the next step is to create an MS-DOS file system on it and specify that the floppy disk is in */dev/fd0*.

```
# mkdosfs /dev/fd0<Enter>
```

Again, we've shown you how to do it as root. The system responds with

```
mkfsdos 2.2 (06 Jul 1999)
```

The next step is to mount the file system—that is, make the newly defined file system (the just-formatted floppy disk, in this case) part of the overall system file hierarchy. Now you can use the `mount` command with one of a choice of options. For example, you can use

```
# mount -t msdos /dev/fd0 /mnt/floppy<Enter>
```

to tell the system to mount the `fd0` device as part of the file system and refer to it as the */mnt/floppy* directory (that is, a subdirectory called */floppy* under a subdirectory called */mnt*, which is under the root directory).

> **NOTE:** *You should do this only as the root user. For security reasons, an ordinary user is not allowed to mount or unmount a file system. An ordinary user can get around this, however, using* `mtools`, *which we discuss later.*

You also told the system that the format of the files in the directory will be DOS but not the type of DOS that supports long file names. If that is not suitable—for example, if you want to mount the type of DOS files developed under Windows 9*x*, which do have long file names—use the following:

```
# mount -t vfat /dev/fd0 /mnt/floppy<Enter>
```

If you've entered everything correctly, the system will do as you command and simply respond with another root prompt.

To check on what has occurred thus far, type the following:

```
# ls -la /mnt/floppy<Enter>
```

If the floppy does not contain any files yet, the system responds with

```
total 8
drwxr-xr-x 2   root root   7168   Dec 31 1969    .
drwxr-xr-x 4   root root   1024   Jan 31 11:31   ..
```

If the floppy contains files, you get the same response along with a listing of those files. Whenever you mount a DOS diskette in this manner, we recommend that you include either the `-t msdos` option or the `-t vfat` option because it is more likely that `ext2` may already be specified in */etc/fstab* if a floppy diskette has ever been used with that system. Specifying `msdos` on the command line here overrides any specification already in */etc/fstab*.

Now you're ready to use the floppy disk as part of your file system, using Linux commands. When you are finished, you can't simply pop out the floppy disk. You must first unmount the file system on the floppy disk from the total file system. Enter the following:

```
# umount /mnt/floppy<Enter>
```

or

```
# umount /dev/fd0<Enter>
```

Again, you must be the root user to unmount a file system, just as you have to be a root user to mount it in the first place. In addition, you can't be in the floppy diskette's own file system when you try to `umount`; if you are, you will get that frustrating *device busy* error message.

The mtools Utilities — *version 3.9.6 installed.*

The `mtools` utilities are a collection of UNIX utilities for creating, accessing, and manipulating DOS disks from Linux/UNIX without having to mount or unmount the DOS file systems (in our case, that means without having to mount and unmount DOS floppy disks). The `mtools` utilities are available in the public domain.

A copy of the `mtools` utilities might be packaged with your Linux distribution. If so, they probably work fine. But in the past, those utilities were unreliable and it was best to get the latest version of `mtools` from one of a few Web sites. If you find that the utilities don't work correctly, check out one of the following sites to download the latest version of `mtools` or the latest patches to your version. Note that more versions are available at the *ftp* site than at the *http* site:

▲ *http://mtools.linux.lu*

▲ *ftp://www.tux.org/knaff/mtools*

We recommend that you download the text files as well because they include the most up-to-date instructions for loading `mtools` on your system and an in-depth discussion of `mtools` in general.

Suppose you download the *mtools-3.9.7-1.i386.rpm* file from among the several formats and versions available. (Version 3.9.7 of `mtools` was released in early June 2000.) You can then install that version by entering

```
# rpm -U mtools-3.9.7-1.i386<Enter>
```

If you use another version, simply follow the instructions in the Internet site's *faq* text file on obtaining and loading alternate versions.

Basic mtools Features

The `mtools` commands are usually identical to DOS commands with the exception of the addition of an *m* prefix. (Some UNIX veterans refer to `mtools` commands as m commands.) The `mtools` commands follow the DOS convention of referring to DOS file systems as drives. For example, the first floppy disk drive is called the a: drive, and the first hard disk drive is customarily called the c: drive. DOS can even refer to a drive by more than one (letter) designation or, in the case of multiple floppy drives, using one drive letter to refer to both drives (in a predetermined search order). Furthermore, DOS file names are generally preceded by the drive letter and a colon; UNIX file names do not have such prefixes.

If you are accessing only the floppy drives, `mtools` allows you to do so without mounting and unmounting their file systems, and you usually don't have to modify the */usr/local/etc/mtools.conf* file. You must ensure that this text file is properly configure, however, if you will be accessing DOS hard disk partitions and DOS emulation image files.

If you find it necessary to use pattern matching, remember that the `mtools` utilities use Linux/UNIX syntax and conventions (for example, use * as a wildcard instead of DOS's *.*). Also, to add options to commands, use a hyphen (-) instead of DOS's slash (/).

mtools Commands

The `mtools` utilities have an extensive `man` page, and a great deal of information is available on the Internet sites listed previously.

We present only a sampling of the commands available in `mtools`. These commands resemble those used frequently by DOS users and DOS file system administrators. (Don't worry, the `mtools` commands are not case sensitive.) The following list provides a quick introduction to the syntax and purpose of these commands:

▲ `mattrib [+/-flags] dosfilename(s)`
   Changes file attributes.

- ▲ `mcd dosdirectory`
  Changes the `mtools` working directory on the DOS drive.

- ▲ `mcopy [options] dossourcefile dostargetfile`
  Copies DOS files to and from UNIX.

- ▲ `mcopy [options] dossourcefile dostargetfile`
  Deletes a DOS file.

- ▲ `mdeltree [options] dosdirectory(ies)`
  Removes a DOS directory and all its subdirectories and their contents.

- ▲ `mdir [-options] dosfilename(s)`
  Displays the contents of a DOS directory.

- ▲ `mformat [-options] dosdrive`:
  Creates a low-level format to a floppy disk and adds a DOS file system.

- ▲ `mmd [-options] dosdirectory(ies)`
  Creates a DOS subdirectory.

- ▲ `mmove [-options] dossourcefile dostargetfile`
  Moves or renames an existing DOS file or subdirectory.

- ▲ `mrd [-options] dosdirectory(ies)`
  Removes a DOS subdirectory.

- ▲ `mren [-options] dossourcefile dostargetfile`
  Moves or renames an existing DOS file or subdirectory.

Refer to the `man` pages and other sources of information for these options. Remember that all pattern matching follows UNIX syntax and conventions, not DOS's. With commands such as `mcopy` and `mmove`, you can determine whether the files are going from a DOS file system to a UNIX file system by seeing if the *sourcefile* or *targetfile* has the DOS letter-drive designation.

touch Command

The `touch` command, which is shown in Example 4.11, has two purposes. If the specified file name does not yet exist, the command creates a *zero-length* (that is, empty) file. If you don't want the creation to take place, use the -c option. If the file or directory does exist, the last modification date and time (displayed with the ls -l command) is updated to reflect the current date and time, unless you specify a preferred time variable. Here is the syntax:

```
touch [-c] filename
```

The touch command can be helpful when you are about to invoke an application against one or more files, and that application checks the files' modification times before taking some action (such as backup or restore) against the files. By using touch alone or with its options, you can alter the dates on certain files so that they will or will not be affected by the application.

Example 4.11 ▼ touch

Assume that you are in the /home/*slatemr*/*pgms* directory (refer to Figure 4.2) and you want to create a zero-length file called *newfile* and change the access date on the existing *suba* file.

First, check the existing situation:

```
$ ls -l<Enter>
-rwxrwxr-x 1 slatemr staff 320 Jan 14 07:30   suba
$ date<Enter>
Wed Aug 3 16:53:46 CST 2000
```

Now make your changes and check your results:

```
$ touch suba<Enter>
$ ls -l<Enter>
-rwxrwxr-x 1 slatemr staff 320 Feb 3 16:54 suba
$ touch newfile<Enter>
$ ls -l<Enter>
-rw-r--r-- 1 slatemr staff   0 Feb 3 16:54 newfile    ▲
```

Exercises

1. Using the `pwd` command, verify that you are in your home directory (the directory you are placed in when you first log in to the system).

   `$ pwd<Enter>`

2. Change your current directory to the root directory.

   `$ cd /<Enter>`

3. Verify that you are in the root directory.

   `$ pwd<Enter>`

   Request a simple listing of the files in that directory.

   `$ ls<Enter>`

   Then request a long listing of the files in that directory.

   `$ ls -l<Enter>`

4. Issue the `ls` command with the `-a` and `-R` options.

   `$ ls -a<Enter>`
   `$ ls -R<Enter>`

   What is the effect of each option?

   NOTE: *The* `-R` *option results in extensive output. After you have seen enough, press* `<Ctrl>-c` *to end command execution.*

5. Return to your home directory and list its contents, including hidden files.

   `$ cd<Enter>`
   `$ ls -a<Enter>`

6. Create a directory in your home directory called *mydir*. Then display a long listing of both */home/directoryname/mydir* and the parent directory of *mydir*. What are the sizes of each directory?

CHAPTER 4: FILES AND DIRECTORIES IN LINUX

7. Change to the */home/mydirectory/mydir* directory. Use the `touch` command to create two zero-length files called *myfile1* and *myfile2* in your *mydir* directory.

   ```
   $ cd mydir<Enter>
   $ touch myfile1<Enter>
   $ touch myfile2<Enter>
   ```

8. Display a long listing of the contents of your *mydir* directory. What are the sizes of *myfile1* and *myfile2*?

   ```
   $ ls -l<Enter>
   ```

   View the long listing again, but this time display the inode numbers too. What are the inode numbers of each file?

   ```
   $ ls -li<Enter>
   ```

9. Change back to your home directory and issue the `ls -R` command to view your directory tree.

   ```
   $ cd<Enter>
   $ ls -R<Enter>
   ```

10. Use the `stat` command to view the inode information in your *mydir* directory. Why might the "Last Accessed" date be more current than the other two dates?

    ```
    $ stat mydir<Enter>
    ```

11. Use the `rmdir` command to remove the *mydir* directory. Does it work?

    ```
    $ rmdir mydir<Enter>
    ```

    NOTE: *To remove a nonempty directory, you must use the* `rm -r` *command, not the* `rmdir` *command. For more on* `rm -r`*, refer to Chapter 5.*

    ```
    $ rm -r mydir<Enter>
    ```

See Appendix B for answers

Quiz

1. Using the directory tree structure shown in Figure 4.2 and using /home as your current directory, how would you refer to the *suba* file in the */pgms* directory using both full and relative path names?

2. When specifying a path name, what is the difference between using double dots (..) and a single dot (.)?

3. What will the following command do?

   ```
   $ cd ../..<Enter>
   ```

4. What conditions must be satisfied for the `rmdir` command to complete successfully?

5. Match the following `ls` command options with their functions.

   ▲ `-a` Provides a long listing of files

   ▲ `-i` Lists hidden files

   ▲ `-d` Lists subdirectories and their contents

   ▲ `-l` Displays the inode number

   ▲ `-R` Displays information about a directory

6. Which of the following are valid file names?

   ▲ *!*

   ▲ *aBcDe*

   ▲ *-myfile*

   ▲ *myfile*

   ▲ *my.file*

   ▲ *my file*

   ▲ *.myfile*

7. Referring to Figure 4.2, assume that your current working directory is */home/flintsfr* and that you entered the following command:

   ```
   $ mkdir test<Enter>
   ```

   What happens? Why?

8. Referring again to Figure 4.2, assume that you are in the directory called */home/rubbleba*. What is the difference in the results after issuing the following commands?

   ```
   mkdir dir1/dir2/dir3
   ```

   ```
   mkdir dir1 dir2 dir3
   ```

See Appendix C for answers.

Chapter 5

Using Files in Linux

THIS CHAPTER DESCRIBES SEVERAL ASPECTS OF FILE MANIPULATION, including copying files, moving files, and referencing a file by more than one name. We also show you how to look at the contents of a file page by page, rather than as a fast-scrolling display on your screen. The chapter closes with that all-important file manipulation function: printing files.

Copying and Moving Files

Users and system administrators alike consider printing to be the most important file manipulation function. That's certainly true from the standpoint of accomplishments in the workplace, but more goes into those accomplishments than simply printing. For example, you might print a draft document for review, finalize it, and then print the document again. But you probably performed a lot of file manipulation before that draft review or crowning moment. And you probably did more file manipulation after; perhaps you copied the document or moved the file in the directory for housecleaning, security, sharing, or collaboration.

Copy a Single File: cp Command

Superficially, the `cp` (copy) command appears to be fairly straightforward:

```
cp source target
```

You follow the command with the source file name (if the file is not in the current working directory, you must specify either the relative or full path name) and the target (also called the destination). See Example 5.1.

WARNING: *If the* cp *target is the name of a file that already exists, the file is overwritten. No error or notification message appears. To prevent this and have the system prompt the user, use the* -i *option (for interactive) with the* cp *command.*

The cp command has many options. We recommend that you check the man pages. Be careful, though: The cp man page states that it is no longer being maintained, so the information could be inaccurate or incomplete. You might want to look at other sources of information as well. For example, you could check out the help utility by typing the following:

```
$ cp -- h | more<Enter>
```

Example 5.1 ▼

cp for Single Files

To create a copy of the */home/slatemr/pgms/suba* file, name the copy *programa*, and install the copy in the */home/flintsfr/doc* directory:

```
$ pwd<Enter>
/home/flintsfr/doc
$ cp /home/slatemr/pgms/suba programa<Enter>
```
▲

Example 5.1 might be a little misleading for new users. You may change the name of the source file in flight, as seen in the example, only if the target directory is also the current working directory. Otherwise, you must execute a separate renaming process (if such is desirable) after the copy of the file has arrived. Renaming files is discussed later in this chapter.

Copy Multiple or Special Files: cp Command

When copying multiple files, the target must be a directory:

```
cp file1 file2 . . . target_dir
```

Chapter 5: Using Files in Linux

Note that the copies will have the same name as the originals.

To recursively copy a directory and its files and subdirectories, including the files within the subdirectories, use the `cp -R` command. For example:

```
$ cp -R /home/flintsfr/mydir /home/flintsfr/newdir<Enter>
```

Using `cp -R` recursively copies the data in the source to the target, thus allowing the replication of complete data trees. As indicated in Example 5.2, this is also an opportunity to use relative path names as well as the . and .. special files mentioned in Chapter 4.

Example 5.2 ▼ cp for Multiple and Special Files

Copy */home/flintsfr/doc/programa* and */home/flintsfr/test1* to the */home/flintsfr/c* directory:

```
$ cd /home/flintsfr<Enter>
$ cp doc/programa test1 c<Enter>
```

Copy */home/flintsfr/doc/trio_ltr* to the */home/flintsfr/c* directory, retaining the same file name:

```
$ cd doc<Enter>
$ cp trio_ltr ../c<Enter>
```
▲

What effect does `cp` have on inode information? All information on the source file remains unchanged, except the last access time and date are updated. New inode numbers and entries are also created for the new files.

Move and Rename Files: mv Command

Like the `cp` command, the `mv` command appears straightforward:

```
mv source target
```

The `mv` command is followed by the source file name (you must specify the relative or full path name if the file is not in the current working directory) and the target. See Example 5.3. If you are moving more than one file, the target *must* be a directory for the command to execute; in addition, the files retain their original names.

WARNING: *If the* mv *target is the name of an existing file and you have the correct permissions set for that file and directory, the file is overwritten. No error or notification message appears. To prevent this and to cause the system to prompt the user, use the* -i *option with the* mv *command.*

Example 5.3 ▼   mv for Moving Files

Move */home/flintsfr/doc/mon_rept* to */home/flintsfr/c* and retain the same file name:

```
$ cd /home/flintsfr<Enter>
$ mv /doc/mon_rept/c<Enter>                                    ▲
```

The mv command has the same effect as cp on inode information. All information on the source file remains unchanged, except the last access time and date are updated. New inode numbers and entries are also created for the new files.

We recommend that you check the man pages for the options to the mv command. Note, however, that the pages are no longer being maintained, so the information could be inaccurate or incomplete. Therefore, you should check out other information sources as well, such as the help utility:

```
$ mv --h | more<Enter>
```

In Example 5.4, note the use of the relative path names in both entries and the use of the special file (.) in the second example.

Example 5.4 ▼   mv for Renaming Files

Move the */home/flintsfr/c/t.letter* file to the */home/flintsfr/doc* directory and then rename it to */home/flintsfr/doc/letter*:

```
$ cd /home/flintsfr/c<Enter>
$ mv t.letter ../doc/letter<Enter>
```

Move the /home/*flintsfr/doc/mon_rept* file to the /home/*flintsfr/c* directory but keep the same file name:

```
$ cd /home/flintsfr/c<Enter>
$ mv ../doc/mon_rept .<Enter>                    ▲
```

Linking Files: ln Command

The `ln` (link) command in its simplest form allows one file to have at least two different names in the tree structure. In other words, one copy of a file is referenced by multiple names. This type of link is called a *hard link*. The owner of the file, the file permissions, and the inode number remain the same for both copies. The syntax follows:

```
ln sourcefile targetfile
```

In Example 5.5, the /home/*flintsfr/manuals* file is linked to the /home/*rubbleba/manfiles* file.

Example 5.5 ▼   ln

The *manuals* file is in the directory /home/*flintsfr*. To refer to it as *manfiles* in the /home/*rubbleba* directory:

```
$ cd /home/flintsfr<Enter>
$ ln manuals /home/rubbleba/manfiles<Enter>      ▲
```

You can create another type of link, the *symbolic link*, by using the `-s` option with the `ln` command. Symbolic links are often used to allow two or more different directories in two or more different file systems to point to the same files. (Symbolic links are not discussed in this book.)

In Example 4.8 in Chapter 4, we briefly mentioned file links. You may want to refer to that example now that we've discussed the linking concept here.

Viewing File Contents

You may view the contents of a file in several ways. In this section, we cover the most popular methods: using the `cat` command and using the `more` and `less` commands.

List File Contents: cat Command

The `cat` (concatenate) command displays the contents of all specified files:

```
cat filename1 filename2 . . .
```

If you want `cat` to number all the lines in a file, use the `-n` option, like this:

```
cat filename -n<Enter>
```

The most obvious problem with `cat` is that with files longer than a single screen, the file scrolls until the bottom of the file is reached. You can mitigate this using

```
$ cat filename | more<Enter>
```

The | `more` (pipe-more) command causes `cat` to display the first screen of the file, and then leaves it to you to proceed line-by-line by pressing <Enter> or screen-by-screen by pressing <Spacebar>. If you choose *not* to use the pipe-more command, you can press <Ctrl>-s to freeze the scrolling of the screen during output and <Ctrl>-q to resume scrolling.

In a later chapter, we discuss how `cat` can read from something called *standard in* and display to something called *standard out*. You can use the `cat` command also to create a file by combining it with the redirect output symbol. Check the `man` pages and other sources for additional options.

Display a File a Page by Page: more and less Commands

The `more` and `less` commands display the contents of a file one page at a time. Both commands pause after each screenful of information is displayed.

When you use the `more` command, the following appears at the bottom of each screen:

```
--more--
```

with the exception of the last screenful of information, when the word *END* appears in parentheses. When `more` is reading from a file, a percentage appears alongside the *more* text indicating the proportion of the file already displayed.

The syntax couldn't be simpler:

```
more filename
```

To maneuver through the file, you use special keypresses, which are shown in Table 5.1.

Table 5.1 Moving through a File Displayed with the more Command

Keypress	Explanation
<Spacebar>	Moves down through the file one screen
<Enter>	Moves down through the file one line
<Ctrl>-c or <Ctrl>-z	Ends `more` and returns to the command line

The `less` command is a more recent (and not as well-known) improvement over `more`, although the syntax is the same:

```
less filename
```

You get more mobility when you examine files with the `less` command, as shown in the additional keypresses listed in Table 5.2.

Table 5.2 Moving through a File Displayed with the less Command

Keypress	Explanation
<Spacebar>	Moves down through the file one screen
<Enter>	Moves down through the file one line
d or u	Moves down or up through the file by half a screen
down or up arrow	Moves down or up through the file one line
<Ctrl>-c or <Ctrl>-z	Ends `less` and returns to the command line

When you use the `less` command, only a colon (:) appears at the bottom of each screenful, again with the exception of the last screenful.

The `more` and `less` commands have several handy options in their man pages. (In fact, the `man` pages themselves use the `less` command.)

Removing Files: rm Command

The `rm` command removes the entries for the specified file or files from a directory:

```
rm [-i] filename1 filename2 ...
```

The `-i` option is the interactive version of the `rm` command. You do not receive confirmation after the files are removed. Example 5.6 shows the `rm` command with and without the `-i` option.

Example 5.6 ▼

rm

Go to the */home/flintsfr/c* directory and remove the *mon_rept* file:

```
$ cd /home/flintsfr/c<Enter>
$ rm mon_rept<Enter>
```

Instead of just removing *mon_rept*, remove it interactively:

```
$ rm -i mon_rept<Enter>
rm: remove 'mon_rept'? y<Enter>
```
▲

You must have the required permissions to remove files and directories. You may remove not only files but also directories with the `rm` command. The syntax is similar:

```
rm [-i][-r] directoryname1 directoryname2 ...
```

You can also use the `-r` option for recursive removal of directories and their respective files. Be careful, though: Removal in this manner does not require directories to be empty before execution.

In Example 4.8 in Chapter 4, we briefly mention the effects of the `rm` command on files with links. You might want to refer back to that example now in light of the discussion here.

Printing Files: lpr, lpq, and lprm Commands

A printer queue mechanism allows more than one user to use the same printer without having to wait for the printer to become available. To queue a file for printing, ordinary users use the `lpr` command. The root user and superuser have additional printing commands at their disposal.

The `lpr` process sends a copy of the file to the */var/spool* directory, where the copy sits for however much time it takes for a free line-printing daemon, called `lpd`, to discover and print it. For a short queue, the timing is almost instantaneous; the print job seems to go straight to the printer.

The `lpr` command has many options and arguments, a few of which are shown in Example 5.7. We recommend that you check the `man` pages and other sources for more information. Two other important print commands, `lpq` and `lprm`, are shown in Example 5.8.

Example 5.7 ▼   lpr

To send a print job to the printer:

```
$ lpr filename1 filename2 ...<Enter>
```

To specify a printer other than the default printer, where `lp1` is the name of the alternate printer:

```
$ lpr -P lp1 filename<Enter>
```

For large files, where copying them to the spool directory would cause memory congestion, you could create a symbolic link between the spool directory and the file. When the print job is to be executed for the specified file name, the `lpd` daemon processes the link, which causes the file to be directly transferred in time for printing:

```
$ lpr -s filename<Enter>
```
▲

Example 5.8 ▼

lpq and lprm

To list print jobs in the print queue, display its current status:

```
$ lpq<Enter>
Rank          Owner        Job     Files        Total Size
active        root         301     walrus       255 bytes
active        Flintsfr     302     mon_rept     2537 bytes
```

To check the status of any queue that is not the default queue and assuming again that `lp1` is the alternate printer:

```
$ lpq -P lp1 filename<Enter>
```

To cancel a print job :

```
$ lprm jobnumber<Enter>
```

To find the job number, issue the `lpq` command beforehand. ▲

CHAPTER 5: USING FILES IN LINUX

Exercises

1. Using the `pwd` command, verify that you are in the home directory, /home/directoryname.

    `$ pwd<Enter>`

2. List the contents of your home directory, including its hidden files.

    `$ ls -a<Enter>`

3. View the contents of the */etc/motd* and */etc/passwd* files. Use the `cat`, `more`, and `less` commands to see how each command handles the output. The */etc/motd* file contains the message of the day (what you see after you first log in). The */etc/passwd* file contains a list of all the users authorized to use the system.

    `$ cat /etc/motd<Enter>`
    `$ cat /etc/passwd<Enter>`
    `$ more /etc/motd<Enter>`
    `$ less /etc/motd<Enter>`
    `$ more /etc/passwd<Enter>`
    `$ less /etc/passwd<Enter>`

4. Turn off the printer attached to your system. Print the */etc/motd* file on the system printer.

    `$ lpr /etc/motd<Enter>`

    Check the status of your print job.

    `$ lpq<Enter>`

    Turn the printer back on.

5. Copy the */bin/cat* file into your current (that is, home) directory.

    `$ cp /bin/cat   /home/teamxx<Enter>`
    or
    `$ cp /bin/cat . <Enter>`

6. Copy the */usr/bin/cal* file into your current (home) directory.

103

```
$ cp /usr/bin/cal /home/teamxx<Enter>
```
or
```
$ cp /usr/bin/cal . <Enter>
```

7. List the files in your current directory. You should see the two files you just copied.

    ```
    $ ls<Enter>
    ```

8. In your home directory, create a subdirectory called *bin*.

    ```
    $ mkdir bin
    ```

9. Move and rename the two files that you copied in Exercises 5 and 6 into your new subdirectory. Name them *mycat* and *mycal*, respectively.

    ```
    $ mv cat bin/mycat<Enter>
    $ mv cal bin/mycal<Enter>
    ```

10. Make the new subdirectory (*bin*) your current directory:

    ```
    $ cd bin<Enter>
    ```

11. List the contents of the directory to verify that the files were copied.

    ```
    $ ls<Enter>
    ```

12. Use the `mycat` command to list the *.bash_profile* file in your home directory.

    ```
    $ mycat ../.bash_profile<Enter>
    ```
    or
    ```
    $ mycat /home/teamxx/.bash_profile<Enter>
    ```

13. Make your home directory the current directory.

    ```
    $ cd<Enter>
    ```

14. Create another subdirectory in your home directory called *goodstuff*.

    ```
    $ mkdir goodstuff<Enter>
    ```

15. Copy a file called */etc/profile* into the new directory and name the new file *newprofile*.

    ```
    $ cp /etc/profile goodstuff/newprofile<Enter>
    ```

16. Use the `cat` command to look at the file.

    ```
    $ cat goodstuff/newprofile<Enter>
    ```

    Is it hard to read? Try the `more` and `less` commands.

    ```
    $ more goodstuff/newprofile<Enter>
    ```
    or
    ```
    $ less goodstuff/newprofile<Enter>
    ```

17. The *newprofile* file name is too long to input time after time. Change its name to *np*. List the contents of the *goodstuff* directory to make sure that you have accomplished the task.

    ```
    $ mv goodstuff/newprofile goodstuff/np<Enter>
    $ ls goodstuff<Enter>
    ```

18. This is a good place to check everything out. Starting from your home directory and working downward, display a hierarchical tree of your files and subdirectories.

19. Ensure that you are in your home directory. Remove the *goodstuff* directory.

    ```
    $ pwd<Enter>
    $ rmdir goodstuff<Enter>
    ```

    Could you do it? Why or why not?

20. Change to the *goodstuff* directory. Request a listing of the contents of the *goodstuff* directory, including any hidden files. Remove the files. Do another listing of the *goodstuff* directory, including the hidden files. Note that the . and .. files are still there. The directory is considered empty if these are the only two entries left.

    ```
    $ cd goodstuff<Enter>
    $ ls -a<Enter>
    $ rm np<Enter>
    $ ls -a<Enter>
    ```

Now remove the directory.

```
$ cd .. <Enter>
$ rmdir goodstuff<Enter>
```

See Appendix B for answers.

Quiz

1. What is the effect of executing the following commands in succession?

    ```
    $ cd /home/flintsfr<Enter>
    $ cp file1 file2<Enter>
    ```

2. What is the effect of executing the following commands in succession?

    ```
    $ cd /home/flintsfr<Enter>
    $ mv file1 newfile<Enter>
    ```

3. What is the effect of executing the following commands in succession?

    ```
    $ cd /home/flintsfr<Enter>
    $ ln newfile myfile<Enter>
    ```

4. List the commands that can be used to view the contents of a file.

5. Which of the commands listed in Question 4 is used automatically when you invoke man pages? How do you know?

See Appendix C for answers.

Chapter 6

Linux File Permissions

ALONG WITH PASSWORDS AND AUTHENTICATION SYSTEMS, file and directory access, or *permissions*, form the basis for system security. Directory permissions and file permissions are not the same, as you will learn in this chapter. We begin with a review of the -ls command, which you issue to view the existing file and directory permissions. In this chapter, we focus on information found in the first column—the permission bits—which provide a summary of the file mode of these entries. Then we focus on the commands and issues involved in setting and changing permissions.

Review of the ls -l Command

We described the output of the ls -l (long listing) command in detail in Chapter 4. Example 6.1 offers the basis for a quick review.

Example 6.1 ▼ ls -l

```
$ ls -l<Enter>
total 5
drwxrwxr-x 2 flintsfr staff 1024 Jan 26 10:18 c
drwxrwxr-x 2 flintsfr staff  512 Feb 21 14:30 doc
-rwxrwxr-x 1 flintsfr staff  320 Mar 14 09:15 manuals
drwxrwxr-x 2 flintsfr staff  512 Feb 18 15:21 test
-rwxrwxr-x 2 flintsfr staff  144 Mar 02 13:29 test1 ▲
```

Following is a description of the different fields of output:

- ▲ *Field 1* consists of the object identifier and file or directory permission bits.
- ▲ *Field 2* is the link count. Ordinary files have a link count of 1. Directories have a link count of 2. The `ln` command can increase the link count by 1; removing a file reduces its link count by 1. When the link count reaches 0, the file is removed.
- ▲ *Field 3* is the user name of the person who owns the entry.
- ▲ *Field 4* is the name of the group for which group protection privileges are in effect.
- ▲ *Field 5* is the character count of the entry.
- ▲ *Field 6* is the date and time the entry was last modified.
- ▲ *Field 7* is the name of the file or directory.

To display information about only a particular directory, use the `-d` option with the `ls -l` command. Directories are treated like ordinary files.

All about Permissions

When a user creates an entry, he or she becomes the owner of that entry. The owner generally wants to control who will have access to or use of the entry. Further, because it is possible to change permissions, the owner has the power to make an entry either more secure or more widely available.

Following is a breakdown of the permission bits:

```
    d      rwx     rwx     rwx
  entry   owner   group   others
```

The single character on the far left identifies the type of entry, or object. Types of entries include file, directory, linked file, block special file, character special file, symbolic link, named pipe, and socket.

The leftmost group of three permission bits—that is, the three next to the object identifier—refer to the permissions the owner has for the entry. The middle three are the permissions that the group has for the entry (the group that the entry will belong to). The rightmost three bits are the permissions held by other users who are not owners and not in the group to which the entry belongs.

For both files and directories, r is read, w is write, and x is execute. Although the names of these permissions are the same for files and directories, the permissions themselves have mean different things.

When viewing or establishing the permissions for an *ordinary file:*

- r permits the viewing of file contents
- w permits the changing and storing of file contents
- x permits the execution of the file (r is also needed)

For a *directory:*

- r permits viewing of files in the directory
- w permits the creation and removal of files in the directory (x is also needed)
- x permits a user to be in the directory (that is, to cd to a directory and to access files from the directory)

The x permission is required to access any files or subdirectories within a directory. This means that the x permission is required on all directories above the specific directory as well.

To remove a file from a directory, you need only w and x permissions for the directory. You don't necessarily need permissions on the file itself.

Changing Permissions: chmod Command

You use the chmod (change permission mode) command along with symbolic notation or numeric notation to specify changes relative to the existing permissions for a file or directory. How? By adding or deleting permissions.

Symbolic Notation

The syntax for changing permissions using symbolic notation with the `chmod` command follows:

`chmod symbolmode filename`

The `symbolmode` parameters are summarized in Table 6.1. You may specify multiple symbolic modes by separating them with commas. The operations are performed in the order in which they appear (from left to right).

Table 6.1 Symbolic Parameters

Mode	Definition	Mode	Definition	Mode	Definition
u	Owner of the file	+	Add permission	r	Read permission
g	Owner's group	–	Remove permission	w	Write permission
o	Other users on the system	=	Clear permission; set to mode specified	x	Execute permission
a	Owner, group, and others				

When you use the symbolic mode to specify permissions, the first set of parameters you specify set the permission field, as follows:

▲ u file owner (when discussing permissions, owner permissions are often referred to as user)

▲ g group

▲ o all others

▲ a owner, group, and all others

Using `a` is the same as specifying the `ugo` option. The `a` option is the default permission field. That is, if you omit the permission field, Linux defaults to the `a` option.

Chapter 6: Linux File Permissions

The second set of flags determines whether permissions are to be added, taken away, or set as specified:

- ▲   +   adds the specified permissions.
- ▲   -   removes the specified permissions.
- ▲   =   clears the selected permission field and sets it to whatever follows on the command line. If you do not specify a permission mode following =, Linux removes all permissions from the selected field.

The third set of parameters determines the permission as shown here:

- ▲   r   read permission
- ▲   w   write permission
- ▲   x   execute permission for files; search permission for directories

To change permissions, you should first issue the `ls -l` command to check the current permission settings (that is, the current file mode). Then you use the `chmod` command to specify the symbolic modes. Finally, it's a good idea to check these new permissions by issuing the `ls -l` command again. Refer to Example 6.2.

NOTE: *With symbolic and numeric notation, you do not separate entries with spaces. This is contrary to your experience with entering commands thus far.*

Example 6.2 ▼ chmod and Symbolic Notation

To add write permissions for the owner's group and other users for the file called *newfile*, first check the initial permissions:

```
$ ls -l newfile<Enter>
-rw-r--r--  1 flintsfr  staff  58 Aug 12 13:05 newfile
```

Then change the permissions:

```
$ chmod go+w newfile<Enter>
```

111

And check the changed permissions:

```
$ ls -l newfile<Enter>
-rw-rw-rw- 1 flintsfr staff 58 Aug 12 13:05 newfile ▲
```

In the example, the permission field begins with go, which breaks down to g and o for group and others, respectively. In the second and third permission fields, we add (+) the write permission (w).

Numeric Notation

The syntax for using the chmod command with numeric notation is similar to that used with symbolic notation:

```
chmod numeric filename
```

With numeric (also called octal) notation, you specify the file or directory permissions that you require. This contrasts with symbolic notation, which requires you to know the existing permissions before specifying new permissions with respect to existing permissions.

Table 6.2 shows the connection between permissions in symbolic form and their binary and numeric counterparts. Note that to translate the permission mode from an alphabetic form to a numeric form, you add the numbers that correspond to the individual permissions required. Refer to the table as you follow along with Example 6.3.

Table 6.2 Numeric Parameters versus Other Notations

Notation	Owner	Group	Others
Symbolic	rwx	rw -	r - -
Binary	111	110	100
Numeric/octal	7 (4 + 2 + 1)	6 (4 + 2 + 0)	4 (4 + 0 + 0)

Example
6.3 ▼   chmod and Numeric Notation

Suppose that you want the owner and group to have read and write

CHAPTER 6: LINUX FILE PERMISSIONS

permissions on *newfile* and others to have only read permission on *newfile*. First first check the initial permissions:

```
$ ls -l newfile<Enter>
-rw-r--r-- 1 flintsfr staff 58 Aug 12 13:05 newfile
```

Then change the permissions:

```
$ chmod 664 newfile<Enter>
```

Finally, check the final permissions:

```
$ ls -l newfile<Enter>
-rw-rw-r-- 1 flintsfr staff 65 Aug 13 11:22 newfile ▲
```

Each permission you set in the nine permission bits is represented by 1 and each lack of permission is represented by 0. For example, rw-r--r-- translates to 110100100 in binary and 664 numeric (octal) notation.

Confused? Refer to Figure 6.1 as you go through the following scenario.

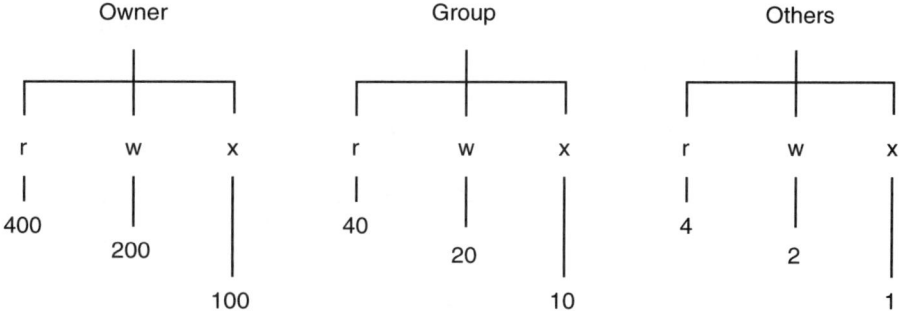

Figure 6.1: Translating binary to numeric.

Assume that you want *newfile* file to be readable and writable by the owner and group, and only readable by all other system users. First, to make the file readable and writable by the owner, you add the r and w permissions, which Figure 6.1 shows to have values of 400 and 200, respectively. Second, to set the same permissions for the group, you add 40 (r) and 20 (w). Finally, to set the read permission for all other system users, you add 4 (r). The result is simple addition:

400 + 200 + 40 + 20 + 4 = 664

The `chmod` command is then

```
$ chmod 664 newfile<Enter>
```

Sometimes, specifying permissions with numeric notation results in safety messages. For example, suppose you are the owner of a file and have no permissions on the file, but you try to remove it. The Linux system asks whether you want to override the protection setting on the file you want to remove. If you respond yes, Linux removes the file. The same would happen if you were a member of the group.

Setting Permissions: umask Command

The real default values for a file in Linux using numeric and symbolic notation are 666 and `-rw-rw-rw-`, respectively. Those for a directory are 777 and `drwxrwxrwx`, respectively. So, why have we listed different figures in Table 6.3? The answer lies in a masking subroutine called `umask`.

Table 6.3 Default File and Directory Values

Entry	ID	Symbolic notation	Numeric notation
File	Root	`- r w - r - - r - -`	644
	User	`- r w - r w - r - -`	664
Directory	Root	`d r w x r - x r - x`	755
	User	`d r w x r w x r - x`	775

Notice how the differences in the default file modes all hinge on the application of the x permission for directories. If there were no x permissions, no one would be able to `cd` into the directories to see, let alone manipulate, other subdirectories or files found therein.

Check Permission Modes

The `umask` command is commonly called a file system option, which restricts access to certain files or directories. However, the command is actually a masking subroutine that creates and applies file modes, or permissions, on files or directories as they are created. The syntax is simply

```
umask<Enter>
```

Example 6.3 shows how you go about checking the permission mode.

Example 6.4 ▼ umask for Checking Permission Modes

Suppose you are an ordinary user and you want to know what modes your files and directories are and will be. To do so, you must find out what your `umask` is:

```
$ umask<Enter>
002
```

Assume the same scenario, but this time as a root user:

```
# umask<Enter>
022
```
▲

When a user logs in, his or her userid, user number, groupid, and group number are input to the */etc/profile* program, which determines whether the user qualifies as a root user or as an ordinary user as far as `umask` is concerned.

If the user is an ordinary user, the program assigns a `umask` of 002. That `umask` is subtracted from 666 from a file permission standpoint and from 777 from a directory standpoint to determine the permissions that will be attributed to files and directories as they are created by that user. The resulting 664 (666 minus 002) for file permissions means that the owner and the owner's group by default have read and write access to files created, but other system users have only read access. The resulting 775 for directory permissions means that the owner and the owner's group have read, write, and execute permissions, and others have only read and execute permissions to any directories created.

If the user qualifies as a root user, the program assigns a `umask` of 022, so the file permissions are 664 and the directory permissions are 755. The owner (as root user) and owner's group have read and write permissions on created files, but others have only read and execute permissions. On created directories, the owner (again, as root user) has read, write, and execute permissions, and the owner's group and others have read and execute.

Those who advocate higher security, especially on a network, recommend a default `umask` of 022 as the absolute minimum, with alternatives such as 027 or even 077. Generally, the higher the `umask` number, the tighter the security.

Change Permission Modes

You may use the `umask` command also to specify the permission bits to be set on any new file or directory created in the same session only. Arguments are numeric:

```
umask numeric
```

Subtracting the new `umask` parameter from the default values of 666 and 777 enable you to determine the new permission bits you want for files and directories, respectively.

Keep in mind the following when changing permission modes:

▲ The `umask` figure, and thus the permission bits, are applicable for only the session in progress and are not in effect after the owner/user logs out and back in. The default values apply upon a new log-in.

▲ The new `umask` affects only files and directories created after the new `umask` parameter is specified. Thus, the command has no effect on existing files and directories. To alter permissions on existing files and directories, you use the `chmod` command.

Example 6.5 ▼ umask for Increasing Security

To check existing permissions in the current directory and the existing `umask`, and then increase security on an ordinary user's file permissions:

```
$ ls -l<Enter>
total 3
drwxrwxr-x 2 flintsfr staff 1024 Jan 26 10:18 c
-rwxrwxr-x 1 flintsfr staff  320 Mar 14 09:15 manuals
-rwxrwxr-x 1 flintsfr staff  144 Mar 02 13:29 test1

$ umask<Enter>
002
$ umask 022<Enter>
```

To create a zero-length file to check your new umask:

```
$ touch tightfile<Enter>
```

To check the new permissions in the current directory:

```
$ ls -l<Enter>
total 4
drwxrwxr-x 2 flintsfr staff 1024 Jan 26 10:18 c
-rwxrwxr-x 1 flintsfr staff  320 Mar 14 09:15 manuals
-rwxrwxr-x 1 flintsfr staff  144 Mar 02 13:29 test1
-rwxr-xr-x 1 flintsfr staff    0 Mar 19 14:34 tight-
   file
```
▲

Remember, in general, the `chmod` command applies permissions and `umask` subtracts permissions. By manipulating these commands, users and system administrators can balance proper security with accessibility.

Creating Personal Directories

In this section, we demonstrate how to create a directory with the appropriate permissions for storing personal documents and data. The command for creating the directory is `mkdir`:

```
mkdir directoryname
```

You change the directory with chmod:

```
chmod numeric directoryname
```

In Example 6.6, the owner/user moves to his or her home directory, creates a directory, changes the mode of the directory, and then checks the permissions on the new directory. With this strategy, the user need not alter the umask and then return the umask to the previous value.

Example 6.6 ▼ mkdir for Personal Directories

To create a private directory called *personal* in your home directory:

```
$ cd /home/flintsfr<Enter>
$ mkdir personal<Enter>
$ chmod 700 personal<Enter>
$ ls -ld personal<Enter>
drwx------ 2 flintsfr staff 512 Mar 19 12:11 personal  ▲
```

The alternative strategy to Example 6.6 is to cd to the home directory, alter the umask, create the personal directory, and then check to ensure that the appropriate permissions were applied. The owner/user would then have to decide whether to return umask to its original value.

Consider the following points when creating personal directories:

▲ Users should maintain their own x values on their personal directories to ensure their own access.

▲ Users should be aware that although the personal directory is invisible to all other users, the root user can still access the personal directory and read the files contained in it.

Giving the Write Permission on Directories

Example 6.7 serves as a cautionary tale regarding security on a file system. Beware of the dangers of giving anyone but yourself write permission on a directory if your intention is to not give anyone but yourself write permission on the files in that directory.

Example 6.7 ▼ Permissions and Security

```
$ whoami<Enter>
rubbleba
$ vi /home/flintsfr/secrets<Enter>
secrets: permission denied
$ ls -l /home/flintsfr/secrets<Enter>
-rw-r--r--1flintsfrstaff2496Nov 23 13:12 secrets
$ ls -ld /home/flintsfr<Enter>
drwxrwxrwx2flintsfrstaff 512Oct 13 08:37 flintsfr
$ vi sneaky<Enter>
Ha! Ha! Fred! I changed your secrets file! How do you
    think I did that?
    Signed, Barney
$ mv sneaky /home/flintsfr/secrets<Enter>
override protection 644 for secrets? Y<Enter>
$ cat /home/flintsfr/secrets<Enter>
Ha! Ha! Fred! I changed your secrets file! How do you
    think I did that?
Signed, Barney                                            ▲
```

In Example 6.7, Barney tries to change Fred's *secrets* file in a straightforward manner, but the system denies him access to the file. Barney checks the permissions on *secrets* and discovers that Fred has not allowed group or others the write permission to the *secrets* file.

Barney then checks the permissions on Fred's home directory, where *secrets* is stored. He discovers that group and others have write permission on Fred's home directory. So Barney creates a file called *sneaky*, in which he leaves Fred the *Ha! Ha!* message. Barney then renames *sneaky* to Fred's *secrets* file. The system sees that Barney has write protection and asks him whether he wants his write permission to the directory to override the lack of write permission on the file itself. Barney replies yes, and *sneaky* becomes *secrets*, overwriting whatever Fred had in *secrets* to begin with. Finally, Barney checks to make sure his piece of skullduggery worked.

If you want to avoid a fate similar to Fred's, make sure you have no similar security issues with your files. Alter your umask and use chmod to alter the permissions on your existing sensitive directories.

Functions and Required Permissions

We provide Table 6.4 as a reference to help you ensure that you set the proper permissions on files and directories to accomplish what you want. Remember that to remove a file, you need write permission on the directory that contains the file; you do not need write permission on the file itself.

Table 6.4 Required Permissions for Selected Files and Directories

Command	Source directory	Source file	Target directory
cd	x	N/A	N/A
ls	r	N/A	N/A
ls -l	r,x	N/A	N/A
mkdir	x,w (parent)	N/A	N/A
rmdir	x,w (parent)	N/A	N/A
cat, more	x	r	N/A
mv	x,w	None	x,w
cp	x	r	x,w
touch	x,w*	N/A	None
rm	x,w	None	N/A

* The write permission is required in the source directory when using the touch command to create a zero-length file but not when using touch on an existing file to update the modification date.

Exercises

1. Change to the *myscripts* directory. Display a long listing of the files in that directory. Note the owner and permissions for the files you copied in the Chapter 5 exercises. Record the permissions for *mycal* and *mycat*.

   ```
   $ cd myscripts<Enter>
   $ ls -l<Enter>
   ```

2. Execute a long listing on the original `cal` and `cat` files in the */usr/bin* directory and compare the permissions to those in the *myscripts* directory.

   ```
   $ ls -l /usr/bin/cat /usr/bin/cal<Enter>
   ```

3. Change the modification time of *mycal* and *mycat* in the *myscripts* directory. Check to see that the time changed.

   ```
   $ touch mycal mycat<Enter>
   $ ls -l<Enter>
   ```

   Describe another use for the `touch` command.

4. Execute the necessary commands so that you can reference the *mycal* file in the *myscripts* directory by the name *home_mycal* in your home directory.

   ```
   $ ls mycal /home/teamxx/home_mycal<Enter>
   ```
   or
   ```
   $ ln mycal ../home_mycal<Enter>
   $ ls -l mycal<Enter>
   $ ls -l /home/teamxx/home_mycal<Enter>
   ```
   or
   ```
   $ ls -l ../home_mycal<Enter>
   ```

   Compare the detailed information for both files. Is there a difference? What is the link count?

5. Change directory to your home directory. Execute *home_mycal*.

   ```
   $ cd<Enter>
   $ ./home_mycal<Enter>
   ```

> **NOTE:** *Because of default path limitations in Linux, simply typing* `home_mycal` *won't work.*

What does the output look like?

Now change permissions on the *home_mycal* file so that you, the owner of the file, have read-only permission. Try running the `mycal` command.

```
$ chmod 455 home_mycal<Enter>
$ ls -l home_mycal<Enter>
$ myscripts/mycal<Enter>
```

Can you do it? Why or why not?

6. Remove *home_mycal*.

   ```
   $ rm home_mycal<Enter>
   ```

   Did that remove *myscripts/mycal*? Why or why not?

   ```
   $ ls -l myscripts/mycal<Enter>
   ```

7. Change directory to the *myscripts* directory. Using symbolic notation with the `chmod` command, remove the read permission on the other permission bits from the *mycat* file. Check the new permissions.

   ```
   $ cd myscripts<Enter>
   $ chmod o-r mycat<Enter>
   $ ls -l mycat<Enter>
   ```

8. Using octal notation, change the permissions on *mycat* so that the owner permission bits are set to read-only with no permission for anyone else. Check the new permissions.

   ```
   $ chmod 400 mycat<Enter>
   $ ls -l mycat<Enter>
   ```

9. Execute the `mycat` command against the *.bash_profile* file.

   ```
   $ mycat ../.bash_profile<Enter>
   ```
   or
   ```
   $ mycat /home/teamxx/.bash_profile<Enter>
   ```

Did it work? What happened?

10. Make your home directory the current directory. Check to see whether you are in your home directory.

    ```
    $ cd<Enter>
    $ pwd<Enter>
    ```

11. Alter the permissions on the *myscripts* directory so that you have read-only access to it.

    ```
    $ chmod u-wx myscripts<Enter>
    ```
    or
    ```
    $ chmod u=r myscripts<Enter>
    ```
    or
    ```
    $ chmod 455 myscripts<Enter>
    ```

12. Use a long list to check that you have set the permissions correctly.

    ```
    $ ls -l /home/teamxx<Enter>
    ```
    or
    ```
    $ ls -ld myscripts<Enter>
    ```

13. Try getting a simple list of the contents of the directory. Try a long list.

    ```
    $ ls myscripts<Enter>
    $ ls -l myscripts<Enter>
    ```

    Did they work? Why or why not?

14. Try to execute *mycal*.

    ```
    $ myscripts/mycal<Enter>
    ```

    Did it work? Why or why not?

15. Try to remove *mycal*.

    ```
    $ rm myscripts/mycal<Enter>
    ```

    Did it work? Why or why not?

INSTALLING AND ADMINISTERING LINUX

16. Return the permissions of *myscripts* back to its original form (`rwxr-xr-x`) and then remove *mycal*.

    ```
    $ chmod 755 myscripts<Enter>
    $ rm myscripts/mycal<Enter>
    ```

17. As time permits, experiment with other permission combinations. When you are through, make sure to change the permissions back to `rwx` for the owner.

See Appendix B for answers.

Quiz

NOTE: *Questions 1, 2, and 3 are based on a file called* reporta, *which has the following set of permissions:* -rwxr-xr-x.

1. What is the file mode expressed in numeric (octal) notation?
2. Change the file mode to `-rwxr--r--` using the symbolic format.
3. Repeat the operation in Question 2 using the numeric (octal) format.
4. Assume that the *jobs* directory contains the *joblog* file.

    ```
    $ ls -lR<Enter>
    total 8
    drwxr-xr-x 2 judy finance 512 June 17 08:09 jobs
    ./jobs:
    total 8
    -rw-rw-r-- 1 judy finance 100 June 18 13:22 joblog
    ```

    Can Fred, who is a member of the finance group, modify the *joblog* file?

5. This question is based on the following listing. Assume that the *jobs* directory contains the *work* directory, which in turn contains the *joblog* file.

    ```
    $ ls -lR<Enter>
    total 8
    ```

124

```
drwxrwxr-x 3 judy finance 512 June 17 08:09 jobs
./jobs:
total 8
drwxrw-r-x 2 judy finance 512 June 17 08:12 work
./jobs/work:
total 8
-rw-rw-r-- 1 judy finance 100 June 18 13:22 joblog
```

Can Fred, who is a member of the finance group, modify the file *joblog*?

6. This question is based on the following listing. Assume that the *jobs* directory contains the *work* directory, which in turn contains the *joblog* file.

```
$ ls -lR<Enter>
total 8
drwxr-xr-x 3 judy finance 512 June 17 08:09 jobs
./jobs:
total 8
drwxrwxrwx 2 judy finance 512 June 17 08:12 work
./jobs/work:
total 8
-rw-rw-r-- 1 judy finance 100 June 18 13:22 joblog
```

Can Fred, who is a member of the finance group, copy the *joblog* file to his home directory?

See Appendix C for answers.

Chapter 7

The vi Editor

LINUX PROVIDES SEVERAL TEXT EDITOR PROGRAMS, from the simplistic vi to the more elegant Emacs. The main reason for discussing vi (the visual front end for the actual editor, ex) in this chapter is that you are likely to run into it no matter what type of UNIX-related system you deal with. The vi is on almost every system because it requires comparatively little space and still does the job adequately. It may not be called vi, but it will be called something similar (such as vim).

The vi editor can be a bit of a tough slog, but you'll need it to deal with Linux, or any other UNIX-based operating system, on a regular basis. Another reason for dedicating a chapter to vi is that it does not have a lot of interactive help (or any other kind). It does have a man page, however. Because vi fronts for ex, you can check the man page for ex as well.

Before you begin editing text, you may want to determine which other text editors are available on your system. Some are installed automatically as part of the base system; others are installed only during custom, or expert, installations. Check your installation or user guide. You will probably find that every Linux distribution has a specific command you can enter to check whether a program has been installed, but you have to be able to enter the precise program name, or something very close to it (using wildcard symbols perhaps).

Other text editors you may have at your disposal are Emacs, ed, joe, jed, or variations on those names, depending on the environment you will be using them in (for example, jed versus jed-xjed) or the extra features one might have compared with another (for example, `vim-minimal` versus `vim-enhanced`).

One last word: `vi` and other text editors are *not* word processing programs, so don't set your expectations too high. They are valuable tools nonetheless because they facilitate administration of UNIX-like operating systems.

An Introduction to vi

As mentioned, `vi` is the standard editor in all UNIX-related systems. The original `vi` editor was distributed with the Berkeley Software Distribution; the various Linux distributions use a form of VIsual editor iMproved (`vim`), which claims to be an improvement over the classic `vi`.

When you enter `vi filename` to invoke the editor, you are actually using a symbolic link to `vim`. `vim` then emulates the classic `vi` editor (an instance of upward compatibility).

The following features are fairly standard across `vi` versions and types:

▲ Full-screen editor

▲ Two modes of operation: Command and Insert

▲ Use of one-letter commands

▲ Unformatted text

▲ Flexible search-and-replace facility with pattern matching

▲ User-defined editing features using macros

This chapter does not pretend to be a comprehensive summary of `vi`. Consult the various Linux information sources for more detailed descriptions of `vi` features. In addition, we have provided a command summary in Appendix A.

We'll be describing and using two `vi` modes: Command and Insert. Some Linux gurus claim that `vi` has three modes: Command, Insert, and Last-line. Users are in Last-line mode when they have used <Esc> to leave Insert mode and then typed a colon (:) so that they can enter specific single-letter commands to quit, save, or so on. In this chapter, we fold the Last-line mode in with Command mode.

Starting vi

Assuming that you have logged in to Linux and are now facing the command-line prompt, enter the following to invoke `vi`:

```
vi filename<Enter>
```

If the specified file already exists, `vi` creates a copy of it and puts the copy into a buffer in the */tmp* directory for you to work on. If the file doesn't exist, `vi` opens an empty buffer in the same directory and gives the file the name specified in your `vi` command.

When invoked, `vi` starts in Command mode and waits for direction from you. What you see on the screen is a flashing cursor and the file name at the bottom of the screen. If the file is new, the editor tells you so on the last line. If the file already existed, Linux gives you the file name in double quotes, as well as the number of lines and number of characters in the file.

The screen on the left in Figure 7.1 is the result of invoking `vi` to edit the existing file called *gearheadlaundry*. As you can see from the bottom of the screen, the file has 8 lines, with 136 characters. If you invoke `vi` to create a new file called *gearheadshopping*, you'd see the empty screen on the right in Figure 7.1. Dashes represent blank lines and the file name appears on the last line.

Figure 7.1: Editing an existing file (left) and starting vi (right).

Exiting vi

To exit from the `vi` editor, you must be in Command mode. To ensure that you are in Command mode before inputting commands at any time, press <Esc>.

You may exit `vi` in one of the following ways (all end with `<Enter>`):

▲ `:q` quits `vi` without saving your file.

▲ `:wq` writes changes and quits.

▲ `<Shift>-zz` writes changes and quits.

The `:q` option works only if you have not made any changes. If you have made changes and you try to quit this way, Linux gives you the following message:

No write since last change (use ! to override).

If you want to exit at this point, type one of the following:

▲ `:q!` quits without writing changes

▲ `:x` writes changes and quits

Adding Text in Insert Mode

After you open a file in vi and want to enter text, you must be in Insert mode (also known as input, or text, mode). Take the following steps to get into Insert mode and then insert text:

1. Using the up and down arrows, position the cursor at the point in a new or existing file where you want to begin inserting text.

2. Use one of the following single-letter commands:

   ▲ a adds text immediately after the cursor

   ▲ A adds text beginning at the end of the line on which the cursor is sitting

   ▲ i inserts text beginning at the same position presently underlined by the cursor

   ▲ I inserts text at the beginning of the line on which the cursor is sitting

3. Add your text.

The difference between a and i will become apparent with practice. Note that while you are adding text, the file name, which was at the bottom of the terminal screen, has been replaced by -- INSERT --. This is a reminder that you are in Insert mode.

If you want to save your text as you go, press <Esc> to reenter Command mode and then type the following

```
w<Enter>
```

This saves the text you have entered thus far, and keeps the file available for input. To resume entering text, use one of the single-letter commands just listed.

When you finish adding text, you need to leave Insert mode by pressing <Esc>. You are returned to Command mode. Your file is still on the screen, but the file name is no longer at the bottom.

Manipulating Text in Command Mode

The first method you need to know to manipulate text is how to move around in the `vi` editor. Table 7.1 provides a list and corresponding descriptions of typical methods for moving your cursor in `vi` while in Command mode. Additional commands are available for moving around; check the `man` pages or other information sources for further help.

Table 7.1 Cursor Movements in vi

Moving within a line	Cursor moves
left arrow or `h`	One character left
right arrow or `l`	One character right
`0`	To the beginning of the line
`$`	To the end of the line
Moving among words	
`w`	To the next word
`b`	Back to the previous word
`e`	To the end of the next word
Moving within the screen	
up arrow or `k`	One line up
down arrow or `j`	One line down
`H`	To the top line on the screen
`M`	To the middle line on the screen
`L`	To the last line on the screen
Scrolling the screen	
`<Ctrl>-f`	Forward to the next screen
`<Ctrl>-b`	Backward to the previous screen
Moving within the file	
`1G`	To the first line of the file
`45G`	To line number 45 of the file
`G`	To the last line of the file

Delete Text

Many commands available for deleting text in Command mode. We list several ways of doing so in Table 7.2, along with two commands to use if you want to undo the deletion. These commands are handy also for moving or copying text, although when copying, the y key is substituted for d. For additional commands, check Appendix A as well as the man pages and other information sources.

Table 7.2 Commands for Deleting and Copying Text in vi

Delete	Copy	Action applied
x		To a single character
dw	cw	To the end of the current word
d$	c$	To the end of the line
d0	c0	To the start of the line
dd	cd	The entire line
dG	cG	To the end of the file
u	u	Undo the last change
U	U	Restore the entire line (only if the cursor has not left the line)

Search and Replace Text

When you're in Command mode, pressing the forward slash (/) automatically puts you in text search forward mode and takes you to the last line on the screen, where vi has placed a forward slash prompt. Similarly, pressing the question mark (?) automatically puts you in text search backward mode and takes you to the last line on the screen, where vi has placed a question mark prompt.

After the prompt, enter the string of text you want to search for and press <Enter>. The search begins in the chosen direction from the position of the cursor. The cursor stops underneath the first character of the first found text string. If you want to continue searching in the same direction, press n. If you want to search in the opposite direction, press N. Eventually, you will reach the bottom or top of the file, and vi will tell you that fact.

To exit from text search, simply enter any other command; you don't press <Esc> first.

In Example 7.1, we present a command to both search and replace text. The example finds all occurrences of the first string *(penguin)* and replaces them with the *Tux* string. Note that the program searches for every occurrence of *penguin* preceded and followed by a space; if the word is found ending a line, beginning a line, or immediately followed by punctuation, it is not replaced.

Example 7.1 ▼ vi for Searching and Replacing Text

To search for *penguin* and replace it with *Tux*:

```
$ vi vifilename<Enter>
<Esc>
:g/ penguin /s// ASCII Tux /g<Enter>
```
▲

The commands work as follows:

▲ The first g (global) tells the editor to perform a search for the first occurrence of the text string in every line of the file.

▲ The two forward slashes bracket the search string (in this case, / *penguin* /; the characters are preceded and followed by a space).

▲ The s means substitute.

▲ The forward slash following the s tells the editor to use the text string preceding the s as the target for the substitution (that is, the preceding text string will be the one replaced).

▲ The next two forward slashes bracket the text string to be substituted for the replaced text string (in this case, / *Tux* /; again the characters are preceded and followed by a space).

▲ The last g tells the editor to make the substitution at every occurrence in each line found by the first g.

An extra feature we could have added to the example is a c before the last g (that is, /cg). The c tells the editor to ask for confirmation before making each change.

Another of many ways you could modify the example command is to make changes to only one line or to the first occurrence on every line. See your information sources for additional ways to carry out a search and replace.

Move Text

The `vi` editor utilizes 36 buffers (numbered 0 through 9 and lettered *a* through *z*) into which you can cut or copy file data. Unless you specify a number or a letter, the data is cut or copied into buffer 0 by default. Example 7.2 is a simplistic example of moving text.

Example 7.2 ▼ vi for Moving or Cutting Text

In Command mode, move the cursor to the line you want to move:

```
This is the first line of text.
This is the second line of text.
This is the third line of text.
```

Press dd. The specified line disappears into buffer 0 (the default buffer) and the cursor moves to the next line. If necessary, move the cursor to the line after which you want to place the specified line. (The cursor is already in the correct place in this example.)

```
This is the first line of text.
This is the third line of text.
```

Press p. The original line appears after the line on which you placed the cursor. Now the cursor is on the newly placed line.

```
This is the first line of text.
This is the third line of text.
This is the second line of text.
```

If you had pressed P instead of p, the orignal line would have appeared above the line on which you had placed the cursor.

If you want to do more complicated moving of text, such as moving several strings at once, try the following. To cut a line into buffer 2, move the cursor to that line and type

```
"2dd
```

To cut a word into buffer 3, move the cursor to that word and type

   `"3dw`

To cut a line and the three lines following it into buffer c, move to that line and type

   `"c4dd`

Move to the various target locations and type `"2p`, `"3p`, and `"cp`, respectively, to place those text strings where you want them. You can do so repetitively, out of order, or however you want because copies of the text strings remain in their respective buffers until they are replaced.   ▲

Note that `"2dd`, `"3dw`, and `"c4dd` are preceded by a double quotation mark. *Preceding the alphanumeric key combinations with one double quote is essential* when specifying buffers. If you don't use the quote mark, the system interprets the rest of the string as some type of bungled command and either does not respond or gives you an error message.

Undo Buffer

If you're deleting, moving, or copying text, the most recent buffer you've put a text string into—whether you have specified it, such as the 2 or 3 or c in the multiple-move example, or whether it's the default 0 buffer if you have not specified a buffer—is the *undo buffer*. Using the multiple-move example, after you have cut the three text strings, the undo buffer is the c buffer, not the 2 or 3 buffer. The only action you would be able to undo with the u command is `"c4dd`.

To undo your last command, simply press u. If you have made several changes on one line *and* you want to undo all of those changes *and* you haven't moved off that line yet, press U.

Copy Text

As mentioned, `vi` utilizes 36 buffers into which you can cut or copy (or, as vi says, *yank*) file data. Unless you specify a buffer number or letter, the data is cut or copied into buffer 0 by default.

Chapter 7: The vi Editor

Example 7.3 illustrates a simple example of copying text. The vi echoes the actions you've taken (for example, *xxx lines yanked; xxx more lines*) as they are completed.

Example 7.3 ▼

vi for Copying Text

In Command mode, move the cursor to the line you want to copy:

```
This is the first line of text.
This is the second line of text.
```

Press yy. The specified line is copied into buffer 0 (the default buffer), but the original line remains on the screen. The cursor stays where you placed it.

Move the cursor to the line below which you want to place the yanked line, which is still in the buffer. (In this case, the cursor is already in the correct location, so it stays where it is.)

```
This is the first line of text.
This is the second line of text.
```

Press p. The yanked copy of the original line appears below the line where you had just placed the cursor. Now the cursor is on the newly placed copy line.

```
This is the first line of text.
This is the second line of text.
This is the second line of text.
```

As with moving text, if you want to do more complicated copying—say, copying several strings at once—do the following.

To copy a line into buffer 2, move the cursor to the line and type

```
"2yy
```

To copy a word into buffer 3, move the cursor to that word and type

```
"3yw
```

To copy a line and the three lines following it into buffer c, move to that line and type

```
"c4yy
```

137

Move to the various target locations and type `"2p`, `"3p`, and `"cp`, respectively, to place those text strings where you want them. ▲

As with moving text, you can copy text repetitively or out of order because copies of the text strings remain in their respective buffers until they are replaced. In the multiple-copy example, just as in the multiple-move example (Example 7.2), `"2yy`, `"3yw`, and `"c4yy` are all preceded by one quotation mark. Remember, you must precede alphanumeric key combinations with one double quote when specifying buffers.

Executing Linux/UNIX Commands in vi

Suppose that while you're working in `vi`, you realize that you need to exit `vi` to run a command. You don't want to exit `vi`, run the command, and then reenter `vi`. Your solution? Using the exclamation point (`!`) command within `vi` creates an appropriate shell to execute the chosen command, prompt you for the command, execute it, and illustrate the results.

In Example 7.4, we show how to copy a file while remaining in the `vi` editor instead of having to exit `vi`, use the cat command on the file, write down the information, reenter `vi`, and type the information in the file.

Example 7.4 ▼ vi for Executing Linux/UNIX Commands

Suppose you are producing a staff notice called *note2stf*. You know that the most up-to-date list of snacks is in the *snacks* file. To copy that file into your notice:

```
$ vi note2stf<Enter>
```

The *note2stf* file on-screen reads:

```
The following should be stocked in the employee break
    room:
Press <Esc> to enter Command mode.
```

Move the cursor down to where you want the new information displayed.

```
The following should be stocked in the employee break
    room:
```

To list the contents of the existing directory:

```
:!ls<Enter>
note2stf file2 file3 snacks
Press RETURN or enter command to continue
```

Now type

```
:r snacks<Enter>
"snacks" 6 lines, 40 characters
Press RETURN or enter command to continue
```

Press <Enter> to insert the contents of the *snacks* file in *note2stf*. By default, the text is inserted just below the cursor's position.

```
<Enter>
The following should be stocked in the employee break
    room:
Coffee
Cream
Sodas
Sugar
Bottled water
Milk
```

▲

If line numbering were set to On in the *note2stf* file, you could have inserted a line number before `:r snacks` to tell the editor to place the contents of *snacks* there instead. (Line numbering is discussed later in this chapter.)

By the way, this is a common method for dumping the output of the `date` command into letters, memos, and other documents.

Do you remember being prompted with *Press RETURN or enter command to continue* in Example 7.4? If you need to run a series of commands without returning to `vi` after the execution of the first command, type `:sh`. Then you can run all your commands in the shell. When you want to exit the shell and return to `vi`, press <Ctrl>-d.

Options for Changing How vi Operates

You can change several appearance and behavior characteristics of vi to make it more useful or convenient. We list some of them in this section, but first we discuss how you change characteristics.

The two basic approaches to changing characteristics are to

▲ Set default options that remain in place after you close the current session

▲ Reset options for single-session use

When you invoke vi, it searches for the user's default characteristics in a hidden file called *.exrc* in the current directory. If vi finds the *.exrc* file, it follows whatever default specifications are located there. If it doesn't find the *.exrc* file in the current directory, it checks the user's home directory for it.

Look in your current directory and home directory for a hidden *.exrc* file. If you can't locate one, you can use vi to create one. Invoke vi, get into Insert mode, and enter any of the options listed in Table 7.3 or in another information source. When you list them in the *.exrc* file, *do not* put a colon at the beginning of any of them. (The colon is used only when you're doing an interactive-style specification in Command mode at the beginning of a vi session.)

Table 7.3 vi Customizing Options

Option	Description
`:set all`	Display all settings
`:set`	Display settings different than the default settings
`:set ai`	Turn on autoindent
`:set noai`	Turn off autoindent
`:set nu`	Turn on line numbering
`:set nonu`	Turn off line numbering
`:set list`	Display nonprintable characters
`:set nolist`	Hide nonprintable characters

Continued

Table 7.3 vi Customizing Options (continued)

Option	Description
`:set showmode`	Show the current mode of operation
`:set noshowmode`	Hide the current mode of operation
`:set ts=4`	Set tabs to four character jumps
`:set ic`	Ignore case sensitivity
`:set noic`	Set case sensitivity
`:set wrapmargin`	Set the margin for automatic word wrapping from one line to the next; a value of 0 turns off word wrapping

You can also set options for a specific session rather than every time you invoke `vi`. For example, to number lines as you enter text, go to Command mode and type

```
:set nu<Enter>
```

At the end of the session, leave `vi`. The next time you invoke the editor, line numbering is off as usual.

The `vi` editor has many options. Some affect the way text is presented; others facilitate editing, especially for new users. Table 7.3 lists commonly specified options. For more exhaustive listings, check your information sources.

Command-Line Editing

Before we discuss editing at the command line, a brief mention of the shells in Linux's basic installation will be useful. Shells, which are Linux/UNIX command interpreters, are described in more detail in Chapter 8. A user can switch from one shell to another by using some simple commands.

For now, we want to simplify the discussion by stating that when a user logs in to Linux, one of the shells is invoked by default. And because many principles, utilities, and commands are similar from shell to shell, we focus on the Bourne Again Shell, or bash shell.

With bash, you can type commands using letters, numbers, and some metacharacters, and then execute the commands by pressing <Enter>. To navigate back and forth along the command line, you can use the right and left arrow keys. To delete text, you use the <Backspace> key rather than the <Delete> key. You can't use a lot of the other handy keys, such as <Home>, <End>, <Shift>, <Alt>, <Ctrl>, and function keys (that is, <F1>, <F2>, and so on), among others.

The up and down keys, however, are powerful enough. You can use them to tap into your command history, starting with the buffer where commands from the current session are saved and including a hidden file called *.bash_history* in your *$HOME* directory. That is, by using the down or up key, you can recall at the command line commands that you have executed previously.

Pressing the up key again takes you into the *.bash_history* file. When you enter it, your initial position in the file is at the bottom, or the most recent command before your last log out. You can move as far into *.bash_history* as the earliest command you executed in the current session. Pressing the up key beyond that results in a beep. After you move at least one command up, you can start pressing the down key, which moves you forward in the history of your executed commands.

The benefit of using the up and down arrow keys at the command line is that you can repeat procedures by recalling their commands and then pressing <Enter> to reexecute. This feature can save you a lot of typing, especially when complicated syntax is involved. You can also do some sensitivity analyses by reexecuting commands while changing options or arguments with each execution to compare results.

Invoke Features of Other Editors

Linux also allows you to invoke at the command line the editing features from its various text editors. For example, if you type the following at the command line, Linux allows you to use some `vi` commands and keystrokes:

```
set -o vi<Enter>
```

Invoking `vi` features also lets you use the h, j, k, and l keys to emulate the left, down, up, and right arrow keys, respectively, to

CHAPTER 7: THE VI EDITOR

navigate the command line or to recall previous commands by tapping into your *.bash_history* file. Other `vi` features, such as `cw` to change a word in the command line, also become available.

This "invoking other editor features" facility can be handy for UNIX-based operating system users and administrators when they find themselves at different locations (especially at different keyboards). The feature brings some predictability to command-line activities.

But be careful with invoking these editor features: With Linux, you might get unpredictable and thus inconvenient results.

> **WARNING:** *If you try to turn off `vi` features (with `set +o vi`, for instance), you might succeed in turning off vi, but you might also turn off previous bash command-line features, leaving you almost helpless at the command line. You would have to log out and log back in again to regain your previous command-line utility.*

Related vi Editors

Here's a quick summary of other editors loaded by Linux that are related to the `vi` editor:

▲ view is the read-only version of vi. Changes cannot be saved unless overridden by using an exclamation mark, !.

▲ ex is a line-oriented text editor, but it can access vi's screen editing capabilities.

▲ ed is a line-oriented text editor with no visual or screen capabilities.

You can experiment with these editors by invoking them at the command line using the following syntax:

```
ex filename
```

You might be fortunate enough to have `Emacs`, an elegant and powerful visual screen text editor. Unfortunately, `Emacs` uses a lot of disk storage, so is not installed universally. It ships with various Linux distributions and is available on the Internet.

Exercises

1. Go to your home directory and create a file in it called *vitest*.

   ```
   cd<Enter>
   vi vitest<Enter>
   ```

2. When you open a `vi` file, you are automatically placed in Command mode. Press the `i` (insert) key to switch to Insert mode. You can also press the `a` (append) key. Use of `i` or `a` simply determines whether typing will start before or after the cursor. Although there is no indicator when you are in Command mode, the text string -- INSERT -- appears at the bottom of the screen when you are in Insert mode.

   Switch from Insert mode to Command mode by pressing the <Esc> key. Press <Esc> a second time. Note that if you press <Esc> twice, you will probably get a beep from your terminal (some ASCII terminals don't beep). The beep indicates that you are already in Command mode. Now press `i` again to go back into Insert mode and continue to the next exercise.

3. Insert the following text *exactly* as it is presented, line by line. Then type in the alphabet, one character per line. The following shows *a* through *c* only, but please continue on to *z* on your terminal. Adding the alphabet, one letter to a line, is an easy way to fill a few screens of information, which you'll need for later exercises.

   ```
   This is a training session about the usage of the vi
   editor. We need some more lines to learn about the most
   common commands of the editor. We are now in the Insert
   mode and we will switch right after this to the Command
   mode.
   a
   b
   c
   .
   .
   .
   ```

4. Return to Command mode. Write and quit this new file. Note that as soon as you press the colon (:) key, it appears below the last line of your input area. After the buffer is empty and the file is closed, you see a message giving the number of lines and characters in the file.

   ```
   <Esc>
   :wq
   ```

   or

   ```
   <Shift>-zz
   ```

5. Open the *vitest* file using `vi`. Note that the bottom line of the screen indicates the name of the file and the number of lines and characters it has found in the file.

   ```
   $ vi vitest<Enter>
   ```

6. Using both the arrow keys and the h, j, k, and l keys, practice moving the cursor down one line, up one line, to the right a couple of characters, and back to the left a couple of characters.

7. You may not want to move the cursor one character or one line at a time throughout an entire file. Practice using cursor movement keys to navigate page by page or line by line. Using the cursor movement keys mentioned in Exercise 6, position your cursor at the first line of the file. While in Command mode, do the following:

   ▲ Move forward one page: <Ctrl>-f or <PgDn>

   NOTE: *There is no <PgDn> key on ASCII terminals.*

   ▲ Move back one page: <Ctrl>-b or <PgUp>

   ▲ Scroll the screen up to one-half the screen size: <Ctrl>-u

   ▲ Move the cursor to the last line in the file: <Shift>-g

   ▲ Move the cursor to the first line in the file: 1<Shift>-g or :1<Enter>

   ▲ Move the cursor to line 4 of the file: 4<Shift>-g or :4<Enter>

INSTALLING AND ADMINISTERING LINUX

- ▲ Move the cursor to the end of the line: $
- ▲ Move the cursor to the beginning of the line: 0 (zero)

8. Move your cursor to the top of the file.

   ```
   1<Shift>-g>
   ```
   or
   ```
   :1<Enter>
   ```

   Search for the word *entry*. Your cursor should be on the *e*. Switch to Insert mode and add the word *text*, with a space after the word.

   ```
   /entry<Enter>
   i
   text
   ```

9. Move the cursor to the space after the word *mode* on the same line. Insert a comma. Remember, you are still in Insert mode.

   ```
   <Esc>
   ```

   Position the cursor to the space after the word *mode*.

   ```
   i
   ,
   ```

10. Enter Command mode. Position the cursor anywhere on the line beginning with *learn the most*. Insert a blank line to form two paragraphs.

    ```
    <Esc>
    ```

    Position the cursor on the line that starts with *learn the most*.

    ```
    o
    ```

    The lowercase *o* opens the blank line following the line beginning with *learn the most*.

11. Opening up a blank line, as in the preceding exercise, automatically puts you in Insert mode. Therefore, return to Command mode. Now save the changes you have made thus far, but do not exit the editor.

    ```
    <Esc>
    :w<Enter>
    ```

12. While still in Command mode, remove the characters *c*, *e*, and *g* but leave the blank lines in their place; in other words, don't delete the entire line, just the characters. Then go back and remove the blank lines. This is an opportunity to use two of the delete functions.

    ▲ Position the cursor on the *c*; press x

    ▲ Position the cursor on the *e*; press x

    ▲ Position the cursor on the g; press x

    ▲ Do the following *twice*: Position the cursor on a blank line and press dd.

13. Now replace the character *h* with *z*.

    ▲ Position the cursor on the *h*

    ▲ Press r

    ▲ Press z

14. Assume that you decided you don't want to save the changes to the characters. Quit the editing session without saving the changes made since the last save.

    ```
    :q!<Enter>
    ```

15. Edit *vitest* one more time.

    ```
    $ vi vitest
    ```

    Do the following:

    ▲ Copy the first paragraph one line at a time to the end of the file:

    Position the cursor on line 1; press yy
    <Shift>-g; press p
    2<Shift>-g; press yy
    <Shift>-g; press p
    3<Shift>-g; press yy
    <Shift>-g; press p

147

▲ When you complete the preceding actions, copy the second paragraph all at once to the end of the file:

4<Shift>-g; press 3yy

<Shift>-g; press p

16. Assume that you decided the lines you just added to the end of the file do not look right. Delete all of them with a single command.

   ▲ Position the cursor on the first copied line to be deleted at the bottom of the file.

   ▲ Count the number of lines to delete.

   ▲ Press 5dd

17. Now, before you do anything else with this file, assume that you need to embed the current date and time as the first line of the file. Do this without leaving the `vi` editor.

   `:!date > datefile<Enter>`
   Press RETURN or enter command to continue`<Enter>`
   `:0r datefile<Enter>`

18. Options can be set temporarily in an editing session using the `set` command. Return to the top of the file.

   `1<Shift>-g`

   Ensure that you are in Command mode and set the following commands:

   ▲ Set automatic word wrap to 15 spaces before the right margin.

   ▲ Display the Insert mode message when in Insert mode.

   ▲ Turn line numbering on.

   ```
   <Esc>
   :set wrapmargin=15<Enter>
   :set showmode<Enter>
   :set number<Enter>
   ```

Chapter 7: The vi Editor

19. Test each of the options set in Exercise 18.

- ▲ You should see that the lines in the file are automatically numbered, just after the command was entered.

- ▲ Try entering Insert mode by typing i or a. You will see the -- INSERT -- message at the bottom left of your screen.

- ▲ Type a few continuous lines of text to test the automatic word wrap feature.

- ▲ Enter Command mode by pressing <Esc>. The -- INSERT -- message disappears from the bottom of the screen.

20. Write the file and quit the editor.

`:wq<Enter>`

21. To set up a command-line editing session, use the `set -o vi` command.

`$ set -o vi<Enter>`

22. Now you can recall previously executed commands, edit them, and resubmit them. Let's build a command history to work with. List the contents of the */usr* directory (do a simple list, not a long list). Display the contents of the */etc/filesystems* file. Echo *hello*.

```
$ ls /usr<Enter>
$ cat /etc/filesystems<Enter>
$ echo hello<Enter>
```

23. Assume you want to edit one of the commands you just executed. Press the <Esc> key to get to vi Command mode. Try pressing the k key several times to go up the list of commands. Try j to go down. This recall of commands is essentially a browse through a buffer of commands that you previously executed in this session. After you log out, the commands are stored in your *.bash_history* file in your home directory.

149

24. Retrieve the `ls` command. Use the `l` key to move your cursor to the slash in */usr*. (Note: The arrow keys tend to wipe out your line. You have to use the `l` key for right cursor movement and `h` for left cursor movement.) Use the `j` key to insert text and change this command to long list, and then execute by pressing <Enter>.

    ▲ k to get to the `ls /usr` command

    ▲ l to get to the /

    ▲ i to get into Insert mode; you could also use an `a` to append if the cursor was on the space before the /

    ▲ -l to change the `ls` to `ls -l`

25. Recall the `cat` command. This time, list the contents of the */etc/passwd* file:

    ▲ Press <Esc>

    ▲ Press k (to get to the previous `cat` command)

    ▲ Move the cursor to the *f* in *filesystems*.

    ▲ Press D (to erase from the *f* to the end of the line; or dw to simply erase the word)

    ▲ Press a (to begin appending text)

    ▲ To execute the */etc/passwd* file, type:

    `passwd<Enter>`

26. Recall the `cat` command. Go to the end of the line (use $). Add to the end of that command by doing this: pipe the output of the `etc/passwd` command to wc, which counts the lines in the */etc/passwd* file.

    ▲ Press <Esc>

    ▲ Press k (to get to the previous `cat` command)

    ▲ Press $ (to get to the end of the line)

    ▲ Press a (to begin appending text)

Chapter 7: The vi Editor

▲ Type the following to execute the */etc/passwd* file again and to get wc to count the number of lines in */etc/passwd* and print the number to the screen:

```
| wc -l<Enter>
```

See Appendix B for answers.

Quiz

1. When using the vi editor, what are the two modes of operation?
2. While using vi, how do you get into Command mode?
3. Which of these single-letter commands could you use to enter text?

    ▲ a

    ▲ x

    ▲ i

    ▲ dd

4. True or False: While in Command mode, pressing u repeatedly will undo all previously entered commands.
5. True or False: The vi editor can be used to globally change the first occurrence of a pattern on every line with a given pattern.
6. Which of these will allow you to quit vi while in Insert mode?

    ▲ :x

    ▲ :qw

    ▲ :wq

    ▲ <Shift>-zz

    ▲ <Shift>-ss

    ▲ :q!

    ▲ All of the above

    ▲ None of the above

See Appendix C for answers.

Chapter 8

Shell Basics

AS SOON AS YOU LOG IN TO A LINUX SYSTEM, you are exposed to a shell—generally the bash variant, which is discussed in detail here. The *shell* program is an interface to the operating system, translating your typed input (or input from other sources) into instructions for the operating system. DOS's *command.com* program does just about the same thing.

This chapter describes the ins and outs of the basic Linux shells. Although the focus is on bash, we introduce elements of the tsch shell and include certain twists on the commands relevant to still other shells.

Knowing what the shell is doing with your input will make you a more efficient and effective Linux user and system administrator. And when you see how you can customize your input with wildcards, metacharacters, and pipelining, you'll begin to understand their power.

The Linux Shells

The shell is but one interface to Linux/UNIX; there are others such as the X Window System. Remember that any shell is just an interface, not the operating system itself.

After you log in, typing your user name and password, the operating system starts the shell program. It's the shell program that responds by giving you a prompt, such as

   [*username*@*hostname* /*directory*]$

In this book, we usually shorten this prompt to $.

The shell is first a command interpreter. When you present a command to the shell, it looks at the command name to see whether it matches an internal shell command that it can execute itself. It checks also to see whether the command is an alias for another command. If the command is not an internal command nor an alias for an internal command, the shell searches the hard disk for the program corresponding to the command name. If it finds one, the shell executes the program and feeds it the arguments (if any) that accompanied the command name entry.

What happens when the shell cannot locate a program? It responds with an error message, such as

```
shellname: commandname: command not found
```

As a job controller, the shell enables multiple task execution. It allows programs (also referred to as processes or jobs) to run in the background (which likely requires no user interaction), while another program runs in the foreground (which likely interacts with the user). The shell switches between these and other multiple tasks as necessary. It can suspend jobs without losing track of where the processes stopped, so that they can begin again at the same point. The shell also allows programs to be piped to achieve complex results with single but perhaps complicated commands. (In *piping*, the output of one program is input to another, which starts automatically.)

The shell also allows you to write scripts. A shell script can invoke other shell scripts as long as their locations are in the search path. Thus, the shell is a comprehensive programming language that does not need a compiler because it interprets the logic itself. Keep in mind, however, that different shells use different syntaxes to execute shell scripts.

Shell Types

The two major UNIX shells are the Bourne shell and the C shell. The Bourne shell is similar to the first UNIX shell developed by Bell Labs. The C shell was developed at the University of California at Berkeley and has a format similar to the C programming language. Another

CHAPTER 8: SHELL BASICS

prominent shell is the Korn shell, developed at the AT&T Bell Labs, which was based on the Bourne shell but also incorporated some C shell functionality.

Your Linux distribution contains several shells. Check your documentation for a complete listing, as well as an indication of which shells are automatically installed as part of the basic installation. Some typical shells follow:

- ▲ *ash* is a Bourne shell clone that supports all Bourne shell commands but is smaller than bash.

- ▲ *ash.static* is a version of ash that is not dependent on software libraries.

- ▲ *bash* stands for Bourne Again Shell, the default Linux shell. An *sh*-compatible interpreter, it reads standard input or input from a file; incorporates features from both Korn and C shells; and is intended to conform with IEEE POSIX Shell and Tools specifications.

- ▲ *mc* is Midnight Commander, a visual shell. It looks like a file manager but has many more features.

- ▲ *pdksh* is a reimplementation of the Korn shell intended for interactive and shell script use.

- ▲ *rsh* is the restricted shell used for network operations.

- ▲ *sash* is a statically linked shell that contains simplified versions of some basic commands. It is useful for system recovery.

- ▲ *tcsh* is an enhanced version of the C shell with additional features and fancier prompts. In Linux, this is the usual choice as the alternative to bash.

- ▲ *zsh* is an enhanced version of the Bourne shell, with most Korn shell, bash, and tcsh features—and more.

You can check to see whether any of the preceding shells (or others) are on your installation medium, as well as which ones were installed with your Linux operating system, by viewing the listing in the */etc/shells* file.

To determine the default shell you log in to, check the listing after your user name in the */etc/passwd* file or check your environment by typing `env` followed by <Enter> to see which directory is listed as the `SHELL=` *variable* value. Although bash is the usual default shell, you can specify which shell you want to use, either by default or for a specific process or task. On some systems, you can change your shell with commands such as `chsh` or `passwd` with the `-s` option. For further help, check your information sources.

Metacharacters and Wildcards

Metacharacters have a special meaning to the shell (although that meaning may vary from one shell to another), so you should never use them as part of a file name. An exception is the hyphen (-), which you can use as long as it is not the first character in the file name. Following is a list of metacharacters:

```
~ ! # $ % ^ & *
( ) { } [ ] | \
; " ' < > ? /
```

Wildcards are a subset of metacharacters used in pattern matching:

```
* ? ! [ ]
```

Linux's shells, like those of all UNIX operating systems, can reference more than one file name using wildcards. This process is called *pattern matching notation for files*.

Asterisk

You can include one or more asterisks (*) with a character or string of characters in a file name specification. The inclusion of the asterisk causes the shell (not the operating system) to initiate a type of pattern matching process called *wildcard expansion*. That process substitutes all possible file names that match the characters included before or after the asterisk. The shell substitutes file names containing zero to any number of additional characters, as long as the specified character or string also appears.

CHAPTER 8: SHELL BASICS

The process is easier to understand through an example, so check out Example 8.1.

Example 8.1 ▼

* Wildcard

To copy all files whose names begin with *n* to the */tmp* directory (refer to Figure 8.1):

```
$ cp n* /tmp<Enter>
ne net new nest
```

Echo all files whose file names begin with *test1* to the screen:

```
$ echo test1*<Enter>
test1 test1.2 test1.3
```
▲

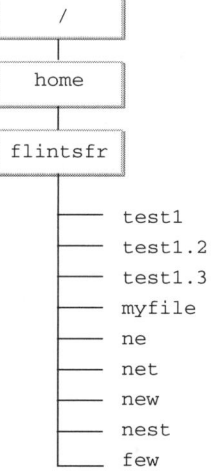

Figure 8.1: Directory structure for Examples 8.1 through 8.5.

Following are additional examples of matches that illustrate asterisk wildcard expansion:

▲ *a* matches any file name containing *a*

▲ a* matches any file name beginning with *a*

▲ *a matches any file name ending with *a*

▲ a*a matches any file name beginning and ending with *a*

The exception to wildcard expansion is that matches will not occur to files beginning with a dot (.)—that is, to hidden files, as well as to current and parent directories—*unless* the dot is included as part of the search string. For example, if you enter the following while in your home directory:

    $ echo *bash* <Enter>

the system will not return the names of hidden *bash* files (for example, *.bash_history* or *.bash_logout*). However, if you entered

    $ echo .bash* <Enter>

the names of all hidden *bash* files (such as the previous two, plus *.bash_profile* and *.bashrc*) are returned to the screen.

Question Mark

A question mark (?) is another wildcard you can use in a file name specification. The shell substitutes file names that have only a single character in the same position as the question mark, as shown in Example 8.2. Thus, the shell still does wildcard expansion, but the expansion goes to only one character instead of from zero to any number of characters,

Example 8.2 ▼   ? Wildcard

Given the directory tree in Figure 8.1, list all files whose file names begin with *ne* and are only three characters long:

    $ ls ne?<Enter>
    net new

Remove all files whose file names are three characters long, with *e* as the middle character:

    $ rm ?e?<Enter>
    few net new

As with the asterisk wildcard, the exception is that matches will not occur to files beginning with a dot (.).

WARNING: *Using wildcards with certain commands, especially the* rm *(remove) command, can be risky. You may get unexpected and unwelcome results. We recommend that you use the interactive form (that is,* rm -i*) when you want to include wildcards. This recommendation is especially helpful when you want to introduce recursive arguments (*-R*) that might alter the contents of directories all the way down the directory tree.*

Square Brackets for Lists

When you want to match only one of several characters, you use the square brackets. Similar to the ? wildcard, the position defined by the location of the brackets is expanded by the shell but to only one character. Unlike with the ? wildcard, however, only file names with the characters specified between the brackets are used as input to the command. Again, this process is easier to see in action, so refer to Example 8.3.

Example 8.3 ▼

[ ] for Lists

Given the directory in Figure 8.1, list all files whose three-character file names begin with *ne* and end with *s, t,* or *w*.

```
$ ls ne[stw]<Enter>
net new
```

Exclamation Point

You use the exclamation point (!) within square brackets as a wildcard to exclude possibilities. Again, the position defined by the location of the brackets is expanded by the shell but to only one character, as shown in Example 8.4. Unlike the square list brackets, however, only file names whose characters in that position are *not* members of the set of characters specified within the brackets are used as input to the command. It might help to think of ! as meaning *not*.

Example 8.4 ▼   ! and [ ] Wildcards

Referring to Figure 8.1, echo all file names that do not begin with *t* or *n*:

```
$ echo [!tn]*<Enter>
myfile few
```
▲

Square Brackets for Ranges

You can use square brackets not only for lists but also for ranges. Here, too, the position defined by the location of the square brackets is expanded by the shell but to only one character. But this time, only file names whose characters in that position are members of the *range* of characters specified in the brackets are used as input to the command. This allows for a much larger list of characters while reducing the amount of typing required to define the list. See Example 8.5.

Example 8.5 ▼   [ ] for Ranges

Given the directory in Figure 8.1, list all files whose file names end with a number from 1 through 5, inclusive:

```
$ ls *[1-5]<Enter>
test1 test1.2 test1.3
```
▲

Standard Files: Redirection and Piping

As mentioned, the shell is the primary interface between the user and the Linux operating system. And the standard shell in Linux is bash, the Bourne Again Shell. For each process in the system, three files are automatically opened:

▲ Standard input (*stdin*) is the location where a command expects to find its input. Usually that location is the keyboard.

▲ Standard output (*stdout*) is the location where the command expects to send its results. Usually, that location is the screen, but it may also be a file.

▲ Standard error (*stderr*) is the location where the command expects to send its error messages. Usually, that location is the screen, but it may also be the system console.

The description of the location is stored in a command's file descriptor table. You can change the defaults (for example, screen, file, or console) using redirection, which we describe shortly.

File Descriptors

Each command or utility opens its own file descriptor to keep track of data files, inputs, outputs, and error messages. File descriptors differ depending on the command or utility that is running. File descriptor entries may refer to special device pointer files that in turn point to system devices, such as a terminal or a disk drive. See Table 8.1. Remember that in Linux/UNIX, not all file names refer to data files.

Table 8.1 File Descriptor Parameters

Descriptor name	Operator	Device pointer	Default device
Standard in (*stdin*)	<	0	Keyboard
Standard out (*stdout*)	>	1	Screen
Standard error (*stderr*)	2>	2	System console

Consider the `cat` command, which we used in Chapter 2 to list the contents of file names we provided on the command line. If you do not specify a file name, `cat` simply echoes back on the screen whatever you type. That's because to `cat`, *stdin* is the keyboard (not a file) and *stdout* is the screen.

Input Redirection

In Example 8.6, we assume that the *fredletter* file has already been created. By using the left angle bracket (<), the `mail` program is instructed to take *fredletter* as the standard input, supplanting `mail`'s expected standard input, which is characters typed at the keyboard. This way, it's easier to format the letter, correct typing errors, or add embellishments to the letter before sending it. The syntax is

```
command < filename
```

With this redirection in place, `mail` does not return the `Subject:` and `Cc:` prompts, unless you add the `-sc` argument to the `mail` command.

Example 8.6 ▼

< for Redirecting Input

The default standard input for the `mail` program is the keyboard:

```
$ mail flintsfr<Enter>
Subject: Letter to Fred
Hey, Fred, this is a letter to YOU.
Signed, Barney
<Ctr>l-d
Cc:<Enter>
```

To redirect input (from a previously created file) and tell the `mail` program to send the *fredletter* file as the letter to *flintsfr*:

```
$ mail flintsfr < fredletter<Enter>
```
▲

NOTE: *Some commands, such as* `ls` *and* `rm`, *do not accept redirected input. Other commands pause and request information from the user if you don't give them a file or data to work with.*

Output Redirection

Redirection allows you to specify where you want standard output to go, if not to the screen, the default location. The syntax is

```
command > filename
```

Chapter 8: Shell Basics

Example 8.7 illustrates the default standard output of the `ls` command, followed by the instruction to `ls` to send its output to the *ls.out* file. If the file does not yet exist, it is created. If the *ls.out* file already exists, its contents are overwritten (called *destructive redirection*).

Example 8.7 ▼ > for Redirecting Output

The default standard output for the `ls` command is the screen:

```
$ ls<Enter>
file1 file2 file3
```

To redirect output and instruct the `ls` command to send the output to the *ls.out* file (new or existing):

```
$ ls > ls.out<Enter>
```
▲

The `ls` command's descriptor table follows:

0   stdin (unchanged)
1   *ls.out* (changed)
2   stderr (unchanged)

If your intention is to add data to a file or simply avoid overwriting existing data, you can append output to an existing file (called *nondestructive redirection*). The syntax is

```
command >> filename
```

This type of nondestructive redirection is shown in Example 8.8.

Example 8.8 ▼ >> and who for Redirecting Output

To redirect output and append it to an existing file, tell the `who` command to send its output to the *whos.there* file, appending the output to any data that is already in the file:

```
$ who >> whos.there<Enter>
```
▲

The file descriptors for the append example follow:

0   `stdin` (unchanged)
1   *whos.there* (changed)
2   `stderr` (unchanged)

 NOTE: *Some commands produce output that cannot be redirected in this way. For example, printing commands write to the printer, period.*

Here's a handy alternate use for output redirection. The first part of Example 8.9 shows a typical use for `cat`. The second part, combining `cat` and redirected output, allows you to create a file quickly, without invoking a text editor. For small files, this procedure might be considered as good as or superior to using a text editor. Note that we use <Ctrl>-d at the end of file. Using <Ctrl>-c would have canceled the command.

Example 8.9 ▼

> and cat for Redirecting Output

The `cat` command is normally used to list the contents of files:

```
$ ls<Enter>
letter acctfile file1

$ cat file1<Enter>
This is file1. This is the first line.
And this is the second line of file1.
```

To instead use `cat` with redirection to create a new file:

```
$ cat > newfile<Enter>
This is line 1 of newfile.
And this is line 2.
Needless to say, this is line 3.
<Ctrl>-d
$ ls<Enter>
letter acctfile1 newfile
```
▲

Following are the file descriptors for the `cat > newfile` example:

0 `stdin` (unchanged)
1 `newfile` (changed)
2 `stderr` (unchanged)

Two more examples of this type of redirection follow:

▲ `> newfile` creates a zero-length file called *newfile*. If *newfile* already exists, this process removes the original contents of the file.

▲ `cat file1 file2 > file3` creates a file called *file3*, which contains the combined contents of *file1* and *file2*.

Error Redirection

Error messages are normally sent immediately to the screen or the system console. Sometimes, however, you want to collect error messages from scripts or shell programs for future reference or troubleshooting. Example 8.10 shows you how. The syntax is

```
command 2> filename
```

Example 8.10 ▼ 2> for Redirecting Error Output

The standard error output of *fileb* goes directly to the screen or system console:

```
$ cat filea fileb<Enter>
```
cat: fileb: Permission denied

To redirect the *fileb* error message to the *errfile* file (new or existing) and then use `cat` to read the error message:

```
$ cat filea fileb 2> errfile<Enter>
$ cat errfile<Enter>
```
cat: fileb: Permission denied   ▲

In Example 8.10, the *fileb* error message is sent directly to the *errfile* file. If *errfile* does not exist, it is created. If *errfile* already exists, its contents are overwritten. (As with output redirection, this overwriting capability is called destructive redirection.) The *filea* results are sent to the screen, but you have to use the `cat` command with *errfile* to see what happened to *fileb*'s results. The file descriptor table follows:

   0 `stdin` (unchanged)

   1 `stdout` (unchanged)

   2 `errfile` (changed)

In Example 8.11, the error message is sent directly to */dev/null*, a special file called the *bit bucket* that remains empty, regardless of what you dump into it. It is used for all sorts of purposes, such as monitoring processes, analyzing network traffic, and collecting error messages you might not want to be bothered with.

Example 8.11 ▼   **2> for Redirecting Error Output to the Bit Bucket**

To redirect the *fileb* error message to */dev/null*, the bit bucket:

   `$ cat filea fileb 2> /dev/null<Enter>`   ▲

The file descriptor table for this second redirection follows:

   0 `stdin` (unchanged)

   1 `stdout` (unchanged)

   2 `/dev/null` (changed)

Following is the syntax for redirecting and appending error output (nondestructive redirection) to a file, which is a similar format to redirecting output un general. The difference is the inclusion of 2 for this process:

   `command 2>> filename`

One application for this type of redirection is system error logging or network analysis.

NOTE: *It is important to remember that the operator symbols for standard error redirection are 2> and 2>>, with no spaces between the characters.*

Combined Redirection

Combined redirection is basically a combination of two or more redirections of input, output, and errors. Following is the syntax for basic but potentially destructive redirection:

```
command < infile > outfile 2> errfile
```

Here is the syntax for nondestructive redirection using the same input file:

```
command >> appendfile 2>> errfile < infile
```

As seen in these two, the order in which the redirections appear does not matter.

To clarify why one redirection is called potentially destructive and the other nondestructive, notice that in the first example, we direct the command output to *outfile* and any error information to *errfile*. If *outfile* and *errfile* already contain information, that information is overwritten (and destroyed) with the new information from this new command. In the second example, the results from command execution are appended to *appendfile*, preserving whatever information may already be in the file. Similarly, error information, if any, is appended to *errfile*, preserving whatever information may be there too.

Association

Association is a type of combined redirection. In the second part of Example 8.12, the syntax differs and the order in which the redirections and associations appear *does* matter.

Example 8.12 ▼ Redirecting to outfile

To redirect process output to the *outfile* file, use the following syntax. Error messages are sent to the standard output location, which is now *outfile* as well:

```
$ command > outfile 2>&1<Enter>
```

In the next example, error messages are also redirected to the standard output location—which is the terminal screen—and *then* standard output is redirected to *outfile*:

```
$ command 2>&1 > outfile<Enter>
```
▲

In the first part of Example 8.12, file descriptor 1 is associated with the specified file, *outfile*. Then descriptor 2 is associated with the file associated with descriptor 1. But file descriptor 1 is now (already) associated with *outfile*. Consequently, error messages are also redirected to *outfile*.

In the second part of Example 8.12, we reverse the order of the redirection. In the first instruction, file descriptor 2 is associated with file descriptor 1. Thus far, file descriptor 1 is by default associated with the terminal screen, and therefore, error messages will go to the screen. Then, the second instruction associates file descriptor 1 with *outfile*. Error messages will ultimately go to the screen and process results will go to *outfile*.

Another example of association, this time for the `ls` command, follows:

```
$ ls -l /*/* > list.file 2>&1<Enter>
```

The file descriptor table for this example is as follows:

0 `stdin` (unchanged)

1 `./list.file` (changed)

2 `./list.file` (changed)

Here's an example of how you might *not* want to execute an association:

```
$ ls -l /*/* 2>&1 >list.file<Enter>
```

0 `stdin` (unchanged)

1 `./list.file` (changed)

2 `stdout` (changed)

Connecting Commands with Pipes

In Linux, as in UNIX, you can connect two or more commands on a single command line using the pipe symbol (|). This concept is called *pipelining* or *piping* and is one of the earliest and most revolutionary aspects of UNIX. Following are the only requirements:

▲ Any command to the left of a pipe must send its output to standard output *(stdout)*

▲ Any command to the right of a pipe must take its input from its standard input *(stdin)*

The output from the command to the left of the pipe is not displayed because it is given straight over to the input of the command to the right of the pipe. You see the results of the final process only, as shown in Example 8.13. The syntax is simply

```
cmd1 | cmd2
```

Example 8.13 ▼ Pipes for Connecting Commands

To count the number of files in the directory you're in using command pipelining:

```
$ ls | wc -w<Enter>
40
```

The piped command line in the preceding example is the same as the following sequence of commands:

```
$ ls > tempfile<Enter>
$ wc -w tempfile<Enter>
41 tempfile
$ rm tempfile<Enter>
```

Why did the word count from the piped commands in Example 8.13 differ from the word count from the sequence of individual commands? In the command sequence, the user created a new file called *tempfile* and its name got caught up in the word count.

NOTE: *If one of the commands in a pipe fails, the entire pipe fails.*

Next, you see how the various elements of a pipe execute in parallel.

Filters

A command is referred to as a *filter* if it can read its input from standard input, alter it in some way, and write the output to standard output. A filter can thus be used as an intermediate command between pipes. When you use filters as intermediate steps in piped commands, you save processing steps and time. The syntax is

```
cmd1 | filter
```

In Example 8.14, the `ls` command lists all files in the directory and then pipes the information to the `grep` command. The `grep` command (covered in more detail in Chapter 13) finds all file names beginning with the letter *n*. The output of the `grep` command is then piped to the `wc -l` command. The `wc` command counts the number of lines—represented by the number of files whose names begin with *n*—of input, and returns with the answer, 4. Thus, the `grep` process acts as a filter because it keeps the four file names (*ne, net, new,* and *nest*) and passes them to `wc`, while discarding the other file names.

Example 8.14 ▼ Using Filters

To use filters to return the number of files in the */home/flintsfr* directory that begin with the letter *n*:

```
$ ls | grep ^n | wc -l<Enter>
4
```

Referring to Figure 8.1, you can see that four file names—*ne, net, new,* and *nest*—begin with *n*, so the preceding result, 4, is correct.   ▲

Here is another way we could have expressed the piped command:

```
$ ls -R /home/flintsfr | grep ^n | wc -l<Enter>
```

CHAPTER 8: SHELL BASICS

However, in this version, we do not assume, as we did in Example 8.14, that the user begins in the /home/*flintsfr* directory.

Split Outputs: tee Command

You can *tap* information from a command pipeline. The `tee` command acts as a filter for capturing a snapshot of information at a specific point in a pipe. The command puts a copy of the data at that point into a file and passes the original data to standard output, which is used through the standard input of the next downstream command:

    $ *cmd1* | tee *filename* | *cmd2*<Enter>

The `tee` command does not alter the data. See Example 8.15.

Example 8.15 ▼   tee

Referring to Figure 8.2, three files are at the beginning of the pipe (*Pebbles*, *Wilma*, and *Fred*) when you issue the following command:

    $ ls | tee ls.save | wc -l<Enter>
    3

By the end of the pipe's execution, there are four files (*Pebbles*, *Wilma*, *Fred*, and *ls.save*), yet the `wc` command reports only three. If the pipes are truly parallel, shouldn't the `wc` command have reported 4? Perhaps, but it reports 3 because it takes longer for a file handle to be given to `tee` than it takes for the entire pipe to run.   ▲

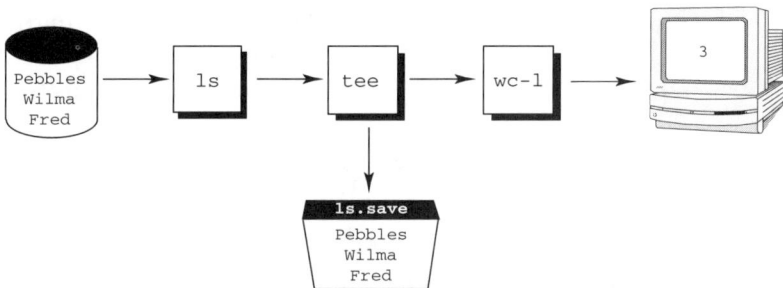

Figure 8.2: The tee *command, as shown in Example 8.15.*

The `tee` command takes its input and routes it to two destinations: by default to the terminal, unless you pipe its output to another command (such as in Example 8.15) and to the file of your choice.

Command Grouping with the Semicolon

The shell can cope with multiple commands on the same line. The semicolon (;) is the metacharacter that facilitates the process. The syntax is

    cmd1 ; cmd2

Placing several commands on the same line, each separated from the next by a semicolon, produces the same result as entering each command on a separate line, as shown in Example 8.16. Relationships between the output of one process and the input to the next are not necessary.

Example 8.16 ▼ ; for Multiple Commands

To issue a sequence of commands on more than one line:

    $ ls -R > outfile<Enter>
    $ exit<Enter>

These two lines are the same as the following single command line:

    $ ls -R > outfile ; exit<Enter>   ▲

One reason you might consider using the semicolon in this way is that some commands (such as the `ls -R` command) might take a while to execute. Separating them with a semicolon allows the next command to execute without delay after the previous one has finished executing.

Line Continuation with the Backslash

Line continuation is a shell feature that is useful when the options and arguments appended to a single command cause you to type past the

CHAPTER 8: SHELL BASICS

length of the single command line. Simply type as far as you can and finish with a single backslash (\) followed immediately by <Enter>—no other character can follow the backslash. The shell takes you to the next line and automatically presents you with an angle bracket (>), called the secondary prompt, which indicates that the shell is expecting more input from you:

```
$ cmd continued_cmd\<Enter>
> continued_cmd<Enter>
```

The secondary prompt does not interfere with the interpretation of the command. Do not confuse this prompt with the redirection prompt angle bracket, which is a key you have to type. See Example 8.17. You can change the secondary prompt from the angle bracket to another symbol or even to a phrase of your choice by changing the value in the PS2 variable.

Example 8.17 ▼   \ for Continuing Command Text

```
$ cat /home/mydir/mysubdir/mydata \<Enter>
> /home/yourdir/yoursubdir/yourdata<Enter>
```

173

Exercises

1. Go to your home directory. Execute a simple `ls` command to list the nonhidden files in your home directory. Now use the `ls` command with a wildcard character to list these files.

   ```
   $ ls<Enter>
   $ ls *<Enter>
   ```

   What is the difference in output of these two commands? Why?

2. Change to the */usr/bin* directory. List the files starting with the letter *a*.

   ```
   $ cd /usr/bin<Enter>
   $ ls a*<Enter>
   ```

3. List all two-character file names.

   ```
   $ ls ??<Enter>
   ```

4. List all file names starting with the letters *a, b, c,* or *d*.

   ```
   $ ls [abcd]*<Enter>
   ```
   or
   ```
   $ ls [a-d]*<Enter>
   ```

5. List all files except those beginning with *c* through *t*. This will be a long list, so you might want to pipe the output to `more`.

   ```
   $ ls [!c-t]* | more<Enter>
   ```

   Did you get any file names that you didn't expect? If so, do you know why?

6. Return to your home directory.

   ```
   $ cd<Enter>
   ```

7. Using the `cat` command and redirection, create a file called *junk* containing a few lines of text. Use <Ctrl>-d at the beginning of a new line when you have finished entering text and want to return to the shell prompt, $.

   ```
   $ cat > junk<Enter>
   ```

CHAPTER 8: SHELL BASICS

```
Type several lines of junk for this file.<Enter>
When you're finished, press the Enter key<Enter>
to go to a new line and then press Ctrl-d<Enter>
to return to the shell prompt.<Enter>
<Ctrl>-d
```

8. Append more lines of text to the file you have created using the `cat` command and redirection.

   ```
   $ cat >> junk<Enter>
   Type some more lines and append them to<Enter>
   junk. When you are fininshed, go to a new line<Enter>
   and press the Enter key and then the Ctrl-d keys.<Enter>
   <Ctrl>-d
   ```

   NOTE: *Remember that there are no spaces between the angle brackets in the command line.*

9. Mail the *junk* file to yourself. Wait several seconds, and then open your mail, delete *junk*, and quit the program.

   ```
   $ mail username << junk<Enter>
   $ mail<Enter>
   ? t<Enter>
   ? d<Enter>
   ? q<Enter>
   ```

10. Using the `ls` command, list the files in your current directory.

    ```
    $ ls<Enter>
    ```

    Make a note of the number of files.

11. List the files in your current directory but this time redirect the output to the *temp* file.

    ```
    $ ls > temp<Enter>
    ```

12. Use the appropriate command to count the number of words in the *temp* file.

    ```
    $ wc -w temp<Enter>
    ```

    Is this the same count as in Exercise 10? If not, why not?

Display the contents of *temp*.

    $ cat temp<Enter>

Then remove the file.

    $ rm temp<Enter>

13. This time, use a pipe to count the number of files in your current directory.

    $ ls | wc -w<Enter>

    Was the result what you expected this time? Is it the same as in Exercise 10?

14. Use the command you created in Exercise 13, but this time insert a `tee` in the middle, trapping the result of the list in a file called *junk2*.

    $ ls | tee junk2 | wc -w<Enter>

    Was the number displayed on the screen? Check the contents of *junk2* to make sure that it contains what you expected.

    $ cat junk2<Enter>

15. Again, using piped commands, list in reverse order the contents of your current directory; send the results of the reverse listing to a file named *junk3* and to a program to count the number of words in the reverse listing; and append the final count to *junk3*.

    Remember to use the append version of redirection. In this particular case, you may get unexpected results if you do not. It might not be a straight overwrite because the file is being used twice in the same command. Experiment if you are curious.

    $ ls -r | tee junk3 | wc -w >> junk3<Enter>

16. A special file in the */dev* directory represents your terminal. Display the file name associated with your terminal. The output will be something like *tty0*, *lft0*, or *pts/x*.

    $ who am i<Enter>

CHAPTER 8: SHELL BASICS

Repeat the command from Exercise 15 with two exceptions: (a) Rather than using *junk3*, `tee` the output to the special file that represents your terminal. (b) Do not append the results of the wc command to *junk3*. Display the count at your terminal.

```
$ ls -r | tee /dev/lft0 | wc -w<Enter>
```

17. On the same command line, display the date, who is logged in, the name of your current directory, and the names of the files in your current directory.

    ```
    $ date ; who ; pwd ; ls<Enter>
    ```

    Do these commands have any relation to each other?

18. The primary purpose of this exercise is to use line continuation with a command that is too long to fit on one command line. The secondary purpose is to test what you have learned so far by letting you create a very long command string. You can choose to break the line anywhere you like. When completed, test your output by displaying the contents of the files that were created. This should be one long command connected by pipes and redirection.

    ▲ Do a long listing of the files in your home directory, including hidden files.

    ▲ Capture the output to a file named *reverse.listing* and send the same output to a program that will count only the number of words.

    ▲ Capture the number of words and place the number in four files named *file1* through *file4*.

    ▲ Finally, send the output to a program to count the number of lines in *file4* and redirect that number to a file named *file5*.

    ```
    $ ls -al | tee reverse.listing | wc -w | tee file1 \
        <Enter>
    > | tee file2 | tee file3 | tee file4 | wc -l > file5
        <Enter>
    ```

See Appendix B for answers.

Quiz

1. What will the following command match?

   ```
   $ ls ???[!a-z]*[0-9]t
   ```

2. Identify the devices for this command:
   ```
   $ cat file1<Enter>
   ```
   ▲ standard input (0)

   ▲ standard output (1)

   ▲ standard error (2)

3. Identify the devices for this command:
   ```
   $ mail tim < letter<Enter>
   ```
   ▲ standard input (0)

   ▲ standard output (1)

   ▲ standard error (2)

4. Identify the devices for this command:
   ```
   $ cat .profile > newprofile 2> 1<Enter>
   ```
   ▲ standard input (0)

   ▲ standard output (1)

   ▲ standard error (2)

   NOTE: *For Questions 5, 6, and 7, first create command lines to display the contents of a file called* filea *using* cat.

5. Place the output of the command in *fileb* and the errors in *filec*.

6. Place the output of the command in *fileb* and associate any errors with the output in *fileb*.

7. Place the output in *fileb* and discard any error messages (that is, do not display or store error messages).

8. What will the following command do?

   ```
   $ banner hello > /dev/tty1<Enter>
   ```

See Appendix C for answers.

Chapter 9

Using Shell Variables

THIS CHAPTER DESCRIBES MANY OF THE VARIABLES found in both the terminal and shell environments. Linux supports three types of variables: terminal environment variables, built-in variables, and user-defined variables. We show you the two principal methods of setting variables: variable substitution and command substitution. Variables can be set so that all or only specified processes can use them. Note, however, that some variable setting commands differ from shell to shell.

Other topics include quoting (disabling the meaning of metacharacters to change the shell's normal operation) and the shell's interpretation, or parsing, of commands, options, arguments, and metacharacters before sending those commands for execution.

Variables and the Terminal Environment

Before we can discuss variables in detail and their influence on the Linux terminal and shell environments, it is worthwhile to first define variables and the terminal environment.

A *variable* is a name that is known to a program and that represents data. Although the value of the data may remain constant, it more likely changes one or more times while the program is running.

The *terminal environment* is basically the set of all variables and shell functions to which all your shells and their commands, utilities, and other processes have access. The terminal environment is thus the set of variables that all those commands, utilities, and processes have in common, but it is not some all-encompassing set of all variables from all shells. This definition varies from the more classic definition of terminal environment, that is, the list of variables pertaining only to your computer terminal (the ones you can see by typing `stty -a` at the command line). For our purposes, the variables in the terminal environment include the `stty` variables and variables exported to the environment by various profiles, daemons, start-up files—even the shells themselves—as your system was configured, as it starts up, and as you log in.

As you learn more about Linux, you will no doubt customize your terminal environment by altering the values of existing variables and by defining and exporting other variables into your environment. You can rely on the variables that shipped with your distribution and were initialized during your installation and configuration, or you can add to or change them as you become more familiar with variable and process functionality.

How do you identify the variables in your terminal environment and their respective values? Go to a command line and type `env`.

At some point, you may decide that one or more of your shell variables should be added to your environment, so that you don't have to keep defining them from session to session or from shell to shell. How do you add variables to your terminal environment? If you're in the bash shell, you first set the shell variable by typing

```
$ var=value<Enter>
```

(See the "Equal Sign" section later in the chapter for an explanation of this syntax.) Then, to export that variable, you type

```
$ export var<Enter>
```

If you're in the tcsh shell, the `export` command is different. After you've set the variable, you type

```
$ setenv var value<Enter>
```

The `set` and `setenv` commands are discussed again later in this chapter. See Chapter 10 for more information about exporting variables.

CHAPTER 9: USING SHELL VARIABLES

Shell Variable Types

As discussed in Chapter 8, the shell is the interface between the user and the operating system, and it passes information about the terminal environment to applications, commands, and processes. Your shell must have access to several variables so that it can control your Linux session. When you check your shell for all its variables, you will find that it has inherited all the terminal environment variables plus all the shell variables that have not been exported to the environment. Thus, the set of shell variables (that is, the shell environment) is larger than the set of terminal environment variables.

Linux supports the following three types of variables:

▲ **Terminal environment variables** are part of the operating system environment. Users do not necessarily have to define these, but they can use them in shell programs; some can be modified within shell programs (for example, PATH, USER, SHELL).

▲ **Built-in variables** are provided by Linux's operating system and automatically set by the shell to make decisions within a shell script or program (for example, $#, $?, $0, $*, $$). Users cannot modify these variables.

▲ **User-defined variables** are defined by a user when a shell script is written. Users can use and modify these variables anytime within a shell program.

The shell uses all these variable types to define a user's Linux session. All shell environment variables are case sensitive. For instance, if you define a variable called *path*, it won't be the same as *PATH*. Built-in variables and terminal environment variables are generally uppercase, and those defined by the user are generally lowercase. This is not a rule, but rather a convention. However, when you observe this convention, user-defined variables will not interfere with the operation of terminal environment or built-in variables, and you will find it easier to keep them straight when reading your variable listings or doing your own shell programming.

Listing Variable Settings: set Command

To identify your shell environment variables, you can type

    `$ set<Enter>`

It may be advisable to type the following instead, in case the listing of variables is longer than a screenful:

    `$ set | more<Enter>`

The customary use of the `set` command is to assign values to variables:

    `set var=value`

However, if you do not use options or arguments with the command, the shell reports back with a listing of all shell variables as well as their values, as shown in Example 9.1.

Example 9.1 ▼ set

```
$ set<Enter>
HOME=/home/username
HOSTTYPE=i386
OSTYPE=linux
PATH=/bin:/usr/bin:/usr/local/bin:/home/teamxx/bin:
    etc.
PS1=$
PS2=>
SHELL=/bin/bash
USER=flintsfr
.
.
.
xy="hello world"
abc=day                                                    ▲
```

The `set` command is a shell-related command and thus provides a different listing according to the shell currently being used. Because the `set` command reports the variables set in the current shell, it also reports the variables from the terminal environment. As mentioned, the terminal environment variables are a subset of the shell environment variables. However, even though your current shell has access to the values of these variables, all your commands might not have the same access because they may be invoked from different shells. The `export` command allows you to export the variables and their values to the terminal environment so that all commands will have that access, too.

> **NOTE:** *If you're in the tcsh shell and you want to export variables and their values to the terminal environment, you have to use* `setenv` *instead of* `export`.

Near the end of the `set` variable listing, you will probably notice a line that begins with an underscore (_). This is related to the command you executed before `set`. The next time you execute `set`, different characters will likely appear following the underscore because you will have entered a different command before executing `set`.

Setting Shell Variables by Variable Substitution

The values of variables can be set by a form of direct definition called *variable substitution*. They can be set also to the output of a command or a group of commands, which is called *command substitution*. Command substitution is discussed later in the chapter.

Equal Sign

When setting the values of variables, the commands differ depending on the shell you are using. To set a variable when you're in the bash or pdksh shell, use the equal sign with the name of the variable (existing or new) on the left side, and the value you want to set for the variable on the right side:

```
var=value
```

There are *no* spaces between the characters. To set a variable in the tcsh shell, use the `set` command:

```
set var = value
```

In this case, spaces appear on both sides of the equal sign. See Example 9.2 for setting variables in all three shells.

183

Example 9.2 ▼   = for Setting Variables

To set a variable in the bash or pdksh shell:

    $ PS2="Continue typing command >"<Enter>

To set a variable in the tcsh shell:

    $ set PS2 = "Continue typing command >" <Enter>   ▲

User-defined variables can hold any type of data (for example, integer numbers, single words, text strings, or complex numbers). It is up to the application referencing the variable to decide what to do with the contents. In contrast, the content of system-defined variables is fairly static and inflexible. For example, the HOME variable can contain only a directory and not a file.

The variable substitution in Example 9.2 is reminiscent of the latter part of Chapter 8, where we used a backslash followed by <Enter> to interrupt a long command on one line so that we could continue typing the command on the next line. We mentioned that the right angle bracket (>) was assigned to the secondary prompt through the value of the PS2 variable.

Thus, in Example 9.2, we change from the secondary prompt > to a text string to avoid confusion with the standard out redirection symbol. Note that to do so, we have to include double quotation marks at each end of the text string. If we didn't use the double quotation marks, we would receive an error message beginning with *bash:syntax error.* In fact, whenever you set a variable with a text string, *always* enclose the text string in double quotation marks.

NOTE: *The* man *page for each shell generally describes the syntax used to set their respective prompts.*

echo $

If you want to check to see what a variable is set to, simply enter the echo command, followed by a dollar sign and the name of the variable. Note that you add a space between the echo command and the

CHAPTER 9: USING SHELL VARIABLES

dollar sign, but *not* between the dollar sign and the name of the variable being referenced.

In Example 9.3, the value of the user-defined variable *xy* is set to the text string `hello world`. The second command line checks to see whether the value of the variable was successfully set.

Example 9.3 ▼ echo $ for Checking Variable Settings

```
$ xy="hello world"<Enter>
$ echo $xy<Enter>
hello world
```
▲

NOTE: *You can also* echo $var *variables set through command substitution.*

unset Command

Example 9.4 shows how to use the `unset` command to unset the value of a variable. To ensure that the value of the variable is no longer the previously set text string `hello world`, the combination of the `echo` command, the dollar sign, and the variable name are again entered. The seeming lack of a response *is* the shell's response— *xy* no longer has a value attached to it.

Example 9.4 ▼ unset for Changing Variable Settings

```
$ unset xy<Enter>
$ echo $xy<Enter>
```
▲

NOTE: *Similar to* echo $var, *you can also* unset var *on variables whose values were set through command substitution.*

Variable Substitution Sample

Example 9.5 illustrates some additional and typical variable definition and substitution scenarios but with unexpected results in one

185

instance. Note that when no space appears *before* the variable, the substitution is not hampered.

When no space is encountered *after* the variable name, however, the shell is tricked into looking for the wrong name. In this case, it searches in vain for `abclong`, which we know does not exist because we did not define it. When the shell can find no definition for the (wrong) variable name `abclong`, it returns with a null string. That is, the shell does not make a substitution but rather removes the portion of the statement containing the wrong or undefined variable name.

Example 9.5 ▼

Character Substitution for Setting Variables

To assign and verify the `abc` variable:

```
$ abc=day<Enter>
$ echo $abc<Enter>
day
```

To substitute the `abc` variable:

```
$ echo Tomorrow is Tues$abc <Enter>
Tomorrow is Tuesday
```

To try (and fail) to substitute:

```
$ echo There will be a $abclong meeting<Enter>
There will be a meeting
```

To try again to substitute, this time successfully:

```
$ echo There will be a ${abc}long meeting<Enter>
There will be a daylong meeting
```
▲

When you can't have a space following the variable name, you can preserve the proper variable name by surrounding it with curly brackets ({ }). Note, however, that $ remains *outside* the curly brackets.

NOTE: *To set a variable equivalent to a string of text, surround the text string with double quotation marks.*

CHAPTER 9: USING SHELL VARIABLES

Setting Shell Variables by Command Substitution

In the preceding discussion of variable substitution, you saw how to specifically place a value into a variable. In this section, we discuss how to place the result of command execution into a variable.

In Linux's bash shell, you can accomplish command substitution using two types of syntax:

cmd1=`cmd2`

and

cmd1=$(cmd2)

The first syntax uses backquotes to surround the command whose output you want to assign to the variable. The backquote key (`) is located immediately to the left of the 1 key. Do not confuse the backquote with single quotation marks.

Backquotes are supported by the classic Bourne and C shells, so they are supported also by the bash and tcsh shells. Backquotes are supported by the Korn shell for backward compatibility.

The second type of syntax—*cmd1=$(cmd2)*—was originally specific to the Korn shell.

Example 9.6 ▼ Command Substitution in Practice

To determine that the command works and to show how it works:

```
$ date<Enter>
Mon Jun 12 16:14:34 CST 2000
```

To set the variable to contain the results of the command:

```
$ now=`date`<Enter>
```

or

```
$ now=$(date)<Enter>
```

To check on whether the variable works:

```
$ echo $now<Enter>
Mon Jun 12 16:14:34 CST 2000
```

187

Note that you can carry out the command only once. The result is then available for use until the variable is removed or reassigned. ▲

Quoting Metacharacters to Disable Shell Interpretation

Quoting is the disabling, overriding, negating, or escaping (you will encounter *all* these terms in reference to this concept) of the special meaning of other metacharacters, variables, or command names. It is called quoting because two of the three methods use single or double quotes.

Basically, these quoting techniques, equipped with their own sets of metacharacters, are used to override or disable the shell's normal interpretation of other metacharacters. Table 9.1 summarizes the functions of the quoting metacharacters and presents simple examples.

The quoting metacharacters cause the enclosed metacharacter to be interpreted literally (for example, the single quotes cause $HOME to be interpreted as just that—$HOME—because the dollar sign becomes just a dollar sign and not a single character command) or to not be expanded in the manner that the shell would have otherwise interpreted and acted upon. For example, `echo "*.*"` returns *.*, not a listing of all files whose file names contain a single dot in any but the first position.

Table 9.1 Quoting Metacharacters and Their Functions

Metacharacter	Instruction to Shell	Examples
Single quotes (' ')	Ignore all metacharacters between quotes	`$ echo '$HOME'<Enter>` `$HOME`

Double quotes (" ")	Ignore all metacharacters between quotes except the dollar sign ($), backquote (`), and backslash (\)	`$ echo "$HOME"<Enter>`
		`/home/flintsfr`
		
		`$ echo "*.*"<Enter>`
		`*.*`

Backslash (\)	Ignore the special meaning of the next metacharacter	`$ echo \$HOME<Enter>` `$HOME`

CHAPTER 9: USING SHELL VARIABLES

 WARNING: *Remember that you must use the single and double quotes in pairs. Otherwise, your secondary command line prompt appears. (In most cases, an angle bracket [>] appears on the next line and the shell expects instructions. To return to the primary prompt, press <Ctrl>-c.)*

The backslash character deserves special scrutiny. If you are using a backslash to continue a command on another line, that backslash disables the special meaning of the pressed <Enter> key that immediately follows, which normally submits whatever is on the line to the shell for interpretation. By using the backslash there, the shell is being told, "The command isn't finished yet; ignore the next <Enter> and let me continue entering instructions." Then, the next <Enter> key submits the command to the shell.

Check out how we use the backslash in Example 9.7. Instead of the shell seeing three double quotes and presenting a secondary prompt (which was not our intention), it presents the statement followed by the double quotation mark (which was our intention).

Example 9.7 ▼ Quoting Metacharacters

```
$ echo "This is a double quotation mark \""<Enter>
This is a double quotation mark "
```
▲

Command Line Parsing

In Chapter 8, we introduced our examination of the Linux/UNIX shells. We defined the shell and its functions as a command interpreter. When a command is presented to the shell, it looks at the command name to see whether it matches an internal shell command that it can execute by itself. It also checks to see whether the command is an alias for another command. If it's not an internal command and not an alias for an internal command, the shell searches for the program according to the command name submitted on that part of the hard disk defined in its PATH environment variable. (See Example 9.1 for an example of the PATH variable.) If it can find the program somewhere in its specified PATH, the shell executes it and feeds it the arguments, if any, provided at the command line.

What if the program cannot be found in the specified PATH? The shell responds with an error message:

`shellname: commandname: command not found`

Please remember that the program may be on the hard disk but not within the PATH. If you suspect that this is the case, try using a command such as the following to find it:

`$ whereis commandname<Enter>`

(The `whereis` command and related commands are discussed in Chapter 13.) If the shell tells you where the program is, reenter the command name at the command line but use the absolute path name as well as the name of the program. For example, in later distributions of Linux, the `banner` command may have to be invoked by using

`$ /usr/games/banner -w40 "hello friends"<Enter>`

(This is handy to remember when doing Exercise 14 at the end of this chapter.)

Before the shell begins searching for the executable (command) program in its various locations, it parses the command line. In other words, the shell effectively examines the command line in the following order:

1. Redirection (<, >, 2>, |, >>, 2>>)
2. Variable and command substitution
3. Wildcard expansion (*, ?, [])

After the shell has examined the command in the preceding order, it submits the command to the operating system to be executed.

Exercises

1. Ensure that you are in your home directory and then display the shell variables.

    ```
    $ cd<Enter>
    $ pwd<Enter>
    $ set<Enter>
    ```

2. Set a variable named `lunch` to `pizza` and a variable named `dinner` to ham. Display the value of the variables using `echo`. Locate them in the list of variables.

    ```
    $ lunch=pizza<Enter>
    $ dinner=ham<Enter>
    $ echo $lunch ; echo $dinner<Enter>
    $ set<Enter>
    ```

3. Using the variables you just defined, display the message *Lunch today is pizza and dinner is ham*.

    ```
    $ echo Lunch today is $lunch and dinner is $dinner
      <Enter>
    ```

4. Using the variables you just defined, display the message *Lunch today is hamburgers*.

    ```
    $ echo Lunch today is ${dinner}burgers<Enter>
    ```

5. Remove the value of both variables. Check to make sure they are no longer included in your list of variables.

    ```
    $ unset lunch<Enter>
    $ unset dinner<Enter>
    $ set<Enter>
    ```

6. Display the value of your primary and secondary prompt strings.

    ```
    $ echo $PS1<Enter>
    $ echo $PS2<Enter>
    ```

7. Change the primary prompt string to *You Rang?*

    ```
    $ PS1="You Rang?"<Enter>
    ```

Why is it necessary to use quotes with *You Rang?*

NOTE: *Single quotation marks will work too.*

8. Change your secondary prompt string to *What Else?* Test it with the `ls` command using line continuation. End the command. Reset both prompt strings back to their original values.

   ```
   You Rang? PS2="What Else?"<Enter>
   You Rang? ls -l\<Enter>
   What Else? <Enter>
   What Else? <Ctrl>-c
   You Rang? PS1= "$"<Enter>
   $ PS2=">"<Enter>
   ```

   Why are quotes needed around the left angle bracket (>) when resetting the `PS2` variable?

9. Check the value of the variable related to your home directory. Reset that variable to change your home directory to */bin*. Use the `cd` and `pwd` commands to test the effects of this change.

   ```
   $ echo $HOME<Enter>
   $ HOME=/bin<Enter>
   $ cd ; pwd<Enter>
   ```

NOTE: *You can check the value also by using* `set`.

10. Log out and then log back in.

    ```
    $ exit<Enter>
    hostname login: username<Enter>
    Password:
    ```

    What is your home directory?

    ```
    $ cd ; pwd<Enter>
    $ echo $HOME<Enter>
    ```

    Why?

CHAPTER 9: USING SHELL VARIABLES

11. Display your list of variables. Reissue the command but send the output to the `wc` command to get the number of variables that are currently set.

    ```
    $ set<Enter>
    $ set | wc -l<Enter>
    ```

12. Using command substitution, `echo` the following:

    ```
    # variables are currently set
    ```

    where # is the number of variables.

    ```
    $ echo `set | wc -l` variables are currently set<Enter>
    ```

13. Each user ID configured on the system is represented by one line in the */etc/passwd* file. Applying your knowledge of command substitution, `echo` a message that displays

    ```
    There are # users created on the system
    ```

    where # is the number of line entries in */etc/passwd*.

    ```
    $ echo There are `cat /etc/passwd | wc -l` users
          created on the system<Enter>
    ```

14. Using all three methods of quoting, `banner` the literal symbol *.

    ```
    $ banner '*'<Enter>
    $ banner "*"<Enter>
    $ banner \*<Enter>
    ```

    Why do all three work?

15. Make sure that you are in your home directory. Create a directory named *quoting* in your home directory.

    ```
    $ cd<Enter>
    $ pwd<Enter>
    $ mkdir quoting<Enter>
    ```

16. Change to the *quoting* directory. Create a zero-length file named *filea* in that directory. Create a variable named n and set it to the value `hello`. Test what you did by displaying the contents of *quoting* and the value of *n*.

    ```
    $ cd quoting<Enter>
    ```

193

```
$ touch filea<Enter>
$ n=hello<Enter>
$ ls<Enter>
$ echo $n<Enter>
```

17. From the *quoting* directory, execute the following five commands. Record the output.

```
$ echo '* $n `ls`'
$ echo "* $n `ls`"
$ echo \* \$n \`ls\`
$ echo * $n `ls`
$ echo * $n "ls"
```

See Appendix B for answers.

CHAPTER 9: USING SHELL VARIABLES

Quiz

For this quiz, assume the following:

▲ The home directory is /home/flintsfr

▲ The current directory is /home/flintsfr/docs

▲ The current directory contains the files aa, bb, and cc

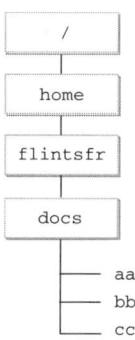

For Questions 1 through 6: What are the results of the following commands?

1. `$ echo "Home directory is $HOME"`
2. `$ echo 'Home directory is $HOME'`
3. `` $ echo "Current directory is `pwd`" ``
4. `$ echo "Files in this directory are *"`
5. `$ echo * $HOME`
6. `$ echo \*`

7. True or False: The listing of terminal environment variables contain all the variables found in your current shell.

8. True or False: When creating built-in variables, you have to ensure that their names are in uppercase. Otherwise, the operating system does not process them properly.

9. What methods can you use to set variable values?

10. Put the following command parsing steps in the proper logical order for the shell to interpret them correctly:

    ▲ Command/variable substitution
    ▲ Command execution
    ▲ Redirection
    ▲ Wildcard expansion

See Appendix C for answers.

Chapter 10

Linux Processes

PROCESSES ARE THE ESSENCE OF COMPUTING. Each command during execution represents at least one process. Some processes run in the foreground, where you can monitor and feed them; some run in the background. Some, like daemons, are initiated at boot time to run all the time or according to an on-demand regime. Batch processes are generally scheduled for execution at a specified time, such as only once, periodically, or somewhere in between.

This chapter describes processes and their environments. Topics also include relationships between processes (for example, how their ID numbers indicate who's who) and the exporting of variables between parent and child processes. Then we take a first look at shell scripts for creating your own processes that you can in turn invoke through the shell. Finally, we discuss return codes, which are used to indicate whether commands have completed successfully.

This chapter does not include exercises. Instead, the concepts in this chapter and Chapter 11 are combined in the exercises at the end of Chapter 11.

Process Environments

A *process* is a single program or task running in its own virtual address space. A command or a job may be comprised of many processes, but (contrary to some opinions), a process is not necessarily the same as a command or a job. Very simple commands, however, can be considered single processes.

From a strict technical interpretation, a program is just a set of instructions, but a process is a dynamic operation that is using the running system's resources.

When you log in, Linux places you in your home (file) directory and initiates a program called a shell. The shell itself is a process. After that, whenever you invoke commands or applications, you are initiating them from within the shell (that is, from within the shell process). In Linux, you can run more than one process at a time, and you can run several copies of the same program simultaneously. You can also track the environments of all the processes while they run.

Table 10.1 summarizes the environment—comprised of variables and parameters—that a typical process may require to run. Some processes require fewer variables and parameters; others require more.

Table 10.1 Process Environment

Field	Explanation
Terminal (TTY)	Terminal ID from which the process was launched
Open files	Files the process is using
Current directory	The directory from which the process was invoked
User ID (UID)	ID of the user who invoked the process
Group ID (GID)	ID of the group that the user belongs to
Process ID (PID)	A unique number that the kernel randomly assigned to the process
Parent process ID (PPID)	A unique number randomly assigned by the process that launched the subject process, if applicable
Flags	Any options and arguments appended to the command that launched the process

We've already mentioned that the shell is a process. Example 10.1 shows you how to check the *process ID,* or *PID,* of the shell process. The built-in variable $ (which, by no coincidence, is also the default user prompt) is the symbol for the current shell.

Example 10.2 ▼ Checking the Shell's PID

To view the PID of the current shell:

```
$ echo $$<Enter>
340
```
▲

Log-in Process

Example 10.2 shows the typical variables and parameters required for the user log-in process, which creates a Linux session that continues until the user logs out. The process environment contains all the information necessary for the process to run. Linux creates the shell environment and initiates the shell process. (By default, users are placed in their own home directories and the bash shell is initiated.)

Example 10.2 ▼ Variables and Parameters for Logging In

Command: `-bash`

UID: `doejane`

GID: `staff`

TTY: `tty1`

PID: 340 ▲

All the information in Example 10.2 is unique to the process environment as long as the user remains logged in. After the user logs out, the information is forgotten. When the user logs in again, the process environment is created anew.

Parent-Child Relationships

When you execute a command, it is important to remember that one or more processes are already running. Thus, every process running in Linux is invoked or managed by another process. This is known as the *parent-child relationship*.

All processes exist in parent-child hierarchies. The process started by a program or command is known as the *parent* process. The parent process may invoke other processes; those processes are called *child* processes. A parent process may have several child processes, but any child process can have only one parent process.

The child process environment is a local one that it has inherited from the parent. That environment tells the child who invoked the child process, how to handle output, and so on. The child can modify its inherited environment and pass the modified environment down to its own children (if applicable), but it cannot pass the modified environment back to its parent. The exception is the child process invoked through the use of a dot (.), which we discuss later. Example 10.3 demonstrates some simple parent and child processes.

Example 10.3 ▼ Parent-Child Processes

To illustrate some parent-child process relationships, suppose that a user named Bob logs in to his terminal and types the following command and options at the command line:

```
$ ps -auxf | less<Enter>
```

The system normally responds with more than one screenful of output, but because the `less` command has been piped to the `ps` command and options, the system stops and waits for user input after each screenful of output is displayed. Let's look at some of the output.

We include the `init` process here to illustrate that it is indeed the parent of all processes. Now let's look at PID 637, which shows us when the root user logged in. The system provided the ability to log in at 09:32, but the root user actually logged in at 12:57. And we see that root's log-in process automatically spawned the child process PID 694, a (default) bash shell, at 12:57. We know that the bash shell is the child of the log-in because of the slash mark(\) that connects the bash command to `login - - root`.

```
USER   PID  %CPU  %MEM  VSZ   RSS    TTY   STAT  START  TIME  COMMAND
root   1    0.0   0.7   1120  472    ?     S     09:31  0:04  init
 .
 .
root   637  0.0   1.6   2224  1036   tty1  S     09:32  0:00  login - - root
root   694  0.0   1.4   1702  944    tty1  S     12:57  0:00  \_ -bash
root   638  0.0   1.7   2232  1128   tty2  S     09:32  0:00  login - - Bob
Bob    749  0.0   1.4   1700  940    tty2  S     14:22  0:00  \_ -bash
Bob    816  0.0   1.2   2488  788    tty2  R     14:37  0:00      \_ ps -auxf
Bob    8170.01.01584   676tty2 S14:370:00\_ less
 .
 .
```

Moving along, we see that our user Bob logged in at 14:22, which caused the spawning of a child process bash shell, too. Notice the same slash connection between that bash shell and Bob's log-in process. Later, at 14:37, we see that Bob entered the ps -auxf | less command. Two child processes were spawned as a result of Bob entering that command: the ps process and the (piped) less process. Those two processes are children of the bash shell because each has a slash connection to it. (We discuss the ps command in more detail in Chapter 11.)

Note that the init process—the first process to start in a system—has a process ID number of 1. When you log in to the system, the kernel assigns the log-in shell a PID of 340. To check the PID number, you use the echo $$ command. The echo command is built into the shell itself, so there is no need to create a subshell to run echo. Although the special $$ variable is used here as an argument to echo, it is mostly used within shell scripts to distinguish between multiple instances of the same shell script. The value of this variable changes as you move from one current process environment to another.

At any rate, here we are in the log-in shell: the PID is 340 and the parent process ID (PPID) is 1 (init process).

To further illustrate parent-child relationships, we start another bash shell. We could have started the tcsh or any other shell, depending on whether we needed a specific shell to run a certain application or shell script, but here we just open another bash session. The PID of the new shell is 382, and the PPID is 340, indicating that the parent process is the previous bash shell. (See Figure 10.1 for an illustration of these concepts.)

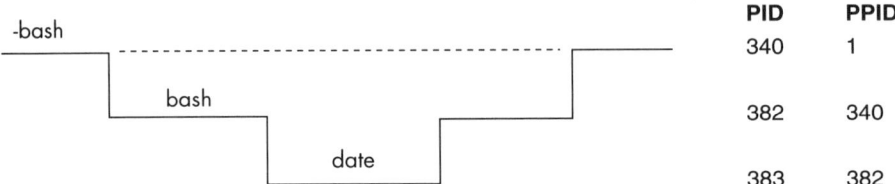

Figure 10.1: Parent-child processes.

While in the second bash shell (that is, the subshell), we invoke the `date` command, which is another process. That process is PID 383, and its parent's PPID is 382, the process ID number of the bash subshell.

NOTE: *While the `date` command executes, you can't interact with the shell. You have to wait until it the commands is finished before running other processes. Thus, the parent (the bash subshell) "sleeps" while the child (`date`) executes. And when the child process terminates, the parent "reawakens."*

Next, we exit from the bash subshell by pressing <Ctrl>-d. We move to the original bash log-in shell, which we verify by executing `echo $$` one last time.

Note that had we invoked more complicated commands or maybe a shell script or two, their processes might have spawned additional child processes. Shell scripts often launch additional shells, in which shell commands are executed.

Processes and Variables

Example 10.4 illustrates that user-defined variables are local to the shell or process in which they are set. Child processes do not automatically inherit user-defined variables and their values. The two basic principles involved here are that variables form part of the environment of a process, and processes cannot access or change variables in the environment of another process.

Example 10.4 ▼ Setting User-Defined Variables

To set the value of x in the bash shell:

```
$ x=4<Enter>
```

To create another bash subshell:

```
$ bash<Enter>
```

Search for the value of x in the subshell.

```
$ echo $x<Enter>
$
```

No record of x is found, so set the value of x to 1:

```
$ x=1<Enter>
```

Exit from the bash subshell to the original bash shell and check the value of x.

```
$ <Ctrl>-d
$ echo $x<Enter>
4
```

The original value of 4 is returned. ▲

Exporting Shell Variables

In Chapter 9, you encountered the `export` command when we discussed how to ensure that variables are inherited from the terminal environment to the shell environment. In this section, we discuss the inheriting of variables and their values from parent processes to their respective child processes—the same principle, only extrapolated.

As stated previously, every process has an operating environment inherited from its parent process. User-defined variables, however, are valid only in their respective processes—they are not by default inherited from parent to child, nor passed back from child to parent. But sometimes you are in one shell and need to set variables so that they can be used by other programs or shell scripts (that is, by other processes). To make one or more variables and their respective values available to any child processes, you export them.

But before you export, you have to set the value of the variable, as shown in Example 10.5. The syntax for the `export` command is

```
$ var=value<Enter>
$ export var<Enter>
```

If you do not specify options after the `export` command, the screen displays the variables that are already exported. This can be handy sometimes. Also handy are the `set` and `env` commands for displaying the shell environment and the inherited environment (referred to as the terminal environment in Chapter 9), respectively.

Example 10.5 ▼ export

`$ echo $$<Enter>`	This command lets us check which process is currently running.
340	The system tells us that the PID is 340.
`$ x=4<Enter>`	We now set the value of the variable x to 4.
`$ export x<Enter>`	We tell the system that any user-defined variables or values, such as x = 4, will be inherited by child processes.
`$ bash<Enter>`	Now we start a bash subshell, which is a child process of the original bash shell.
`$ echo $$<Enter>`	Here, we check the PID of the new bash subshell.
395	The system tells us that the subshell has a PID of 395.
`$ echo $x<Enter>`	The moment of truth: We ask what the value of the user-defined variable x is.

CHAPTER 10: LINUX PROCESSES

4	The value of x has indeed been inherited by this child process.
`$ x=400<Enter>`	At the subshell process level, we change the value of x to 400.
`$ echo $x<Enter>`	As a check, we request the value of x.
400	As expected, the value in this subshell is now 400.
`$ <Ctrl>-d`	We leave the bash subshell and return to the parent bash shell.
`$ echo $$<Enter>`	We check to see whether we have indeed left the subshell by requesting the PID of this shell.
340	No surprise; we are back in the parent bash shell.
`$ echo $x<Enter>`	Now we request the value of x to see whether the 400 has been inherited upward to the parent process.
4	No, the value of x in the parent process is still 4. Thus, variable values are inherited from parent to child but not vice versa. ▲

NOTE: *The* `export` *command (alone) and the* `env` *command show all inherited variables. Use* `set` *to show all shell variables.*

In Example 10.5, the value of x is set to 4 in the log-in shell and then exported to the terminal environment. Another bash subshell is then created. The inherited value of x, as predicted, is 4 here too. But we change the value of x to 400 in the subshell, to see whether it will affect the value of x in the parent log-in shell. Then we exit to the log-in shell and check the value of x. We discover that, despite the fact that we changed x from 4 to 400 in the bash subshell, the value of x remains unchanged in the log-in shell: It's still 4. Thus, changing the value of a variable in a subshell does not affect the parent process.

Assume that you are still in the bash subshell and have just changed the value of *x* from 4 to 400. If you open up another subshell within this subshell, will the value of x be 4 or 400? The answer is 400: The child process inherits the parent process value in this case. After a variable has been exported, it doesn't have to be exported again. If you continued to open subshells within these, the value of x would remain 400 until you saw fit to change it.

If you exit from the string of subshells back to the log-in shell and then open subshells below the log-in shell, the value of x returns to 4. Changes made by a child process to an exported variable are available only to subsequentchild processes. The variable value is not inherited back up to the log-in shell or down any other process. ▲

Shell Scripts

A *shell script* is a collection of system commands stored in a text file that the shell reads and executes in sequence. Such a script contains at least one Linux/UNIX command, as shown in Example 10.6. When the shell processes a shell script, it reads the script file one command at a time, parses the commands, and sends them to the operating system for execution. The commands are executed in turn, just as if you had typed them at the terminal command line.

You can execute any Linux command in a shell script. In fact, some shell features that you can use in a script can't be accessed at the command line. They are built-in facilities that allow more complicated functions to be performed. You can use any text editor to create a shell script.

Example 10.6 ▼ Creating a Shell Script

Assume that you want to execute the `date` command, but you do not want to enter it on the command line. Create a shell script called *script1* using a text editor:

```
$ cat > script1<Enter>
$ date<Enter>
<Ctrl>-d
```

In Option 1 of the next section, "Invoking Shell Scripts," we show you what happens when we execute *script1*.

Assume also that you want to execute `date`, `pwd`, and `ls -l`, but you don't want to enter them at the command line one after the other. Create another shell script called *script2* to handle this:

```
$ cat > script2<Enter>
$ date<Enter>
$ pwd<Enter>
$ ls -l<Enter>
```

In Option 2 of the next section, "Invoking Shell Scripts," we show you how to execute *script2*. ▲

Invoking Shell Scripts

Option 1: Subshell Executes Only One Command

Option 1 invokes a subshell that runs only one command. For this method, the script file does not have to be an executable file but must be readable:

```
$ bash script1<Enter>
```

Invoking the `bash` command within the log-in shell invokes another bash subshell that runs just one command: the execution of the readable *script1* file (see Figure 10.2). In other words, the file has the read permission, even if it doesn't have an execute permission. (Normally, we might expect an x permission, but in this case, we don't need one.)

Another subshell is invoked to run the commands found within the *script1* file. When that subshell has finished executing the commands in the *script1* file, it terminates. The bash subshell that is executing *script1* also terminates, and control is passed back to the log-in shell.

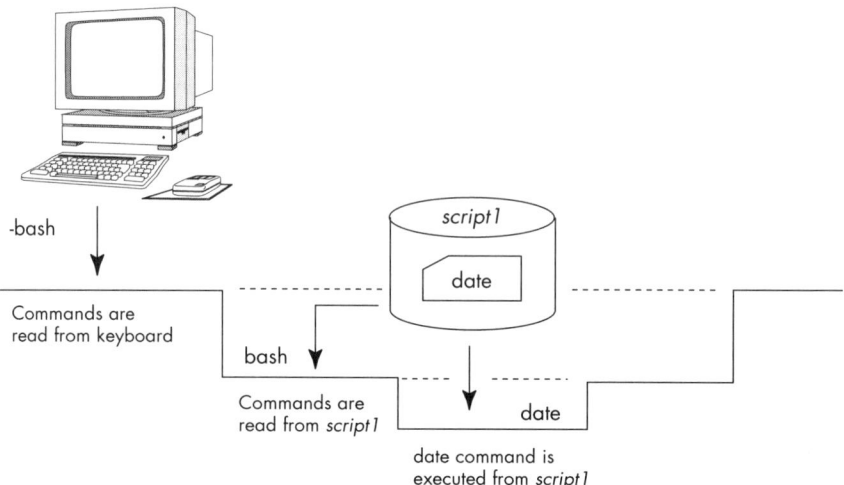

Figure 10.2: Invoking shell scripts using Option 1.

Option 2: Executable Shell Script Files

Option 2 relies on the owner of the shell script first making that file an executable file with the `chmod` command. The owner can use either of the following two formats:

```
$ chmod ugo+rx script2<Enter>
```
or
```
$ chmod 755 script2<Enter>
```

Users of this shell script file must have both read and execute permissions for the shell script file. Why? Because the shell needs to open the script file to read the commands within it. In addition, the script file has to be in a directory to which there is a path, so make sure its directory is listed in the `PATH` environment variable. If there is no path to the directory, you'll get a message from Linux similar to the following:

bash: script1: No such file or directory

After you complete all these steps, you can invoke the *script2* shell script as if it were an ordinary command, like this:

```
$ script2<Enter>
```

Chapter 10: Linux Processes

The processes invoked are similar to those of Option 1 (as illustrated in Figure 10.2) in that a subshell is invoked to execute the shell script file. The processes differ from Option 1, however, in that separate processes are invoked in succession to execute the multiple commands found in *script2*.

What would be the effect of the following command?

    $ chmod +x script1

Answer: The execute (x) permission is given to user, group, and others for the *script1* file. Therefore, this is a third way of ensuring that everyone could execute the shell script file.

Option 3: Dot (.) or source Commands

The previous two methods of executing shell scripts involve the creation of subshells in which to run the commands. Using those methods, any changes to environment variables are local to the script itself and are forgotten when execution of the script ends.

Option 3 involves using the dot (.) command to execute the script file in the current bash or pdksh shell (or using the `source` command when in the tcsh shell). With this method, the dot or `source` command allows you to retain changes in the parent shell, if you want. Both commands ensure that the script file is executed in the current shell (see Figure 10.3). Anyone using this method need only have read permission to the shell script file.

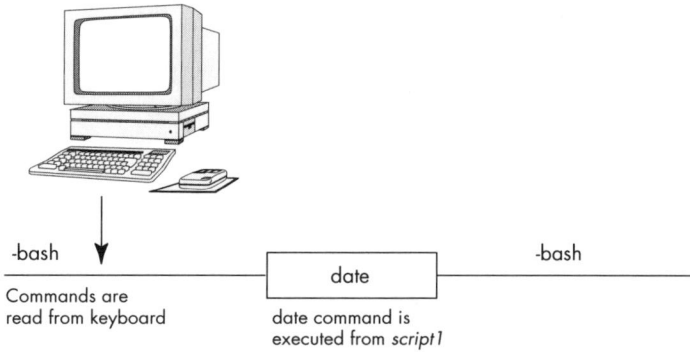

Figure 10.3: Invoking shell scripts using Option 3.

Where do you think this method could be useful? Assume that you have just made changes to the *.profile* file. The shell could reexecute the user profile without logging out. You could type either of the following:

    $ . .profile<Enter>

or

    $ source profile<Enter>

WARNING: *If you are contemplating using this method by default, be aware that after settings are made in the current shell (you're usually in the log-in shell), the only way of returning to the original default settings is to log out and log back in again.*

Return Codes from Commands

After a command has attempted or completed execution, it sends a *return code* (also known as an *exit code*) to its parent process. Note that a return code is a return message from a command, *not* from each individual process within the command. Also note that piped commands (discussed in Chapter 8) send only one return code to their parent.

The return code is stored in the parent process environment as a value for the built-in question mark (?) variable, as shown in Example 10.7. Successful completion of a command returns a value of 0; unsuccessful completion returns a value ranging from 1 to 255.

How do you find the return code to a command? After sending the command for execution, type:

    $ echo $?<Enter>

Example 10.7 $? for finding a Command's Return Code

    $ date<Enter>
    Fri Mar 19 12:05:39 CST 1999
    $ echo $?<Enter>
    0   ▲

Quiz

1. When would you execute a shell script using the dot (.) command? Why?

2. Which command is used to pass the value of a variable from a parent shell to a subshell?

3. Determine the value of *x* at the end of the following procedure:

   $ (... *starting in the log-in shell...*)
   $ x=5<Enter>
   $ bash<Enter>
   $ x=50<Enter>
   $ export x<Enter>
   $ <Ctrl>-d

4. True or False: Each process returns an exit code to its parent process after successful completion.

5. Which of the following is the proper syntax for checking a shell's process identification number?

   $ echo $$<Enter>
   $ echo $?<Enter>
   $ echo $pid<Enter>
   $ ps ef<Enter>

6. When you export a variable, the variable and its value become part of what environment?

7. When invoking shell scripts using Option 1—that is, by invoking a script file in a subshell—which permissions among the following must be given to the script file?

   ▲ drwsxrwxrwx
   ▲ r but not necessarily w or x
   ▲ x and r
   ▲ 755
   ▲ -rw-r-xr-x

- ▲ r but not necessarily w or x; and `-rw-r-xr-x`
- ▲ r but not necessarily w or x; x and r; and
  `-rw-r-xr-x`

See Appendix C for answers.

Chapter 11

Controlling Linux Processes

IN THIS CHAPTER, WE DISCUSS MONITORING and controlling processes as well as foreground and background processes. We then turn to elegant and brutal process termination. The exercises at the end of the chapter cover concepts and procedures discussed in both this chapter and Chapter 10.

Process Monitoring: ps Command

Users (occasionally) and system administrators (more frequently) have to check how their Linux processes are running. The ps (process status) command is commonly used to see how many processes are running, whether a specific process is running or has hung, and how many resources the various processes are using. In addition, the command checks priorities, who's doing what, and so on. A frequent use of the ps command is to monitor background jobs and other processes that do not regularly communicate with your terminal. The syntax is

    ps options

You used the ps command in Chapter 10 when we illustrated parent-child process relationships. At that time, the ps command, with its a, u, x, and f options, showed us which processes were running, who they belonged to, and which processes were children of other processes.

The default ps listing, illustrated in Example 11.1, displays only minimum information about the processes started from your terminal. These processes are described in Table 11.1. On a system with more than one terminal, the TTY field indicates which terminal initiated the process.

Example 11.1 ▼ ps

```
$ ps<Enter>
PID  TTY STAT  TIME  COMMAND
340  1   s     0:00  -bash
356  1   S     0:00  bash
363  1   S     0:00  ls -R /
364  1   S     0:00  ps
```
▲

Table 11.1 Output of the ps Command

Field	Description
PID	Process identification number assigned by the kernel
TTY	Terminal where the process originated
STAT	Current status of the process (for example, S = Asleep, R = Runnable)
TIME	Cumulative execution time for the process (min:sec)
COMMAND	Name of the process being executed

The ps command options are fully detailed in the man pages and other information sources. A few options are explained in Table 11.2.

Table 11.2 Selected Options for the ps Command

Options	Description
e	Environment of the process
f	Processes and subprocesses spawned from the parent processes
l	Long listing (along with basic ps flags, including FLAGS, UID, PPID, PRI, NI, SIZE, RSS, WCHAN)
j	Jobs format (along with basic ps flags, including UID, PPID, PGID, SID, TPGID)
a	Other users' processes too
u	User's name and start time
x	Processes without an associated terminal

Invoking Foreground and Background Processes

Typically—and so far in this book—you invoke processes interactively from the command line. However, you may also invoke processes from the foreground and background states.

Processes that are started and require interaction from the terminal are called *foreground processes*. They are invoked in the foreground when you are fairly sure that they will finish in a short time or when you have to interact with them before and during execution. The processes themselves take over the terminal while they run. The syntax for a foreground process is

    command [-] options arguments

Processes that run independently from the initiating terminal are called *background processes*. You run processes in the background when, for example, you want to use your terminal for other tasks. But they are most useful for executing commands (or scripts or batch files containing numerous commands) that will take a long time to run, regardless of whether or not you are using your terminal. The syntax for a background process is

    command [-] options arguments / > backfile &

NOTE: *A process can be run in the background only if it does not require keyboard input and only if you observe the invocation syntax—the ampersand (&) at the end of the command line.*

Terminating Processes

You might want to terminate a foreground or background process for several reasons:

▲ You no longer need the program or process, and there is no other way to stop it.

▲ You are not getting the results you expected.

▲ You are not getting any results, and your system seems frozen.

▲ Conversely, your output facilities (screen or printer) are overwhelmed by program or process output.

▲ The process or program is using too many system or network resources (such as memory, CPU usage, or bandwidth usage).

▲ The process or program is not behaving properly or predictably.

The first reason likely affects an advanced user or system administrator who may have altered the configuration of one or more systems and now finds that daemons or other background processes are no longer relevant to the system. The other reasons noted are self-explanatory.

Termination Methods

Foreground processes run on the user's terminal and can usually be terminated by some type of quit signal. The most common is <Ctrl>-c, which stops a foreground process and returns you to a shell prompt, generally a dollar sign ($) for users or a pound sign (#) for the administrator, root, and superuser.

Remember that <Ctrl>-c doesn't work with man; use q or <Ctrl>-z instead. Also, some shell scripts or other programs may ignore the quit signal. In cases like these, you may have to enter the `kill` command, which we discuss in detail in the next section. You always have to use `kill` to terminate background processes.

Powering down a local system is a reasonably sure way of terminating foreground or background processes running on the system. However, you should always be concerned with the effects that suddenly powering down might have on individual files or programs, file systems, other system features or processes, and even other users. Powering down should be an alternative of last resort.

The kill Command

An ordinary user has the ability to kill any process that he or she has initiated. By comparison, a root user can kill *any* process. The syntax is

    kill PIDs

or

    kill signal PIDs

CHAPTER 11: CONTROLLING LINUX PROCESSES

If a process is successfully terminated, you get no message from the shell except a prompt. If you try to kill a process that you have no right to terminate or if you try to kill a process and the process you specify doesn't exist, you will see error messages.

WARNING: *Be careful when specifying PIDs with the* `kill` *command: If you kill the wrong process by mistake, you may end up in a lot of trouble.*

In Example 11.2, the `yes` command is invoked in the background. Then the `ps` command finds its PID, and a `kill` command is sent to the yes PID.

Example 11.2 ▼ kill

```
$ bash<Enter>
$ yes > /dev/null &<Enter>
$ ps f<Enter>
PID  TTY STAT TIME    COMMAND
201  1   s    0:00    -bash
206  1   S    0:00     \_ bash
209  1   R    0:00         \_ yes
210  1   R    0:00         \_ ps f
$ kill 209<Enter>
```
▲

NOTE: *Another way to kill a process is* `kill %jobnumber`. *This method is discussed later in the chapter.*

If your terminal hangs, locks, or freezes (all these names describe the same affliction) and <Ctrl>-c doesn't work, you may have to log in to a different terminal (or to a different virtual terminal) and use the `kill` command from there on the log-in shell of the hung terminal. This is just one advantage of UNIX operating systems over a popular GUI-related operating system we all know.

kill Command Signals

With the `kill` command, you can specify one of several signals to terminate processes in a prescribed manner. Table 11.3 shows just a few of the 30-odd signals available. To get a complete listing of Linux `kill` command signals, type the following at the command line:

```
$ kill -l<Enter>
```

Table 11.3 Selected kill Command Signals

Numeric signal	bash signal	tcsh signal	Description
1	SIGHUP	HUP	Hang-up signal sent to a process if its parent is terminated (such as logging off while the process is running). The process can terminate gracefully.
2	SIGINT	INT	Interrupt signal sent when <Ctrl>-c is sent from the keyboard.
3	SIGQUIT	QUIT	Quit signal sent when <Ctrl>-\ is sent from the keyboard.
9	SIGKILL	KILL	Unconditional kill, which cannot be caught or ignored. Stops processes before they have completed.
15	SIGTERM	TERM	Termination signal, which is the default that instructs a process to terminate.

As stated previously and as can be seen in the `kill -l` listing, these signals are used to communicate a change of state to running commands. Depending on the signal used, the change of state ranges from an orderly stop, to an immediate stop, to a stop with the dumping of information to a file for debugging, or even to a rereading of parameters.

Let's discuss the signals tabulated here in a little more detail. First, the *hang-up signal* (that is, 1, SIGHUP, or HUP) is sent to a process if its parent process is terminated. For example, when you log out—that is, when you terminate the log-in shell—a hang-up signal is sent to any running background processes.

CHAPTER 11: CONTROLLING LINUX PROCESSES

The *interrupt* signal (that is, 2, SIGINT, or INT) is sent when a user presses the interrupt key sequence <Ctrl>-c. A process running in the foreground stops unless its program is such that interrupts are ignored. Then a more drastic step may be required. Interrupts don't work on background processes.

The *quit* signal (that is, 3, SIGQUIT, or QUIT) is sent when the quit key is pressed. Generally, the quit key sequence is <Ctrl>-\ but it may vary by system. This signal produces a core file.

The *unconditional kill* signal (that is, 9, SIGKILL, or KILL) is sent when no other signal can stop the process. No process can catch, or ignore, this signal. It should be used with caution because the target process stops immediately. It doesn't finish what it was intended to do, which could cause loss or damage to files or information already generated by the process. For example, if you unconditionally kill a process that is updating a file, the updated material or even the entire file could be lost.

The *termination* signal (that is, 15, SIGTERM, or TERM) is the default signal that tells the command it should proceed with an orderly shutdown. However, some commands or shell scripts may be waiting for device operations to finish, may be attempting to interact with unavailable NFS resources, or may contain statements that allow them to continue executing despite being sent a kill signal (that is, they contain statements that allow them to catch the kill signals). In those cases, a more drastic kill -9 may be necessary.

You can specify any one of several signals, using the syntax we show you in Example 11.3. But if you'd don't specify a signal, kill sends the default -15 (also called SIGTERM in the bash shell or TERM in the tsch shell) to instruct all processes to terminate themselves.

Example 11.3 uses the unconditional -9/KILL/SIGKILL to show you the two basic ways to specify kill signals: using their numeric names or using their shell-specific names.

Example 11.3 ▼ kill Signals

Numeric signals, bash or tcsh shell:

    $ kill -9 PID<Enter>

The bash shell signal name:

    $ kill SIGKILL PID<Enter>

The tcsh shell signal name:

    $ kill KILL PID<Enter>

NOTE: *The number assigned to a signal by Linux/UNIX has no bearing on its strength or priority. This means that a higher or lower number does not indicate potency.*

WARNING: *Sometimes when a process is killed—especially if it has been terminated with a* `kill -9`*— a child process may be terminated but the parent process, although notified of the child's termination, does not acknowledge the termination. The now-dead child process becomes what is called a zombie and will appear as* `defunct` *under the COMMAND column when you issue a* `ps` *command. You may or may not be able to* `kill` *a zombie; it will continue to be listed in the COMMAND column because it holds onto a process slot (that is, a record in the process table) until its parent process acknowledges its termination. A few zombies do not present a major problem, but if the* `ps` *table begins to fill up with them, your ability to execute legitimate processes declines. Zombies can be eliminated by a system reboot or, occasionally, by a* `cleanup` *initiated by the* `init` *process.*

Running Long Processes: nohup Command

The `nohup` (no hang-up) command tells a background command or process to ignore `kill` signals 1 (hang-up) and 3 (quit). This command allows the background process to continue executing after the owner logs out of the system. The nohup command itself takes over control of the command. The syntax is

```
nohup command -option argument > filename &
```

Because the nohup command is designed to shepherd a process *after* the user/owner has logged out, output from the command cannot go to the terminal screen. Therefore, the user/owner should redirect the output to a destination of his or her choice. If the user/owner does not redirect output, nohup automatically redirects the output to the *nohup.out* file in the directory in which the nohup command was originally invoked. See Example 11.4 for both types of redirection.

Example 11.4 ▼ nohup

When the user redirects output:

```
$ nohup ls -R > fileout &<Enter>
[1] 384
```

When the nohup command redirects output:

```
$ nohup ls -R &<Enter>
[2] 574
nohup: appending output to 'nohup.out'
```
▲

NOTE: *If more than one background process is started with* nohup *in the same current directory and the owner/user has not deliberately redirected output, the* nohup.out *file contains the output from all those processes (either mixed or appended). This may create unpredictable results. If no output is required, the output could be directed to a log file or even to the null device (/dev/null).*

Because all processes require affiliation with a parent process, commands started with nohup are affiliated with the init process as their parent after the owner/user logs out of the system.

After the nohup command is sent for execution, the shell replies by displaying numbers, such as [1] 384 in Example 11.4. In this case, the numbers translate to: This is the first command this user is running in the background, and the PID is 384."

Job Control in the bash and tcsh Shells

Creating a List of Background or Suspended Jobs

When you're running multiple processes, it is important to be able to identify which processes are running in the background. You can't always determine which jobs are in the background with the ps command; that's where the jobs command comes in handy.

Looking at Example 11.5, you can see that the results from the jobs command indicate that there are two jobs and that each has been given a job number (in square brackets). The first is still running, and the second has run and completed. (If we invoked jobs again, the second job would not appear.) The jobs command does not list jobs that were started with the nohup command if the user has logged out of the system and then logged back in. However, if the user invokes a nohup job and issues the jobs command before logging out, that nohup job is displayed.

Example 11.5 ▼ jobs

```
$ jobs<Enter>
[1]- Running    yes >/dev/null
[2]+ Done       nohup ls -R
```

Suspending and Resuming a Foreground Task

<Ctrl>-z is used to suspend, not terminate, a foreground process. No CPU resources are used for the suspended process, although it is still a process—it still occupies system memory and is subject to swapping to the hard disk. In other words, the suspended process's data, functions, scripts, and so on remain mapped in RAM until higher priority processes are invoked that will occupy the same RAM space and cause the suspended process's attributes to be saved in the swap space on the hard disk until the suspended process is resumed or terminated. You can tell the job to continue as needed in the foreground or background.

On some older ASCII terminals, <Ctrl>-z may not be able to suspend a foreground task. If that's the case, try entering the following to force the shell to use the key sequence to suspend processes:

```
$ stty susp <Ctrl>-z<Enter>
```

As seen in Example 11.6, to resume a foreground suspended task, simply enter `fg` at the prompt.

Example 11.6 ▼ Foreground Task Control

In this example, we use the `yes` utility which, in this case, simply enters the characters y and `newline` (that is, <Enter>) ad infinitum, using up system resources until it is deliberately terminated. Thus, we're using `yes` as a utility with predictable and controllable outputs. If you're curious about more useful ways to use `yes`, consult your information sources.

To suspend a foreground task:

```
$ yes >/dev/null<Enter>
<Ctrl>-z
[1]+ Stopped    yes >/dev/null
```

To resume a suspended task:

```
[1]+ Stopped    yes >/dev/null

$ fg<Enter>
yes ./dev/null
```
▲

Suspending and Resuming a Background Task

If the job you want to suspend is running in the background, you'll find that <Ctrl>-z doesn't work because it is strictly a foreground-related command. In this case, use the `fg` command to bring the command into the foreground and then suspend it with <Ctrl>-z. You may have to use the job number as supplied by the `jobs` command.

As shown in Example 11.7, you would issue fg %*jobnumber*, press <Enter>, and then press <Ctrl>-z.

Assume that you want to resume a suspended job and return the job processing to the background. Simply type bg (background) at the prompt. The shell returns a job number in square brackets followed by a plus sign (+). The plus sign indicates that the job is the most recently started or stopped. The returned display also includes the ampersand (&) at the end of the listed job name, indicating that the job is in the background.

Example 11.7 ▼ Background Task Control

To suspend a background task, use the fg command to move it to the foreground. Then suspend it:

```
$ fg %jobnumber<Enter>
<Ctrl>-z
[1]+ Stopped   yes >/dev/null
```

To resume the same suspended task and move it to the background:

```
[1]+ Stopped   yes >/dev/null
$ bg<Enter>
[1]+ yes >/dev/null &
```
▲

NOTE: *When you execute* jobs *to check background processes, the shell assigns a job number (in square brackets) to each job. With the* kill *command, you can use the job number or the PID. With the* bg *or* fg *command, you must use the job number;* the *PID will not work.*

More Job Control Examples

Example 11.8 illustrates how a job can be created and controlled using the commands covered in this chapter.

Example 11.8 ▼ Job Creation and Control

A job is initiated in the background, and the shell assigns it job number 1 and PID 273.

```
$ ls -R > out &<Enter>
[1] 273
```

The jobs command indicates that the job is running in the background:

```
$ jobs<Enter>
[1]+  Running    ls -R > out &
```

The job is brought to the foreground:

```
$ fg %1<Enter>
ls -R > out
```

The job is stopped with <Ctrl>-z, and the shell reports that it has indeed stopped:

```
<Ctrl>-z
[1]+  ls -R > out &
```

Again, jobs indicates that the job is running in the background:

```
$ jobs<Enter>
[1]+  Running    ls -R > out &
```

kill terminates the job in the background:

```
$ kill %1<Enter>
```

The jobs command verifies that the job has terminated:

```
$ jobs<Enter>
[1]+  Terminated ls -R > out
```
▲

Daemons: Never-Ending System Processes

Daemons are constantly running processes that were not started by the user nor associated with the terminal. They start when you start your system and run until you shut down your system.

Daemons wait for a specific event to take place, such as the submission of a print job to a print queue. The printing daemon detects the event and then takes responsibility for the task, seeing that it gets processed. More specifically, Linux's printing daemon, called `lpd`, tracks print job requests as well as the printers available to handle those requests. The daemon maintains queues (that is, spool directories) of outstanding requests and sends each request to the appropriate device at the proper time.

In Linux, most of the file names associated with daemons end with *d* and are found in configuration file directories (such as */usr/bin*). You can usually view them by entering the following command:

```
$ ps -guax<Enter>
```

If you have a moment, take a look at them. You will see common daemons such as `lpd`, `syslogd`, `inetd`, and `crond`. These directories and files are typically maintained by system administrators.

Exercises

1. Ensure that you are in your home directory, and then display your current process ID (PID).

    ```
    $ cd<Enter>
    $ pwd<Enter>
    $ echo $$<Enter>
    ```

2. Create a subshell by entering `bash` at the prompt, and then request the PID of the subshell. Is the subshell PID different than your log-in process?

    ```
    $ bash<Enter>
    $ echo $$<Enter>
    ```

3. Enter the `ls -R / > outfile 2> errfile &` command and then execute the command that displays all your running processes. (The `ls` command terminates when it gets to the end of the file system.)

    ```
    $ ls -R / > outfile 2> errfile &<Enter>
    $ ps a<Enter>
    ```

4. Terminate your child shell.

    ```
    $ exit<Enter>
    ```

    What happens if you type `exit` from your log-in shell?

5. Display all variables in your current process environment.

    ```
    $ set<Enter>
    ```

6. Create a variable named x and set its value to 10. Check the value of the variable. Again, display all current variables.

    ```
    $ x=10<Enter>
    $ echo $x<Enter>
    $ set<Enter>
    ```

7. Create a subshell.

    $ bash<Enter>

    Check to see what value the x variable holds in the subshell.

    $ echo $x<Enter>

    What is the value of x? List the subshell's current variables.

    $ set<Enter>

    Do you see a listing for x?

8. Return to your parent process.

    $ exit<Enter>

    Set the value of the x variable so that its value will be inherited by your child processes.

    $ export x=10<Enter>

    Verify by creating a subshell and checking the value of x in the subshell.

    $ bash<Enter>
    $ echo $x<Enter>

9. Change the value of x in the subshell to 200.

    $ x=200<Enter>

    Verify that the value was changed.

    $ echo $x<Enter>

10. Return to the parent process.

    $ exit<Enter>

    Check the value of x in this environment.

    $ echo $x<Enter>

    Was the change in the subshell exported back to the parent?

CHAPTER 11: CONTROLLING LINUX PROCESSES

11. Create a shell script and name it *sc1*. It should read:
    pwd, cd /, pwd

    ▲ `$ vi sc1<Enter>`
    ▲ `i` (to enter Insert mode)
    ▲ `pwd`
    ▲ `cd /`
    ▲ `pwd`
    ▲ `<Esc>` (to leave Insert mode)
    ▲ `:x<Enter>` (to save `sc1` and leave vi)

12. Make *sc1* executable and run the program.

    `$ chmod 700 sc1<Enter>`
    `$ sc1<Enter>`

    NOTE: *If you received a response such as* bash: sc1: command not found, *rerun the program with the command* /home/username/sc1. *It is likely that* /home/username *was not in your* PATH *environment variable, so the shell couldn't find the* sc1 *command.*

    What directory are you in now? Why?

    `$ pwd<Enter>`

13. Create another shell script and name it *sc2*. Have it read
    var1 = hello; var2 =$LOGNAME; export var1 var2.

    ▲ `$ vi sc2<Enter>`
    ▲ `i` (to enter Insert mode)
    ▲ `var1=hello`
    ▲ `var2=$LOGNAME`
    ▲ `export var1 var2`
    ▲ `<Esc>` (to leave Insert mode)
    ▲ `:x<Enter>` (to save `sc2` and quit vi)

14. Make *sc2* executable and run the program.

    `$ chmod 700 sc2<Enter>`
    `$ sc2<Enter>`

When the script has finished, examine the values of the `var1` and `var2` variables.

`$ echo $var1 $var2<Enter>`

What values do `var1` and `var2` have? Why?

15. Run the *sc2* program again, this time by forcing it to run in the current shell.

    `$ . sc2<Enter>`

    When it is finished, check the values for `var1` and `var2`.

    `$ echo $var1 $var2<Enter>`

    What values do `var1` and `var2` have now? Why?

16. Execute the `ls -R / > outfile 2> errfile` command in the foreground.

    `$ ls -R / > outfile 2> errfile<Enter>`

17. Suspend the job you just started.

    `$ <Ctrl>-z`

18. List all the jobs that you are running on the system and restart the preceding job in the background.

    `$ jobs<Enter>`
    `$ bg %jobnumber<Enter>`

19. Bring the job back to the foreground.

    `$ fg %jobnumber<Enter>`

20. After the `ls` command finishes executing, restart it again in the background. Display the process ID and log out.

    ▲ `$ ls -R / > outfile 2> errfile<Enter>`
    ▲ `$ ps a<Enter>`
    ▲ `$ exit<Enter>` (You will see a message telling you that you have jobs running.)
    ▲ `$ exit<Enter>`

Chapter 11: Controlling Linux Processes

21. Log in. Check to see whether the process is still running.

    Login: *username*<Enter>
    Password: <Enter>
    $ ps a<Enter>

22. Create a shell script and name it *sc3*. It should read:
    sleep 60; ls -R / > outfile 2> errfile &.

    ▲ $ vi sc3<Enter>
    ▲ i (to enter Insert mode)
    ▲ sleep 60
    ▲ ls -R / > outfile 2> errfile &
    ▲ <Esc> (to leave Insert mode)
    ▲ :x<Enter> (to save *sc3* and quit vi)

    Make the script executable.

    $ chmod 700 sc3<Enter>

    Start the script with the nohup command, reference it using an explicit path, and put it in the background. Don't forget to redirect the output from *sc3*, and then log out.

    ▲ $ nohup ./sc3 > sc3.out 2> sc3err &<Enter>
    ▲ $ exit<Enter> (You will see a message telling you that you have jobs running.)
    ▲ $ exit<Enter>

23. Log in. Check to see whether the process is still running.

    Login: *username*<Enter>
    Password: <Enter>
    $ ps a<Enter>

24. When the process has finished, display the file that contains your output. (Hint: If you did not specify an output file, nohup sends the output to *nohup.out*.)

    $ more /home/directoryname/sc3.out<Enter>

25. Use the `ls -R /` command to start a long-running job in the background.

    `$ ls -R / > outfile 2> errfile &<Enter>`

    Note the process ID that is provided when you begin the background process.

26. If you did not record the process ID when you first started the command in the background, how would you find it?

    After you know the process ID, `kill` the process. Check to be sure it was killed.

    ```
    $ ps a<Enter>
    $ kill PID<Enter>
    ```

    (For this step, enter the PID you recorded in Exercise 25 or found with the `ps a` command you just executed.)

    `$ ps a<Enter>`

27. Repeat Exercise 25. Kill the process using the job number rather than the process ID. Check to be sure the job was killed.

    ```
    $ ls -R / > outfile 2> errfile &<Enter>
    $ jobs<Enter>
    $ kill %jobnumber<Enter>
    $ ps a<Enter>
    ```

    or

    `$ jobs<Enter>`

See Appendix B for answers.

CHAPTER 11: CONTROLLING LINUX PROCESSES

Quiz

1. What option would you use with the `ps` command to show the relationships between your running programs and their parent processes?

2. True or False: As an ordinary user, you can `kill` only your own jobs and not those of other users.

3. Which of the `kill` command signals is strongest and cannot be caught or ignored?

4. It is always a good idea to start long jobs in the background with the `nohup` command. Give two reasons why.

5. What are never-ending Linux/UNIX processes called?

6. True or False: When users execute a command in the normal way and the command involves navigation of the directory structure, they will find themselves in the last directory mentioned in the command, unless some type of return command (such as `cd`) is included in the program or script.

See Appendix C for answers.

Chapter 12

Customizing the User Environment

AT TIMES, YOU MAY WISH YOU HAD MORE CONTROL over your Linux/ UNIX environment. Perhaps you would like to execute some commonly used commands but would rather use the DOS names because, well, you know them already. Or perhaps you'd prefer to use a different default shell at log-in than bash. How could you do that?

In this chapter, we begin with a discussion of the evolution of your Linux environment, to set the stage for where and why you might, or might not, customize it. Topics covered include techniques to undertake any desired Linux environment customization, the use of aliases for certain commands so you can remember or execute them more easily, and methods for manipulating and re-executing previously executed commands in a fast and easy manner.

Setting Default Shell Variables

In this section, we describe the sources of most environment variables and mention the roles of several programs, initialization scripts, and other files you use from the time you boot your system until you successfully log in. We focus on logging in to a bash shell; the other shells use a slightly different but similar process. The illustration of the environment files shown in Figure 12.1 presents a rough outline of the environment-building process for an introductory-level discussion.

(Here we use the broadest definition of *files* as collections of data or byte streams; some of these files are programs, scripts, and the like, and not strictly data files.)

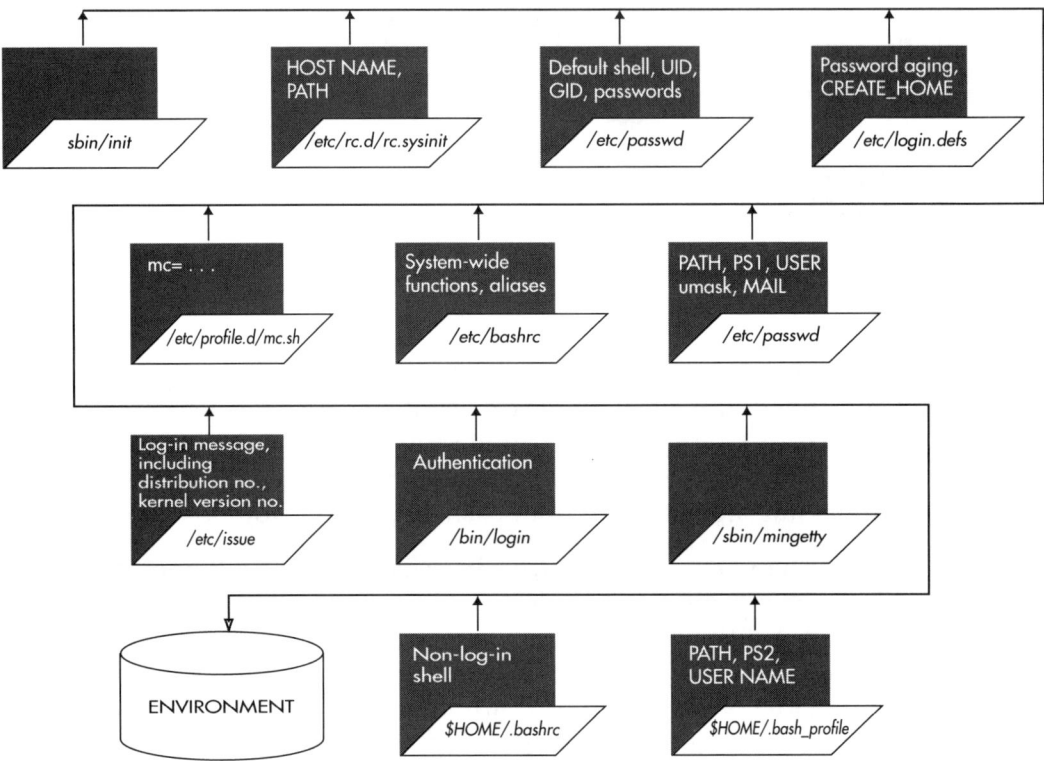

Figure 12.1: Default shell variables.

Assume that you are logging in at your terminal, which you have already booted. But, during the course of booting, the `init` program—commonly regarded as the parent of all system processes because it is the first program that the kernel executes (it's even given the PID of 1)—has already executed, or caused to be executed, several system initialization scripts. Those scripts—the primary one is */etc/rc.d/rc.sysinit*—define the system initialization environment (and other parameters regarding security and other system features) that reflect your or your company's policies. The */etc/profile* shell script, which contains system-wide environment variables and commands, and its companion, the */etc/bashrc* shell script, which contains system-wide functions and aliases, can be changed by only the system administrator or root user. The `init` program has also provided a `getty` program, which in turn has supplied a log-in message and prompt (*/etc/issue*). (If you use the `ps a` command at your terminal, you will see copies of */sbin/mingetty* waiting at your other virtual terminals).

When you log in by supplying your user name, the */bin/login* program runs, carrying out a number of functions and prompting you for a password. If you provide a password that matches the now-encoded password on file for you, *login* authenticates you and then runs the `login` command in the */etc/passwd* program. Now that you have been authenticated, your log-in shell—the one listed alongside your user name in */etc/passwd*—is invoked.

Your *$HOME/.bash_profile* and *$HOME/.bashrc* shell scripts are used to initialize the bash shell and add variables and values to your shell environment. The environment variables in those scripts override any of the same variables set in previous scripts (for example, `PATH` as it may have been defined by */etc/profile* or */etc/rc.d/rc.sysinit*). In addition, you can change or add to the *$HOME* script files to customize your environment.

The difference between *.bash_profile* and *.bashrc* is that *.bash_profile* is used when you are in your log-in shell, and *.bashrc* is read when you invoke any other child process (such as a subshell) that is *not* your log-in shell. Both bash and tcsh distinguish between the log-in shell and other invocations of the shell. If *.bash_profile* is not present at log-in, *.profile* is used if it exists.

Now that you are authenticated and your shell is initialized, *login* displays the message of the day (*/etc/motd*), if there is one, checks for any email messages awaiting you, and notifies you if email messages are available.

Sample /etc/profile File

The */etc/profile* file is the default initialization file for the bash, ksh, and sh shells. Because it contains the environment commands and variables that are invoked when every user logs in to the system, this file is also called the *global profile*. Only the system administrator can change the file, but individual users can override the variables by modifying them in their own *$HOME/.bash_profile* files. However, the */etc/profile* file is *not* intended to replace the individual user's *$HOME/.bash_profile* script file. All customizing should be performed in those individual scripts.

The */etc/profile* should be kept as small as possible because it is used by other scripts as well as by users. Example 12.1 shows the contents of a sample global profile file.

Example 12.1 ▼ etc/profile

```
# cat /etc/profile<Enter>
# /etc/profile
# System-wide environment and startup programs
# Functions and aliases go in /etc/bashrc

PATH="$PATH:/usr/X11R6/bin"
PS1="[\u@\h \W]\\$ "
ulimit -c 1000000
if [ `id -gn` = `id -un` -a `id -u` -gt 14 ]; then
      umask 002
else
      umask 022
fi
USER=`id -un`
LOGNAME=$USER
MAIL="/var/spool/mail/$USER"
HOSTNAME=`/bin/hostname`
HISTSIZE=1000
```

CHAPTER 12: CUSTOMIZING THE USER ENVIRONMENT

```
HISTFILESIZE=1000
export PATH PS1 HOSTNAME HISTSIZE HISTFILESIZE USER
    LOGNAME MAIL
for i in /etc/profile.d/*.sh ; do
    if [ -x $i ]; then
        . $i
    fi
done
unset i
```

▲

> **NOTE:** *The* etc/profile *file is also the home of the default* umasks. *The* export *command is invoked within the file to allow those variables to be used by other shells.*

Selected variables in Example 12.1 are described in Table 12.1. The PATH variable lists the directories through which the shell will look for commands that have been issued to it. Note the format of PATH in Example 12.1, especially $PATH, which tells the shell to include all directories listed in previous initialization scripts. Notice also that the shell was told to add the */usr/X11R6/bin* directory to those directories.

Table 12.1 Selected Variables in the Global Profile File

Number	Variable or command name	Description
1	PATH	List of directories the shell will look through for commands
2	PS1	Primary system prompt
3	ulimit	Upper limit on system resources that a file or command can use
4	umask 002; umask 022	Permissions on new files or directories for the root user (002) and the ordinary user (022)
5	USER	Format of user's name as it is applied to commands and scripts
6	LOGNAME	Format of expected log-in name
7	MAIL	Directory where the user's mail messages are found
8	HOSTNAME	Name of the computer

Table 12.1 Selected Variables in the Global Profile File (continued)

Number	Variable or command name	Description
9	HISTSIZE	Maximum number of previous commands displayed in response to the `history` command
10	HISTFILESIZE	Maximum number of commands kept in the *$HOME/.bash_history* file before the earliest ones are discarded

The `PS1` variable, as discussed previously, sets the format of the primary shell prompt. In Example 12.1, the shell is told to put the user name, the name of the user's computer, and the user's default home (file) directory in square brackets. The dollar sign (outside the brackets) is the prompt symbol.

With the `ulimit` command, the shell is provided with the upper limit on system resources that commands and files can use. Check the `ulimit` man pages or other sources for further information.

As discussed in Chapter 6, `umask` sets the user's default permissions as owner, group member, and member of others for user-created files and directories. In the example, the user ID is subjected to an if-then-else process to set the `umask` for a root user to `002` and for an ordinary user to `022`.

Next, the shell is told that the format for the user account name will be the user's name on the system, not the user's ID number as found in */etc/passwd*. This means that any command or script that calls for the variable `USER` will be given that name in the format specified here.

The `LOGNAME` variable tells the shell that the user's log-in name will be the same as the user's name stipulated by the `USER` variable.

The `MAIL` variable tells the shell where to look for mail messages for `USER`. The mail will be found in the directory whose name is the same as the `USER`, within the */var/spool/mail* directory.

The `HOSTNAME` variable tells the shell where to find the name of the computer, in this case, */bin/hostname*.

The `HISTSIZE` variable sets the number of lines of command history (that is, the number of previous commands) that the shell will display when the user types `history`. This can be handy, as discussed previously, for retyping previous commands, doing sensitivity analyses around command arguments, or even troubleshooting. As seen in Example 12.1, the default is 1,000 commands!

The `HISTFILESIZE` variable sets the maximum size of the *$HOME/.bash_history* file (that is, the maximum number of previous commands that the shell will keep a record of before it starts dumping the commands, earliest commands first). The user accesses this command history by using the up and down arrows on the command line or by listing the *$HOME/.bash_history* file. Like `HISTSIZE` in Example 12.1, the maximum is set by default to 1,000 commands.

Sample /etc/bashrc File

The *etc/bashrc* file is another system initialization script invoked by `init`. It is the companion to */etc/profile*, but where */etc/profile* is intended to hold environment variables and commands, */etc/bashrc* is intended to hold other system functions and aliases for commands or procedures. Remember that a *function* is a procedure that transforms a value or performs other actions and returns the results. Invoking the action or transformation is generally referred to as *calling* the function.

In Example 12.2, we see a reminder that environment information will be placed in */etc/profile*. We then ensures that the primary system prompt for users will be consistent no matter where the user is operating. Finally, an alias is defined (discussed later in this chapter), which allows any user to use the newly defined command when trying to determine the absolute path location of any command they name. For example, `which man<Enter>` returns `/usr/bin/man`, the location of the executable that invokes `man` pages.

Example 12.2 ▼ /etc/bashrc for System Initialization

```
# cat /etc/bashrc<Enter>

# /etc/bashrc
# System wide functions and aliases
# Environment stuff goes in /etc/profile
```

```
# Putting PS1 here ensures that it gets loaded every
  time.
PS1="[\u@\h \W]\\$ "

alias which="type -path"
```
▲

Sample $HOME/.bash_profile File

In Example 12.3, we see the variables set for an individual user in his or her personal *.bash_profile* script file. Every time the user logs in, this script is read and its variables and commands are adopted or executed.

Example 12.3 ▼ Setting Variables for an Individual User

```
$ pwd<Enter>
/home/flintsfr
$ cat .bash_profile<Enter>
# .bash_profile
# Get the aliases and functions
if [ -f ~/.bashrc ]; then
     . ~/.bashrc
fi
# User-specific environment and start-up programs
PATH=$PATH:$HOME/bin
BASH_ENV=$HOME/.bashrc
USERNAME=""

export USERNAME BASH_ENV PATHs
```
▲

The first conditional if-then-else decision structure calls for the shell to check whether a hidden script file called *.bashrc* (containing aliases and functions specific to this user only and not all users, such as those in */etc/bashrc*) exists in this directory, and if so, to execute it. Note that the *.bashrc* file, which contains user-specific functions and aliases, could be called anything, but the convention is to name it similarly to the */etc/bashrc* file, which has global functions and aliases.

Next, the user's PATH statement is modified. The existing PATH directories are adopted, and the */bin* directory in the user's home directory is added to them. If you want to ensure that the current directory is included in the PATH variable, verify that the variable contains two or more adjacent colons or a colon followed by a period.

The BASH_ENV variable causes the *.bashrc* script in the user's home directory to run every time another new bash shell is invoked. This is not exported because that the settings, aliases, and other functions in *.bashrc* may not be variables and thus are not subject to export.

Discussion of the USERNAME=" " variable (where the double quotes indicate a null string) is beyond the scope of this book.

Note that the USERNAME, BASH_ENV, and PATH variables are exported so that these variables and their respective values will be adopted by child processes.

Just as */etc/profile* has a companion in */etc/bashrc* for system functions and aliases, so *$HOME/.bash_profile* has, by convention, its companion *$HOME/.bashrc* for user-defined functions and aliases.

Sample $HOME/.bashrc File

Example 12.3 contains the BASH_ENV=$HOME/.bashrc variable, which causes *$HOME/.bashrc*, with its extra specifics, to be executed every time the users starts a new bash shell. The *$HOME/.bash_profile* file is executed only once, when the user logs in.

In Example 12.4, we see that aliases and functions specific to the user are recommended, and then the global aliases and functions are searched for and invoked by the if-then-else decision string. Otherwise, those functions, aliases, and so on would not be invoked.

Example 12.4 ▼ Script for User-Defined Functions and Aliases

```
$ pwd<Enter>
```
/home/flintsfr
```
$ cat .bashrc
```

```
# .bashrc

# User-specific aliases and functions

# Source global definitions
if [ -f /etc/bashrc ]; then
    . /etc/bashrc
fi

# Begin aliases written by Fred
# Number 1 - Alias similar to old DOS command; written
  on April 13
alias dir-p="ls -l | more"
# End of aliases written by Fred                          ▲
```

In Example 12.4, we see how Fred has written his own alias. It appears that Fred is a DOS veteran, preferring the dir style of commands to the UNIX ls style. Note that he cannot use dir /p, the proper DOS syntax. He has to modify the command. Why? The shell would not interpret the forward slash in the same way as DOS, and so would return an error message.

Linux/UNIX Shortcut: alias Command

You would probably appreciate being able to execute frequently used commands with fewer keystrokes. Or there may be long-winded commands, frequently used or not, for which you would *really* appreciate using fewer keystrokes.

Enter the alias command, which you can use to create an abbreviated command name—or perhaps some kind of mnemonic sequence—that becomes a new internal shell command that will accomplish the same effects as the longer command it replaces. We've already seen examples of the use of aliases in Examples 12.2 (the *etc/bashrc* file) and 12.4 (the *.bashrc* file).

An alternative to creating command names using alias is to write a shell script to do the same thing. However, because a new alias-created command is an internal shell command, the shell gives it precedence over any script you may have created to do the same thing. In addition, creating shell scripts involves using a text editor such as vi, and testing and using shell scripts requires you to give the script files the proper permissions. Then you have to make sure that the PATH variable includes a reference to the location of the shell script so it can be found and executed. Of course, sometimes a shell script is just what you want, or need, especially when you want to do something more complex (for example, execute a sequence of commands automatically when you log in). Still, from the standpoint of creating, testing, and executing, the use of the `alias` command is a more simple and straightforward technique.

In Example 12.5, we first use the `alias` command alone to view the aliases that have already been defined in our profile, function, and alias files. We find two: `dir-p`, created by Fred in a previous section, and `which`, the default alias that helps us identify commands. Next, we use the `alias` command with arguments to create three new aliases. Two of them perform listing functions: `alias l='ls -l'` creates a long listing of the nonhidden files and subdirectories in your current directory, and `alias p='ps f'` creates a list of processes and indicates which child processes were spawned by which parent processes. The last alias (`alias r='fc -e -'`) is a shorthand form for: Repeat the last or immediately previous command. Finally, we use the `alias` command by itself again to verify that the three new aliases were created.

Example 12.5 ▼   alias

To find existing aliases:

```
$ alias<Enter>
alias dir-p='ls -l | more'
alias which='type -path'
```

To create three new aliases for common functions to reduce lengthy keyboarding:

```
$ alias l='ls -l'<Enter>
$ alias p='ps f'<Enter>
$ alias r='fc -e -'<Enter>
```

To check that the new aliases are listed with the original two:

```
$ alias<Enter>
alias dir-p='ls -l | more'
alias which='type -path'
alias l='ls -l'
alias p='ps f'
alias r='fc -e -'
```
▲

You can use the new alias by itself as a command. Or you can add arguments to it, but the arguments must pertain to the command (if there is more than one command within the alias, the arguments must pertain to the last command). For instance, assume that you have a new alias, l, which is equivalent to ls -l. If you want to see hidden files too, you should type l -a at the prompt.

NOTE: *Keep in mind that these aliases will work only in the shells in which they were created. If you want them to work elsewhere, you have to enter them in your $HOME/.bashrc file (or whatever file you use for the BASH_ENV variable) or into function or alias files for your other shells.*

By adding aliases to global function and alias files, the system administrator can make those aliases available to all or specific groups of other users.

Using and Removing Aliases

Suppose you no longer need an alias you have been using and want to delete it. To do so, you use the `unalias` command. Its syntax is

```
unalias aliasname
```

In Example 12.6, we check for existing aliases, verify that the alias we created in Example 12.5 works, remove that alias, and then verify that it no longer works.

CHAPTER 12: CUSTOMIZING THE USER ENVIRONMENT

Example 12.6 ▼ Identifying and Removing an Alias

To identify existing aliases:

```
$ alias<Enter>
alias dir-p='ls -l | more'
alias l='ls -l'
alias p='ps f'
alias r='fc -e -'
alias which='type -path'
```

To verify that the `l` alias works:

```
$ l<Enter>
-rw-r--r- 1 flintsfr staff   524 Jun 13 12:45 xfile1
-rw-r--r- 1 flintsfr staff  1455 Jul 15 14:13 xfile2
```

To remove the `l` alias and then check to see whether it works:

```
$ unalias l<Enter>

$ l<Enter>
bash: l: command not found
```
▲

You can remove more than one alias at a time by entering their names in a list after the `unalias` command; be careful to separate each name with a space.

> **NOTE:** *Remember that `unalias` removes the alias from the current shell's alias list, but if the alias appears somewhere in the definition of the `BASH_ENV` variable file, it will be back the next time you log in and will also appear in any subshells you create (even now). So you must take care to remove it, if that's your intention, from all definition files where it may be found.*

247

Shell History Commands

history Command

The `history` command reads, numbers, and displays the text of the previous commands from the buffer and also from the *.bash_history* file in the user's home directory or from whatever file is named as a value for the `HISTFILE` variable. The default is HISTFILE=*$HOME/ .bash_history*, but you can change the default by adding or modifying `HISTFILE=filename` to your *$HOME/.bash_profile* file.

The maximum number of commands that `history` can access is the number of commands already in the buffer from the current session plus the number of commands stored in the *$HOME/.bash_history* file. The maximum size of that file is specified in the `HISTFILESIZE` variable. However, the maximum number of previous commands that `history` can display is the number specified in the `HISTSIZE` variable. If no number is specified, the default is 17 (although all reference materials say 16).

The `history` command has several options and arguments. For example, `history -a` appends the current session's commands to the *.bash_history* file immediately and not at your log out. Another example is `history n`, which displays only the previous *n* commands, as long as *n* is less than or equal to the value of the `HISTSIZE` variable. For further information, check your information sources.

fc Command

You can also use the `fc` command to display your command history, as well as edit those commands. Used with its options and arguments, `fc` can be handier than `history`. For example, `fc -l 5 120` lists all previous commands in your history list sequentially from number 5 to number 120. To list the same commands but in reverse order, use `fc -l -r 5 120`. The limitations on this maneuverability are that `HISTSIZE`, `HISTFILESIZE`, and other variable values must accommodate what you want to do.

You can also use `fc` to edit any of your previous commands by invoking the editor of your choice. An example is `fc -e vi 68`, which means: Edit previous command number 68 with the `vi` editor. The shell responds by opening `vi` and displaying the command corresponding to number 68 on the top line. You do whatever editing you want and then exit `vi`, after which the shell executes the newly modified command.

Here's another example. Assume that your previous command number 68 is set | more. You want to change it quickly to set | cat and then execute it immediately, without going into or exiting from a text editor. Just type the following:

```
fc -s more=cat 68
```

and press <Enter>. The default text editor is automatically invoked and changes command number 68 to what you want, and then the shell executes it.

You might ask how you can control which text editor the shell uses. Set the `FCEDIT` variable to the name of your preferred text editor. If nothing is specified for `FCEDIT`, `vi` is used by default.

One thing you will probably notice after using `fc` is that when you display your command history, you never see the `fc` command. All you see is the proper or revised command. The only time the `fc` command and its options are displayed is when command execution did not occur, which means you made a mistake.

For other `fc` options and arguments, refer to your sources for additional information.

Bang Command

Regardless of the form of `fc` or `history` command you use to display your previous commands, you can re-execute any displayed commands using the bang symbol (!), as follows:

```
!commandnumber
```

or

```
!textstring
```

The command number is obvious after the listing of the previous commands. However, the text string option can be handy if you don't want to do a history listing and you remember the first few unique characters in the text of the desired command.

Recall that command number 68 was set | more in the preceding example. Assume that you want to set a variable, FCEDIT=vi, and you want to verify that the variable has indeed been set to vi:

```
$ FCEDIT=vi<Enter>
$ !68<Enter>
```

Your environment variables are listed.

You could also have input the following and obtained the same result:

```
$ FCEDIT=vi<Enter>
$ !se<Enter>
```

You don't even need the whole word *set,* but only *se.* A word of caution: If another set command was in your history list, the shell would be confused and you would likely end up with unanticipated results.

The bang command can save you a lot of typing. But when you examine a command history, you never find a ! command per se, just the command that you invoked by using ! (just like with the fc command). Again, the only exception is when you make a mistake.

NOTE: *Some information sources indicate that a space is required between the exclamation point and the command number or text string, and some indicate that there should be no space between them. The correct syntax is no space between ! and the command number or text string.*

The ! command has other handy arguments and options, such as the inclusion of extra arguments with previous commands or the mixing of arguments from one previous command to another before re-execution. Again, consult your sources for more information.

Exercises

1. To customize your environment and have that customized environment take effect every time you log in, you must incorporate your modifications in a file that is read at log in. First, log in to the system and ensure that you are in your home directory.

   ```
   $ cd<Enter>
   $ pwd<Enter>
   ```

   Now edit your *.bash_profile* file as follows: Change your primary system prompt string to reflect your current directory; display a message at every log in that contains your log-in name and the time of your log-in; and define an alias named `dir` that invokes the `ls -l` command.

   ```
   $ vi .bash_profile<Enter>
   i    (to enter Insert mode)
   PS1='$ PWD =>'<Enter>
   echo User $LOGNAME logged in at `date` <Enter>
   alias dir='ls -l'<Enter>
   set -o vi<Enter>
   <Esc>   (to enter Command mode)
   :wq<Enter>   (to save .bash_profile and leave vi)
   ```

2. Test your customization by re-executing your *.bash_profile*. You can do that by logging out and then logging in or by simply rerunning the file using dot notation.

   ```
   $ logout
   Login: username
   Password:
   or
   $ . .bash_profile<Enter>
   ```

   Execute and answer the following:

   ▲ Did your message appear?
   ▲ Is your prompt identical to the name of your home directory?
   ▲ Change to the */etc* directory. Did your prompt change?
   ▲ Use `dir`. Did you get a long listing of your current directory?

Installing and Administering Linux

If you answered no to any of these questions, edit your *.bash_profile* and correct it.

3. After your customized *.bash_profile* is set up and functioning properly, open a subshell.

   ```
   /home/teamxx => bash<Enter>
   ```

   Is your prompt identical to the name of your current directory? Does the `dir` alias still work the way you set it?

4. Exit from the subshell and return to your home directory.

   ```
   $ <Ctrl>-d
   /home/teamxx => cd<Enter>
   ```

   Most settings, with the exception of system variables, apply only to the current environment they are set in and are not passed to subshells (which are child processes). To pass customized settings down to subshells, you must set the BASH_ENV variable appropriately in your *.bash_profile*, and you must have a properly customized *.bashrc* file.

   Revise your *.bash_profile* and create the appropriate *.bashrc* file to support the customization you implemented in Exercise 1.

   Remove *only* what you previously added to the *.bash_profile* in Exercise 1, except for the `echo` statement and the `PS1` variable assignment. Add the BASH_ENV variable assignment. Export both the PS1 and BASH_ENV variables and their values.

   ```
   /home/teamxx => vi .bash_profile<Enter>
   i    (to enter Insert mode)
   BASH_ENV=/home/teamxx/.bashrc<Enter>
   export PATH PS1 BASH_ENV<Enter>
   <Esc>   (to enter Command mode)
   :wq<Enter>  (to save .bash_profile and leave vi)
   /home/teamxx => vi .bashrc<Enter>
   i  (to enter Insert mode)
   alias dir='ls -l'<Enter>
   <Esc>   (to enter Command mode)
   :wq<Enter>    (to save .bashrc and leave vi)
   ```

5. Test your customization by re-executing your *.bash_profile* file. Open a subshell.

   ```
   /home/teamxx => . .bash_profile<Enter>
   /home/teamxx => bash<Enter>
   ```

   Is your prompt identical to the name of your current directory? Is the value of the `dir` alias still working?

6. Exit the subshell and return to your log-in shell. Display a listing of all currently set alias names and locate the `dir` alias.

   ```
   /home/teamxx => <Ctrl>-d
   /home/teamxx => cd<Enter>
   /home/teamxx => alias<Enter>
   ```

7. Temporarily "unalias" `dir` without editing the *.bashrc* file. Then display the list of alias settings again and ensure that `dir` is no longer defined. Try executing `dir`.

   ```
   /home/teamxx => unalias dir<Enter>
   /home/teamxx => alias<Enter>
   /home/teamxx => dir<Enter>
   ```

8. The `dir` alias is still in your *.bashrc* file, but it is not set. The `unalias` command removed it from the list of current alias names. Invoke *.bashrc* to automatically add `dir` back to the alias list.

   ```
   $ logout
   Login: teamxx
   Password:
   ```
   or
   ```
   $ . .bashrc<Enter>
   ```

   Execute `dir`.

   ```
   /home/teamxx => dir<Enter>
   ```

See Appendix B for answers.

Quiz

1. What are the differences between the *.bash_profile* and *.bashrc* files?
2. True or False: You have to have a *.bashrc* file when you are using the bash shell.
3. True or False: The `init` process is considered the parent of all processes.
4. Which file is called the global profile? Why?
5. Define the following:
   - ▲ HISTSIZE
   - ▲ HISTFILE
   - ▲ HISTFILESIZE
6. True or False: After an alias is defined in your *.bashrc* file, you cannot undo its functionality with `unalias`.
7. Fill in the blanks. In the bash shell, _____ is to */etc/profile* as _____ is to *.bash_profile*.

See Appendix C for details.

Chapter 13

Basic Linux Utilities

THE COMMANDS COVERED IN THIS CHAPTER are useful for various practical administrative tasks such as finding and manipulating files and the text within files. Specifically, we discuss the `find` command, several `find`-like utilities, and the `grep`, `head`, `tail`, and `sort` commands. These commands are powerful and handy but also a bit more complicated than commands discussed previously. However, keep their respective purposes, principles, and syntaxes in mind, and with experience you will find that these utilities will enhance your efficiency and overall effectiveness.

Searching Directories for Files: find Command

In this section, we introduce the basic uses and syntax of the `find` command. The `find` command is a powerful utility because it can find files and automatically perform actions on those files. We will use Barney's sample directory structure in Figure 13.1 in the examples in this section and in the rest of the chapter.

The `find` program searches recursively downward through the file structure, starting in the directories you specify. The syntax is particular (some believe it's more like *peculiar*) and can generally be expressed as follows:

```
find [where to start looking?] [what to look for?]
    [what to do with it when it's found?]
```

Installing and Administering Linux

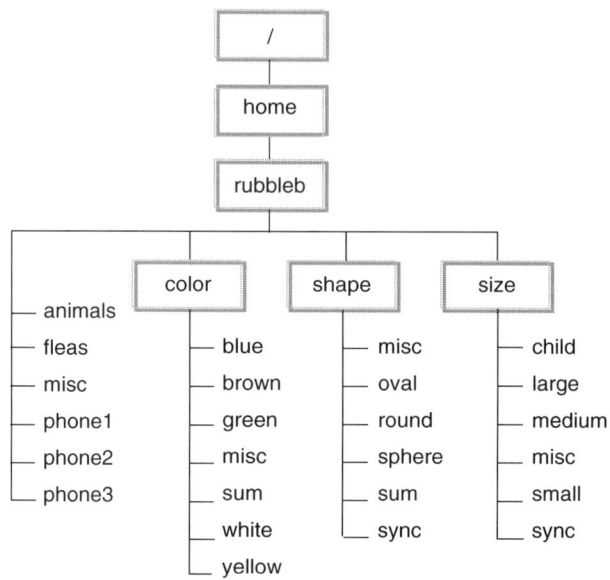

Figure 13.1: Sample directory structure.

In Example 13.1, our first `find` example, we use the following syntax:

```
find directory(ies) conditions
```

The *conditions* could include or be called options, match criteria, actions, arguments, and all sorts of other designations. Nearly all information sources seem to have a different interpretation of what to call the required parameters but their examples all look similar. Luckily, even though no agreement exists on how to express the parameters for the `find` command, overall agreement does exists on how to use it.

Example 13.1 ▼ find with Conditions

To change to Barney's home directory:

```
$ cd /home/rubbleb<Enter>
```

To search for all occurrences of files named *misc* from the current directory down through the file structure:

```
$ find -name misc -print<Enter>
./misc
./color/misc
./shape/misc
./size/misc
```

We start at the top of Barney's home directory, as shown in the sample directory structure in Figure 13.1, and ask for a list of all occurrences of files named *misc* within that file structure. The shell returns the correct list: four files called *misc*, each in a separate subdirectory.

Two additional considerations are worthy of mention:

▲ In the example, the `find` utility found the four *misc* files. Had there also been one or more *misc* subdirectories somewhere in Barney's file structure, `find` would have returned a reference to them as well. However, `find` would have returned references to only the subdirectories, not to files within them that are not called *misc*.

▲ File and directory permissions apply to `find`, as they do to other commands. If you have no business in certain directories or no permissions to certain files, `find` will not find them. You can't use the command to circumvent permission requirements. If you lack appropriate permissions, you get an error message similar to the following on the terminal screen: *find: /directoryname: Permission denied.*

In Example 13.1, we specify `-print` at the end of the command line, which is interpreted as printing to `stdout` (that is, printing to the terminal screen). If we had not specified anything, the output would have printed to the terminal by default. In earlier versions of UNIX and UNIX-like operating systems, though, this was not the case. You had to explicitly tell the shell what to do with the output.

The find Command with a Noninteractive Single Action

Example 13.2 illustrates how you can execute a single command, or *action*, with `find`. The syntax is

```
find directory(ies) conditions -exec commandname
     options { } \;
```

Example 13.2 ▼ find with a Noninteractive Action

```
$ find . -name 'm*' -exec ls -l { } \;<Enter>
-rw-rw-r-- 1 rubbleb staff 59 Apr 19 13:48 ./misc
-rw-rw-r-- 1 rubbleb staff 27 Apr 19 13:54 ./color/misc
-rw-rw-r-- 1 rubbleb staff 32 Apr 19 11:37 ./shape/misc
-rw-rw-r-- 1 rubbleb staff 75 Apr 19 11:39 ./size/medium
-rw-rw-r-- 1 rubbleb staff 37 Apr 19 13:55 ./size/misc
```
▲

Loosely speaking, Example 13.2 states: Start in the current directory and, working downward, find all entries that begin with *m*. As you find each entry, present its data on the screen in long list format.

Here is a breakdown of each element in the command:

▲ . (the dot) means to start in the current directory, which in this example is */home/rubbleb,* and move recursively through the file structure.

▲ -name means that the names of the entries you want to find follow.

▲ 'm*' indicates that the first character in each entry is *m*. The asterisk (*) indicates that subsequent characters do not matter. This part of the command is in single quotes because the asterisk is a metacharacter, and if it were not surrounded in single quotes, it would have a different effect on the command.

▲ -exec means that after finding each entry, execute the following command on it in turn.

▲ `ls -l {}` requests a long listing of the entry. The `{}` argument means that as each entry is found, its name should be substituted here so that `ls -l` can be executed on it.

▲ `\;` is called an *escaped semicolon*. It indicates that we have reached the end of the `find` and `exec` command sequences.

▲ `<Enter>` submits the command sequence for parsing and execution.

Note that because of the way we have coded the `find/exec` command combination, no interaction occurs between the process and the terminal. This may or may not be desirable. For instance, what if you wanted to remove the entries that `find` found? In this case, interaction may be useful.

Note also that the `\;` sequence must be part of the command line when `find` is combined with the `-exec` and `-ok` actions. (We discuss the `-ok` action in the next section.)

In Linux and other more recent versions of UNIX, you can use `ls` as an option with `find`. Thus, you can use an abbreviated syntax to get the same results as in Example 13.2. Try the following:

```
$ find . -name 'm*' -ls<Enter>
```

The find Command with an Interactive Single Action

This section focuses on how to add an interactivity to the `find` command with the `-ok` action. This time, instead of just going ahead and performing the second command, the shell prompts the user for verification before proceeding, as shown in Example 13.3. The prompt is a basic yes or no; the user types y, yes, n, or no and then presses <Enter>.

The advantage here is that the user has the ability to monitor the action and prevent execution of the action. The syntax is

```
find directory(ies) conditions -ok commandname options
    { } \;
```

Example 13.3 ▼ find with an Interactive Action

```
$ find . -name 'm*' -ok rm { } \;<Enter>
< rm ... ./misc >  ?        y<Enter>
< rm ... ./color/misc >  ?  y<Enter>
< rm ... ./shape/misc >  ?  y<Enter>
< rm ... ./size/medium >    y<Enter>
< rm ... ./size/misc >  ?   y<Enter>
```
▲

Consider using -ok with `find` in the following situations:

▲ *When your search pattern may not be or cannot be absolutely accurate* (or absolutely surgical, if you are only trying to affect some entries and not all of them), and you don't want to affect any entries unnecessarily.

▲ *When your second command is fairly final.* (In Example 13.3, we are removing the successful `find` candidates; that's pretty final. If we were doing this noninteractively and something were to go wrong, we would have to find a way to restore the entries we did not want to remove. This could prove costly in some situations.)

▲ *When the number of files to be located by `find` is relatively small.* No one really wants to sit at a terminal for a long time typing y<Enter> or n<Enter> repeatedly. This activity is tedious, and tedious activities can lead to mistakes.

Table 13.1 lists some other common options that you can specify with the `find` command. For even more options, consult your information sources.

Using Additional Options with the find Command

This section includes four examples of `find` command options. Most of these options were described in the preceding section.

In Example 13.4, we split the command so that one part is written opposite the primary prompt and the rest is written opposite the secondary prompt. We did this to show how this command form works (and to show that it *will* work).

Table 13.1 Selected find Options

Option	Description
`-type c`	Find files of type c (character-special file). The type can also be `b` (block special file), `d` (directory), `f` (plain file), `l` (symbolic link), `p` (fifo or a named pipe), or `s` (socket).
`-size n[c]`	Find files containing *n* blocks or, if c is specified, *n* characters long (1 block = 512 bytes).
`-mtime +n|n|-n`	Find files that were last modified more than (+*n*), less than (–*n*), or exactly (*n*) days ago.
`-perm nnn`	Find files whose permissions are set to octal number *nnn*.
`-user user`	Find files belonging to user (*username* or *userid*).
`-o`	Find files that match condition *a* or condition *b*.
`-newer file`	Find files that have been modified more recently than *file*. Note the similarity to `mtime`.

What is the command requesting? Starting from the current directory, find all files that begin with the character *s* and larger than two blocks (approximately 1 KB). Then, as each successful file is found, create a long listing of it and present the long listing on the terminal screen.

Example 13.4 ▼ find with a Split Command

```
$ find . -name 's*' -type f -size +2 \<Enter>
> -exec ls -l {} \;<Enter>
-rw-rw-r-- 1 rubbleb staff 1380 Apr  2 14:49 ./shape/sum
-rw-rw-r-- 1 rubbleb staff  808 Apr 20  4:44 ./size/sum
```
▲

Example 13.5 requests that the system find and display, again from the current directory downward, the names of all files that have their permissions set to 644 (that is, `-rw-r--r--`) and have not been modified in more than four days.

Example 13.5 ▼ find with Complex Options

```
$ find . -perm 644 -mtime +4 -print<Enter>
./shape/misc
```
▲

This example is a little tricky. Only files can have the octal number permission 644. If a directory were to have a permission of 644, it would be difficult to access and manipulate files in it.

Example 13.6 requests that the system find and display the names of all files named *fleas* or *sum* from the current directory downward.

Example 13.6 ▼ find with OR

```
$ find . -name fleas -o -name sum<Enter>
./fleas
./color/sum
./shape/sum
./size/sum
```

Example 13.7 requests that the system find, from the root directory downward (that is, through the entire system file structure), file names containing the *security* text string as part of their path name. The successful path names are displayed on the screen. Errors are not displayed on the screen, but they are listed in the *errfile* file in the current directory. If such a file does not exist, the command creates it.

Example 13.7 ▼ find with Error Redirection

```
$ find / -name "security" -print 2> errfile<Enter>
/usr/include/security
/usr/lib/per15/i386-linux/5.00404/security
/etc/security
/lib/security
```

Be careful with commands like this one. If the command does not appear to provide the expected output, it may be because of errors. But you won't know about the errors unless you check the *errfile* file. Even if it does seem to respond, there may still be errors. An ordinary user (as opposed to a superuser or a root user) is likely to encounter more errors in these situations due to a lack of permissions on directories or files.

Locating Commands: whatis, whereis, and which Commands

What if you are trying to execute a program and the shell tells you it can't find the file or directory you refer to when you use the name of the command? Or what if you are writing a program that will invoke a command and you need the full path name of the command, but you don't know where it resides? Here are three quick find-like utilities that can help.

The whatis command searches the whatis database, a file found in the */usr/man* directory, for the command name you want to investigate, and then prints a brief summary of what that command does when invoked. This command can be helpful when you are not sure of a command name, when you are not sure of exactly what the command will do, or even when you want to resolve arguments among colleagues. The syntax for whatis is straightforward:

    whatis commandname

Be sure to use a complete word—no partial text strings are allowed. Example 13.8 shows the simple response sent to stdout. If more information is required, you can search the man pages or other information sources. Thanks to whatis, you may now at least have the correct command name to search for (even though you may have to enter whatis several times to nail down the correct name).

Example 13.8 ▼ whatis

```
$ whatis find<Enter>
find (1)- search for files in a directory hierarchy
find (3) - traverse a file tree                        ▲
```

The whereis command is a little different. The syntax is

    whereis commandname

You can use it to find commands, command sources, and manual pages. This command searches a standard built-in list of directories (*/bin*, */etc*, */usr/bin*, */usr/local/bin*, among others) to find and print all matches of the specified command name. However, `whereis` does not search your search path (that is, as spelled out in your PATH variable), so it may not find your shell scripts if they are in your local system directories or in your own *$HOME/bin* directory (assuming you have created one).

The `whereis` command in Example 13.9 is simplified compared with the syntax you will find in your information sources, wherein you can specify the type of file to look for, where to look for it, and so on. For instance, if you want to find all files in */usr/bin* that are not documented in */usr/man/man1* but have a source in */usr/src*, you might enter the following:

```
$ whereis -u -M /usr/man/man1 -S /usr/src -f *<Enter>
```

So, you can see that `whereis` is not quite as simple as `whatis`. As always, consult your information sources for further details.

Example 13.9 ▼ whereis

```
$ whereis find<Enter>
```
find: /usr/bin/find /usr/man/man1/find.1   ▲

The `which` command is different than both `whatis` and `whereis`. Its syntax is

```
which commandname
```

It lists the path names of the files that will be executed if you run the specified command. Unlike `whereis`, `which` searches your PATH variable. The major drawback to `which` is that it stops searching after finding and reporting on the first occurrence of the command name you specify.

An advantage to `which` is that, if you are working in a C shell environment, it also checks the *.cshrc* file, if one exists, for aliases.

Example 13.10 ▼ which

```
$ which find<Enter>
/usr/bin/find
```
▲

Locating Data in a File: grep Command

You can use the `grep` (global regular expression parsing) command alone or with other commands. We mentioned this command briefly in Chapter 8 in the discussion of commands used as filters to other commands. The syntax is

```
grep [options] regular expression [file1 file2 ...]
```

Generally, the `grep` command searches for a regular expression—a specified pattern of text, logical constructs, and metacharacters—within specified files. If and when such expressions are found, it takes one or more slices (each line in the text file that contains the regular expression is a slice) from the files and writes the slices to `stdout`.

The syntax for `grep` is

```
commandname [options] | grep [options]\<Enter> > |
    commandname [options]
```

Example 13.11 will be more meaningful if you take the time to create the following files with the `vi` text editor:

Filename: *phone1*
Cottage - 416-555-0123
Office - 780-555-1234
Pager - 780-555-2345
Home - 780-555-3456
Field Office - 604-555-5678
Publisher - 307-555-6789
Editor - 403-555-7890

Filename: *phone2*
Ms. Smith - 780-555-4567
Ms. Brown - 502-555-8901

Filename: *phone3*
Emergencies - 800-555-0987
Human Resources - 800-555-8765
Mail Room - 800-555-3210

Filename: *animals*
```
mice    .3
cats    .2
horses  .1
pigs    .0
dogs    .4
rabbits .6
fish    .5
```

Filename: *fileaswritten*
```
file<Spacebar>file4
file<Spacebar>file7
file<Tab>file8
file<Tab>file1
file<Spacebar>file3
```

NOTE: *In the* fileaswritten *file,* <Spacebar> *indicates that you should press the* <Spacebar> *between the end of the word* file *and the beginning of the word* file4. *for example.* <Tab> *indicates that you should press the* <Tab> *key between the end of the word* file. *for example. and the beginning of the word* file1.

Example 13.11 ▼ grep

```
$ grep 780 phone1 phone2<Enter>
phone1:Office - 780-555-1234
phone1:Pager  - 780-555-2345
phone1:Home   - 780-555-3456
phone2:Ms. Smith - 780-555-4567
```
▲

In Example 13.12, we list all the files (in the current directory), grep all files whose name begins with *p*, and count the number of lines in the output to the grep command.

Because grep found two files, *phone1* and *phone2* (see Example 13.11), its output would have two lines. The wc command counts those lines and reports a 2 to the screen, which is the default stdout. The grep command is used most often in this capacity, to extract certain specified information from stdin for further processing. In the next section, we examine grep's metacharacters used in its regular expressions.

Example 13.12 ▼ grep for Extracting Data

```
$ ls | grep ^p | wc -l<Enter>
2
```
▲

The syntax for the basic use of `grep` looks a lot like the syntax for any command:

```
$ grep [options] regular expression [filename1
    filename2 ... filenameN]<Enter>
```

As mentioned, the regular expression can be a text string or can utilize metacharacters. Note that the symbols `grep` uses may be identical to some used by the shell, but they may mean different things to `grep`. Consequently, sometimes symbols should be surrounded by single quotation marks (preferably) or double quotation marks. The `grep` command's metacharacters are discussed in the next section.

You usually specify a file name with `grep`. If you don't, `grep` searches `stdin` for its input. It is acceptable to alter `stdin` to accommodate that (that is, you can use the technique shown in Chapter 8 to designate files or directories for `grep` to search).

If you have not altered `stdin`, the shell takes you to the next line on the screen and leaves you with a flashing cursor (no prompt, even) and waits for you to enter input there. Remember, to `grep`, the terminal is the default `stdin`. If you execute `grep` and want to do that, fine. If and when you enter a text pattern that matches the specified search text pattern, `grep` will echo that text pattern to the screen. To stop the echoing, press <Ctrl>-c. The process terminates and returns a prompt.

Assume that you have entered a search text pattern and a single file name to search through, and `grep` finds your text pattern one or more times in that file. It returns copies of those lines to your screen but it does not display any lines that do not match the text pattern. If you have entered more than one file name to search and `grep` has found your text pattern in more than one file, however, it returns each line it found and also precedes each line with the name of the file in which it found the text pattern. (Example 13.11 illustrates this type of response.)

Take another look at Example 13.12. You could get the same results by entering the following:

```
$ grep 780 phone*<Enter>
```

In Barney's file structure, the asterisk wildcard points to the same two files. However, what if you have more than two files that begin with *p*, and you want to check only those two files? How would you restrict the search? Besides listing the two files explicitly, can you think of any other syntax that would work? The next section should help answer these questions.

Regular Expressions with Metacharacters

We have discussed how `grep` searches in specified files for specified regular expressions, which can include text patterns and metacharacters. In Example 13.12, you saw a metacharacter used with `grep` to search for every file that begins with the character *p* (`grep ^p`).

We also mentioned how the metacharacters used with `grep` may or may not mean the same as the metacharacters used by the shell. Take a look at Table 13.2. Can you see how `grep` metacharacters might cause confusion as well as unreliable and undesirable results? This is why we recommend that you surround `grep` expressions containing metacharacters with single quotes. Double quotes may be acceptable in some situations, but you will get the most reliable performance by using single quotes.

Table 13.2 Metacharacters in grep and the Shell

Metacharacter	Meaning in grep	Meaning in the shell
.	Match any character	If followed by *filename*, execute *filename*
*	Match zero or more preceding	Match zero or more
^	Match beginning of line	Bourne shell pipe symbol
$	Match end of line	Variable (generally, the user prompt)
\	Escape the character following	Escape the character following
[ ]	Match one from this set or range	Match from this set or range
{ }	Match this range of instances	
+	Match one or more preceding	
?	Match zero or one preceding	Match zero or one

Following are three examples of `grep` metacharacter usage:

- ▲ `[a-f]` means any *one* character from the range *a* through *f*
- ▲ `^a` means any lines beginning with *a*
- ▲ `z$` means any lines ending with *z*

grep Options

Table 13.3 presents some of the more common grep options. All these options are used in Example 13.13, where we present the poem titled "Fleas." Barney has installed the poem in his home directory.

Table 13.3 Selected grep Options

Option	Description
`-v`	Print the lines that do not match the specified pattern
`-c`	Print only a count of the matching lines
`-l`	Print only the names of the files with matching lines
`-n`	Print matching lines and their line numbers in the respective files
`-i`	Ignore the case of the letters when making comparisons
`-w`	Perform a whole word search

Example 13.13 ▼ fleas

```
$ cat fleas<Enter>
```

Fleas
```
You bite those fleas and give a yelp
You scratch as though you thought that'd help
You chase your tail, you drag your butt
You're bound to fail, ya mis'rable mutt

Alright, c'mere, I'll scratch your head,
Such fleas as these can cause such dread!
I'll rub your belly and your back
To stem that burning itch attack

You sense what's up? You see, ol' friend?
To get the fleas, to write "the end"
```

```
            If you want to escape their wrath,
            Well, first ya gotta take a bath!
                                        Al McKinnon, July 2000
```

To search for all lines that contain the word *you*, in both uppercase and lowercase variants of *y*:

```
$ grep -i you fleas<Enter>
```

To perform the search using only metacharacters:

```
$ grep '[Yy]ou' fleas<Enter>
```

To perform the search using the `egrep` command (discussed later):

```
$ egrep 'you|You' fleas<Enter>
```

To search for all lines that contain at least one character but return only a line count of those lines:

```
$ grep -c '.' fleas<Enter>
14
```

To search for all files that contain the word *you*, whether in uppercase or not:

```
$ grep -li you *<Enter>
```

This one illustrates how you can combine options. Note that when subirectories are encountered during the search, the following message appears:

grep: *directoryname*: Is a directory

To search for all lines that do not contain the word *you*, uppercase or not:

```
$ grep -vi you fleas<Enter>
```

This one illustrates the combination of options but the displayed output includes all blank lines as well.

To search for all lines in the *fleas* file, number them, and send the output to the *fleas.num* file:

```
$ grep -n '.*' fleas > fleas.num<Enter>
```

Chapter 13: Basic Linux Utilities

Note how this one uses `grep` options and metacharacters and then uses redirection to send the output to the *fleas.num* file. To view the results, type

```
$ cat fleas.num<Enter>
```

To search for all occurrences of the whole word *you* in the poem:

```
$ grep -w 'you' fleas<Enter>
```

Note the words *your* and *You're* are also in the poem. If whole word had not been specified by the -w option, the occurrence of those words would also have been displayed. ▲

Regular Expressions with Metacharacters

In this section, we provide more examples of `grep` in action to help ensure that you understand how to use this powerful command. These examples are representative of the tasks that administrators typically encounter.

▲ Display all processes belonging to *username:*

```
$ ps ua | grep -n username<Enter>
```

This is a request for a listing of nonblank lines. You can apply such a procedure in several situations, such as stripping comments from a file.

▲ Select all lines (blank lines and nonblank lines) from the *phone1* file.

```
$ grep '.*' phone1
```

When you ask for this type of output, you are probably assuming that the file has blank lines. Single quotes surround the regular expression because without them, the shell will interfere with `grep`'s execution by imposing the shell's interpretation on the asterisk.

▲ Select only the blank lines in *phone1*:

```
$ grep '^$' phone1<Enter>
```

271

▲ Select all the lines in the *phone2* file that begin with the letter *M* and end with the number 7, with any number of characters in between.

```
$ grep '^M.*7$' phone2
```

This request asks for lines that have a particular pattern within a file.

▲ Select all the lines in the *phone2* file that contain an asterisk:

```
$ grep '\*' phone2<Enter>
```

Other grep Commands: egrep and fgrep

We have already discussed how `grep` can be extremely useful when you have to extract text from a data stream, such as a text file. (Yes, `grep` can be used for other types of data streams, but this usage is not covered here.) The command's functionality or performance for extracting text in particular situations is further enhanced by the `egrep` and `fgrep` commands.

Search for Alternates

The `grep` command itself cannot be used for the type of search request where you want to find all strings containing this or that. The extended `grep` command, `egrep`, allows OR searches by letting you put a pipe symbol (|) between your specified alternate search expressions, as shown in Example 14.14. The `egrep` command also works with `grep`'s metacharacters and options. The `egrep` command is a little slower than a normal `grep`, mostly because it executes more than one `grep` process.

Example 13.14 ▼ egrep

```
$ egrep '800|900' phone3<Enter>
Emergencies        800-555-0987
Human Resources    800-555-8765
Mail Room          900-555-3210
```

▲

Faster Search for Fixed Strings

The `fgrep` command is similar to `grep` but does not provide the regular expression capability. Instead, you are limited to searching for fixed text strings, as shown in Example 13.15. This command allows you to use the same options as `grep`, with the exception of any that deal with metacharacters or other aspects of regular expressions. Because `fgrep` does not require the extra translation, it requires fewer processor resources.

Example 13.15 ▼ fgrep

```
$ fgrep 'Brown' phone2<Enter>
Ms. Brown     502-555-8901
```

Sorting Output: sort Command

You use the `sort` command to sort the output of a file or the `stdout` of a process before it is sent to the screen or wherever you want it to go. Thus, `sort` helps to ensure that the output is in an acceptable order or presented as you want. It works by reading `stdin` (which may be the `stdout` of another process), processing the data, and sending it to `stdout` or wherever you designate. The `sort` command's syntax follows:

```
$ sort [-t delimiter] [+field[.column]] [options]
  [file(s)]<Enter>
```

The processes of the `sort` command use dictionary or ASCII ordering by default, which you can override with options, several of which appear in Table 13.4. For information on `sort`'s many other options, consult your information sources.

Table 13.4 Selected sort Options

Option	Description
-b	Ignore leading spaces and tabs
-c	Check whether data in the file is already sorted; if so, produce no output
-d	Sort in dictionary order

Continued

Table 13.4. Selected sort Options (continued)

Option	Description
-f	Ignore differences in uppercase and lowercase
-n	Sort in arithmetic order
-o*file*	Place output in *file*
-r	Reverse the sort order

NOTE: *The* sort *command uses <Tab> or <Spacebar> as the default delimiter between fields. If the input to* sort *consists of a combination of spaces and tabs throughout the data being sorted, the tabs and spaces are subject to the sorting process. This can result in what appears to be incorrect processing (as shown in Example 13.16).*

In Example 13.16, we first use the cat command to display the contents of the *fileaswritten* file. Then, by adding +1 in the +field position (see the syntax), we sort the contents according to the second field of each line. Look at how tabs have priority over spaces.

Example 13.16 ▼ sort with Spaces and Tabs

```
$ cat fileaswritten <Enter>
file<Space>file4
file<Space>file7
file<Tab>file8
file<Tab>file1
file<Space>file3

$ sort fileaswritten +1<Enter>
file<Tab>file1
file<Tab>file8
file<Space>file3
file<Space>file4
file<Space>file7
```
▲

Chapter 13: Basic Linux Utilities

Example 13.17 presents several instances of the `sort` command in action. We use the *animals* file, which as you may have noted in Figure 13.1, is in Barney's home directory.

Example 13.17 ▼ sort in Action

To display the *animals* file as written:

```
$ cat animals<Enter>
mice      .3
cats      .2
horses    .1
pigs      .0
dogs      .4
rabbits   .6
fish      .5
```

To sort *animals* into dictionary order:

```
$ sort animals<Enter>
cats      .2
dogs      .4
fish      .5
horses    .1
mice      .3
pigs      .0
rabbits   .6
```

To sort by the second character in the first word:

```
$ cat animals | sort +0.1<Enter>
rabbits   .6
cats      .2
mice      .3
pigs      .0
fish      .5
dogs      .4
horses    .1
```

275

The t option tells sort which character in the file to recognize as the field separator. The most common separators are colons, tabs, or \n (new line character). To sort on the second field, numerical, using the dot (.) as the field delimeter:

```
$ cat animals | sort -t. -n +1<Enter>
pigs      .0
horses    .1
cats      .2
mice      .3
dogs      .4
fish      .5
rabbits   .6
```
▲

NOTE: *This command's line options are unique to* sort. *If you were using the* cut *command, for example, the delimiter would be* d, *not* t.

Displaying Parts of Files: head and tail Commands

You use the head and tail commands when you want to view only parts of a file.

The head Command

In this section, we discuss only the simplest applications of the head command. Refer to your sources for further information regarding this command's additional options.

The head command is used to display the first *n* number of lines in a file, as shown in Example 13.18. The syntax is

```
head [-number of lines] [file(s)]
```

If you do not specify a number, the default value of 10 is used. If no files are specified, head reads from stdin. If head is combined after another command, head still reads from stdin, although it appears that head is reading from the stdout of the previous command. If more than one file is read, a header of the type ==> *filename* <== is displayed before the respective lines of text.

The second part of Example 13.18 shows how you can pipeline to head the output of one process to display only a specified number of lines.

Example 13.18 ▼ head

```
$ head -5 animals<Enter>
mice     .3
cats     .2
horses   .1
pigs     .0
dogs     .4
$ ls -l | head -12<Enter>
-rw-rw-r--   ...   15:27 animals
drwxrwxr-x   ...   12:54 color
    .
    .
    .
drwxrwxr-x   ...   14:49 shape
```
▲

The tail Command

The tail command performs a bit differently than head. Its syntax is

```
tail [-number of lines | +number of lines] [file(s)]
```

In Example 13.19, note that you may specify a positive or negative number. (For other options, see your information sources.) The negative number tells tail to display text beginning at the nth line from the end of the file, so you get n lines of text. The second part of Example 13.19 illustrates this type of output.

The positive number specification tells tail to display text beginning at the nth line from the beginning of the file and to continue from there. That's why, in the first part of Example 13.19, you see only two lines of output. The *animals* file is only seven lines long.

Example 13.19 ▼ tail

```
$ tail +6 animals<Enter>
rabbits    .6
fish       .5

$ tail -6 animals<Enter>
cats       .2
horses     .1
pigs       .9
dogs       .4
rabbits    .6
fish       .5
```

One interesting option with the `tail` command is the `-f` option. With this option, `tail` continues reading additional lines from the input file as they become available. For example, suppose you have a file called *accts_recvble* that you know will keep growing. You can monitor its growth by entering the following:

```
$ tail -f accts_recvble<Enter>
```

The result is the last ten lines of the file at the moment the command is processed. Then additional lines are displayed as they are added to the file. How do you stop it? Press <Ctrl>-c.

Exercises

1. Log in to the system and ensure that you are in your home directory. Find and display all files in the */tmp* directory.

    ```
    $ cd<Enter>
    $ pwd<Enter>
    $ find /tmp<Enter>
    ```

2. Find all files in your home directory that begin with the letter *s* and then have `ls -l` automatically execute on each file name found as a result of the search operation.

    ```
    $ find . -name 's*' -exec ls -l { } \;<Enter>
    ```

3. Repeat the search in the preceding step but interactively prompt the user to display a long list on each file.

    ```
    $ find . -name 's*' -ok ls -l { } \;<Enter>
    ```

4. Find all files starting from the */usr* directory owned by the *uucp* userid. Modify the command line to count the number of files owned by *uucp*. You probably do not have read permission for some directories, which would result in a *permission denied* message on your terminal screen. Because you anticipate this, redirect all error messages to a file called *errfile*:

    ```
    $ find /usr -user uucp 2> errfile | wc -l<Enter>
    ```

5. Display the *errfile* file from the preceding instruction to see whether any error messages were written.

    ```
    $ pg errfile<Enter>
    ```

6. To demonstrate that `find` recursively searches all directories and subdirectories from the search path down, do the following. First, ensure that you are in your home directory:

    ```
    $ cd<Enter>
    ```

    Next, make a subdirectory called *level1*:

    ```
    $ mkdir level1<Enter>
    ```

Create a zero-length file named *letter1* in the *level1* subdirectory:

`$ touch level1/letter1<Enter>`

Change to the *level1* subdirectory:

`$ cd level1<Enter>`

Make a subdirectory under *level1* called *level2*:

`$ mkdir level2<Enter>`

Create a zero-length file named *letter2* in the *level2* subdirectory:

`$ touch level2/letter2<Enter>`

Change to your home directory:

`$ cd<Enter>`

From your home directory, issue the command to list all files starting with the letter *l*.

`$ ls l*<Enter>`

Record the names displayed.

From your home directory, issue the command to find only files starting with the letter *l*.

`$ find . -name 'l*' -type f<Enter>`

Finally, record the names displayed.

7. Find all lines in the */etc/passwd* file for user names that start with *team*.

   `$ grep team /etc/passwd<Enter>`

8. Find all lines in the */etc/passwd* file that begin with the letter *t*.

   `$ grep '^t' /etc/passwd<Enter>`

9. Find all lines in */etc/passwd* that contain a digit from 0 through 9.

   `$ grep [0-9] /etc/passwd<Enter>`

10. Repeat the search in the preceding step, but this time display only the number of lines that contain the pattern.

    ```
    $ grep -c [0-9] /etc/passwd<Enter>
    ```

11. Use the `ps` and `grep` commands to display the processes that have been initiated by users other than yourself.

    ```
    $ ps ua | grep -v username<Enter>
    ```

12. Display the contents of the */etc/passwd* file in alphabetical order.

    ```
    $ sort /etc/passwd<Enter>
    ```

    Display the contents of the same file, but in reverse order.

    ```
    $ sort -r /etc/passwd<Enter>
    ```

13. Display the first ten lines of */etc/passwd*.

    ```
    $ head /etc/passwd<Enter>
    ```

14. Display the first five lines of */etc/passwd*.

    ```
    $ head -5 /etc/passwd<Enter>
    ```

15. Display the last ten lines of */etc/passwd*.

    ```
    $ tail /etc/passwd<Enter>
    ```

16. The `tail` command is handy also for stripping header information from the output of a command. First, list all processes currently running on your system. Note the headings.

    ```
    $ ps ua | less<Enter>
    ```

    Next, display all processes running on your system, excluding the header information.

    ```
    $ ps ua | tail +2 | less<Enter>
    ```

See Appendix B for answers.

Quiz

1. Which command would you use to locate all the files in your system that begin with the string *mis*?

2. Explain the following command:

   `$ ps ua | grep -w root | grep -w /sbin*<Enter>`

3. Explain the following command:

   `$ ls -l /home/teamxx | egrep 'um$|isc$|ync' | sort -r +8 | tail +2 | head -7<Enter>`

See Appendix C for answers.

Chapter 14

Advanced Linux Utilities

IN CHAPTER 13, WE DISCUSSED CERTAIN BASIC Linux utilities. This chapter continues that discussion and broadens your ability to perform file system administration. In several of the sections and examples in this chapter, we refer once again to Barney's file structure shown at the beginning of Chapter 13 (in Figure 13.1).

Maximizing Work per Command: xargs

The `xargs` command is one of the best you can use to execute commands and programs efficiently. This command reads arguments one line at a time from `stdin` and then assembles as many of them as possible into a single command line, until it determines that the command has reached its capacity, meaning that it cannot execute if any more arguments are added. Then, after `xargs` has filled the input to this capacity, the commands are executed. If there are still more arguments in the source, `xargs` assembles more of them into another single command line until it, too, is filled to capacity, and then the command is executed again. The `xargs` command continues to do this until it exhausts the given supply of arguments. The syntax is

```
commandname [options] | xargs [options]
```

There is a second use for `xargs`. But first, note that some commands are smart enough to take input from a parameter line and execute with it. Moreover, if the parameter line is empty, the command is again smart enough to take input from `stdin`, which is often a pipe.

Unfortunately, not all commands are smart enough to take input from a pipe. For example, `rm` is one of those not-so-smart commands. Faced with this situation, what can you do? Your options are to invoke `rm` several times manually; to use some type of automated loop to invoke `rm` for every file, which causes a subprocess every time `rm` is invoked; or to use `find` to identify the input file names and then execute `cat`, `xargs`, and `rm` in tandem. The third option is the right choice. And that is `xarg`'s second and very valuable use: taking `cat`'s output and passing it to `rm`. Let's take a close look at how this option works in Example 14.1.

Example 14.1 ▼ xargs

Collect the names of existing phone-list-type files into a single file called *oldphonelists*. Then `cat` it to be sure it is correct:

```
$ find . -name 'ph*' -print > ./oldphonelists<Enter>
$ cat oldphonelists<Enter>
./phone1
./phone2
./phone3
```

Use `xargs` and `rm` against *oldphonelists* to remove the original files:

```
$ cat oldphonelists | xargs -t rm<Enter>
rm ./phone1 ./phone2 ./phone3
```
▲

The first step is relatively simple: `find` identifies all the old phone-list-type files and puts their names into the aptly named *oldphone-lists* file. Then `cat` passes the list of file names to `xargs` through `stdout/stdin`. Next, `xargs` translates the information from the `stdin` pipe and passes each parameter (in this case, each file name) to the parameter line following the subsequent `rm` command. The `xargs` command is smart enough to know the length of the parameter line it can produce before `rm` has to be invoked. Thus, `rm` is invoked the optimum number of times, which illustrates why this is the most efficient way of handling this procedure.

Chapter 14: Advanced Linux Utilities

Why did we use the -t option with xargs? The -t option, which is commonly called verbose mode, causes the command line to be printed to stderr just before executing the command. It allows the user to monitor the number of times that rm is invoked. That is why, in Example 14.1, the line rm ./phone1 ./phone2 ./phone3 appears while the tandem cat, xargs, and rm commands are executed. In this case, rm was executed only once. After you get used to xargs and trust it, you will probably no longer use -t.

In Example 14.2, we illustrate two fairly simple cases of xargs usage.

Example 14.2 ▼ Using xargs

To print a large number of file names:

```
$ cd fruits_vegs<Enter>
$ ls > print_list<Enter>
$ vi print_list<Enter>
apple
banana
carrot
   .
   .
   .
yam
zucchini
:q<Enter>

$ xargs -t lpr < print_list
lpr apple, banana, carrot ... pomegranate
lpr rhubarb, strawberry ... yam, zucchini
```

To change the names of multiple files:

```
$ cd fruits_vegs<Enter>
$ ls | xargs -t -i mv {} {}.old<Enter>
mv apple apple.old
mv banana banana.old
mv carrot carrot.old
```

-
-
-

```
mv yam yam.old
mv zucchini zucchini.old
```
▲

In the first part of Example 14.2, we illustrate printing a number of file names at once. In the first step, we move to a directory called *fruits_vegs*. The next step illustrates the creation of a file named *print_list*, consisting of the names of all the files in the *fruits_vegs* directory. These are the names we want to print. The `vi` text editor is invoked for two reasons: to examine the file names in the new file and to add or remove names as we see fit. In this case, we do not add any names, so we just `q` out of `vi`.

The next step shows the combined `xargs` and `lpr` commands and the results. We try to indicate that `xargs` was able to fill the command line with arguments from *apple* to *pomegranate* before `lpr` was executed. Then `xargs` was able to pass the rest of the files, from *rhubarb* to *zucchini*, to `lpr`. Note that we are still using the `-t` option to ensure that `xargs` has passed the input to `lpr` and that `lpr` is indeed executing.

The second part of Example 14.2 shows how to insert file names in the middle of a command line. Our objective is to rename all the files in the *fruits_vegs* directory by adding the *.old* suffix to each. We again move to the *fruits_vegs* directory, invoke a short listing of the files in that directory, and then pipe the file names from `stdout` to `xargs`, which then instructs that each file name, in turn, be inserted (the `-i` option inserts each line of standard input) between the curly bracket placeholders following the `mv` command. This form of `mv` is used to rename files. Because we have also specified the `-t` option, we also get to monitor the execution of `mv` as each file name is passed to it. After the last file, *zucchini*, has its name changed to *zucchini.old*, the combination command finishes and the primary shell prompt returns.

Combining xargs, find, and grep Utilities

Combining the `find`, `grep`, and `xargs` utilities has its benefits. All are powerful and efficient in their own right, but combining them multiplies their usefulness and can make you an even more efficient system user.

The objective of Example 14.3 is to remove from the current directory all files whose modification times are older than 30 days. If we did not use `xargs`, we would have to enter:

```
$ find . -type f -mtime +30 -exec rm {} \;
```

That may not appear inefficient or objectionable at first glance, but it means that `rm` would be invoked every time a file was found that matched the `find` criteria, four times in this case. But how many times would it have to be invoked if you were examining a much larger file system?

On the other hand, using `xargs` allows you to pass multiple parameters to be `rm`, so `rm` is invoked far fewer times (in our case, just once) to remove all the candidate old files. In addition, the `xargs` syntax may be easier to remember than the combined `find`, `exec`, and `rm` syntax. Note that in Example 14.3, we are continuing to use the `-t` `xargs` option, so that you see how many times `rm` was actually invoked.

Example 14.3 ▼ Combining find and xargs

To find and remove files with modification dates older than 30 days:

```
$ find . -type f -mtime +30 | xargs -t rm <Enter>
rm ./file1 ./file2 ./file3 ./file4
```
▲

In Example 14.4, we want to examine the current directory and find all the files containing the word *Hello* (irrespective of case). First, `find` passes a list of the files in the current directory to `xargs`. The `xargs` command invokes `grep` to look into all the files for the entire word *hello* (-w option) regardless of case (-i option), and list the names of the files containing *hello* (-l option). The output list is handed to lpr, which prints the list of file names to the screen. After that, we get the names of the files that contain *hello*: *file5* and *file10*.

Example 14.4 ▼ Combining find, xargs, and grep

To find all files that contain the word *hello*, beginning with an uppercase or lowercase *h*:

```
$ find . -type f | xargs -t grep -lwi 'Hello' lpr
    <Enter>
grep -lwi Hello lpr ./file5 ./file7 ./file10
./file5
./file10                                                ▲
```

We can see that grep was invoked only once because the example file structure contains a small number of files. If there had been many more files to examine, invoking grep more often might have been necessary.

Comparing find Functions and Shell Functions

In this section, we illustrate the difference between the functionality of certain shells and the find command. We have discussed the capability of the find command to travel down through directories (meaning, to search recursively), which is one of its primary benefits.

During most routine operations, the shell interprets the command line and then provides the appropriate arguments to an executable command. Thus, the commands do not understand directory structures and rely on the shell to expand wildcards and then provide the full directory or path name of candidate files for execution.

The sample directory structure in Figure 14.1 is used in this section for demonstration. The comparison of the find command and the shell in Example 14.5 references this figure.

CHAPTER 14: ADVANCED LINUX UTILITIES

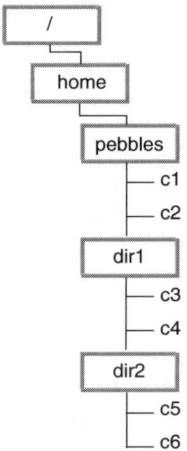

Figure 14.1: Sample directory structure used in Example 14.5.

Example 14.5 ▼ Shell versus find

To ask the shell to find all file names that begin with *c*:

```
$ cd /home/pebbles<Enter>
$ ls c*<Enter>
c1  c2
```

To ask `find` to find all file names that begin with *c*:

```
$ cd /home/pebbles<Enter>
$ find . -name 'c*'<Enter>
./c1
./c2
./dir1/c3
./dir1/c4
./dir2/c5
./dir2/c6
```
▲

Unfortunately, in situations such as Example 14.5, where you try to enter a fairly simple search command, the shell does not look any further than the current directory. To get the shell to look beyond the current directory and traverse the three-tiered directory structure in this example, you have to enter the following:

```
$ ls c* */c* */* /c*<Enter>
```

This is tedious and confusing to type; moreover, you would have to investigate the structure beforehand to know how many arguments to enter so that all directory levels are searched. Finally, the shell does not allow `ls` to check any hidden directories (those beginning with a dot).

That's why you should use the `find` command. The syntax is easier, subdirectories are searched, hidden directories (if applicable) are searched, and you do not have to know beforehand the depth of the file structure under the initially specified directory. For these reasons, many administrators and programmers consider `find`'s recursive search capability its best characteristic.

The find command with the -links option

In this section, we discuss the use of the `-links` option with `find`. As demonstrated in Example 14.6, there are two reasons to use this command combination. First, if you can have the same file referenced by two separate names, the only way you can tell if they are indeed the same file is by examining the inode number. If the inode numbers are identical, they are the same file.

The second reason is probably most important: For security reasons, you do not want outsiders linking to insider programs or files. You must have a way of seeing and confirming where all links are pointing to evaluate if they are necessary and legitimate. Therefore, it is important to conduct a `find -links` check periodically to search for such potential infiltration.

The syntax is

```
find directory(ies) -type [options] -links +[options]
    | xargs ls -li
```

Example 14.6 is typical of a `find -links` check. Note that you should be certain to perform `-links` checks on only *files* because directories by their nature have at least two links (their own and their

CHAPTER 14: ADVANCED LINUX UTILITIES

link with the parent directory). Note that the linked files' inode numbers, link counts, and file sizes are the same. The only difference among the three is their respective file names. Rest assured that they all refer to the same file, regardless of their names.

Example 14.6 ▼ Find -links

```
$ find /home/team01 -type f -links +1 | xargs ls -li
  <Enter>
6289 -rw-r--r--3 team01 staff 1574 May 21 15:35/home/team01/myfile
6289 -rw-r--r--3 team01 staff 1574 May 21 15:35/home/team02/akafile
6289 -rw-r--r--3 team01 staff 1574 May 21 15:35/home/team03/3rdfile
```
▲

Example 14.6 uses `xargs` in tandem with `find -links`, but we could have also used a pure `find`, such as the following:

```
$ find /home/teamxx -type f -links +1 -exec ls -li {} \;
```

Your choice is a matter of syntax preference.

Reducing Keystrokes: Using find with alias

In this section, we show aliases being used to simplify and substitute for certain long commands that are used periodically for system monitoring and maintenance. The syntax is

```
alias shortcommand='longcommand [options]'
```

Remember, when you set aliases from the command line, as we do in Example 14.7, those aliases are effective only for the current log-in session. Use the technique we showed you in Chapter 12 to ensure that the alias survives from session to session.

Example 14.7 ▼ alias for Shortening Commands

To create an alias to check for file links:

```
$ alias linkcheck='find . -type f -links +1 | xargs ls -li'
  <Enter>
```

```
$ linkcheck<Enter>
6289 -rw-r--r--3 team01 staff 1574 May 21 15:35/home/team01/myfile
6289 -rw-r--r--3 team01 staff 1574 May 21 15:35/home/team02/akafile
6289 -rw-r--r--3 team01 staff 1574 May 21 15:35/home/team03/3rdfile
```

To create an alias to remove dated files:

```
$ alias oldrm='find . -type f -mtime +30 | xargs rm'
  <Enter>
$ oldrm<Enter>                                                    ▲
```

Recall that these and any aliases can be undefined using the `unalias` command. Meanwhile, the two cases in Example 14.7 illustrate how to set aliases for commands we discussed previously in this chapter. In the second case, note that we did not add the `-t` option to `xargs`, indicating that we do not need to minutely monitor the `rm` process.

Determining File Types: file Command

The `file` command is used to classify a file according to its content. This command uses up to three tests: a file system test, a magic number test (using the */usr/share/magic* file), and a language test. The syntax follows:

```
file [options] /path/filename(s)
```

The output from `file` is usually some variation of `text`, `data`, or `executable`, unless it cannot find the file. If there is no such file, `find` returns an error message:

```
$ file nonexistentfile<Enter>
Nonexistentfile: can't stat 'nonexistentfile' (No such
    file or directory)
```

Why is `file` beneficial? It can give you a quick indication of whether a file is the type of file that you can more easily display on your terminal screen or send to a printer. Or it can tell you that a file is an executable file; attempting to display an executable file on your screen could cause confusion or even hang your terminal.

The `file` command has its own set of options; check your information sources. The one we use in Example 14.8 is `-f`. This option tells file to check the list of files specified immediately after the -f (that is, in the file called *listoffiles*). Note that when using an argument file to list files for file to check, you should ensure that each file name appears alone on a single line in that argument file.

Example 14.8 ▼ file

```
$ cd /home/rubbleba<Enter>
$ ls > listoffiles<Enter>
$ file -f listoffiles<Enter>
color: directory
fleas: English text
listoffiles: ASCII text
   .
   .
   .
```
▲

For binary files, file can provide an indication of the operating system and the version used to compile the file, as seen in Example 14.9.

Example 14.9 ▼ file for System Information

```
$ file /bin/vi<Enter>
/bin/vi: ELF 32-bit LSB executable, Intel 30386,
    version 1, dynamically-linked, stripped

$ file /home/rubbleba/color/white<Enter>
/home/rubbleba/color/white: English text
```
▲

We suggest that you take the time to check the file man page and also scroll through the */usr/share/magic* file to understand more fully how file checks for "magic numbers" coded within files.

Comparing Text Files: diff Command

Occasionally, you may want to determine the differences between two text files. For example, two users may be working on different sections of the same report at the office, or on the same sections of the same report, or even on the same report at different times. These are times when the `diff` command comes in handy. This command can compare the lines of text in two files or even compare all similarly named pairs of text files in two directories (if the arguments are directory names instead of file names). The syntax is

```
diff [-options] file1 file2
```

The `diff` command has numerous options; check your information sources. In Example 14.10, we use two common options: the `-q` option, which gives you a quick report on whether two files actually differ; and the `-y` option, which prints the two files side by side on the screen so that you can compare them yourself.

Example 14.10 ▼ diff

```
$ diff c3 c6<Enter>
1c1
< This file is called c3.
- - -
> This file is called c6.
3,4c3
< Has to be different from c6 and c9.
- - -
> Has to be different from c3 and c9.
$ diff -q c3 c6<Enter>
Files c3 and c6 differ
$ diff -y c3 c6<Enter>
This file is called c3.| This file is called c6.
Why this name?         | Why this name?
It's not from c6.      | It's not from c3.
```
▲

Depending on your preference, instead of entering

```
$ diff -y file1 file2<Enter>
```

you can enter the equivalent:

```
$ sdiff file1 file2<Enter>.
```

Other valuable options are listed in Table 14.1.

Table 14.1 Selected diff Options

Options	Description
-b	Ignore leading, repeating, and end-of-line spaces, tab characters, and so on.
-e	Print a text editor script, which you might use to modify the first file so that it would be identical to the second file.
-w *n*	For two-column output, the total number of characters used for both columns must have a maximum *n* characters. (The default is 130 characters, but most users prefer to set it to 80 or so.)

It's not uncommon in everyday life to have several versions of (essentially) the same document floating around your system. In the scenario in Example 14.12, in the period between September 1999 and September 2000, ABC Company's Web site development team lost one member, Marie Freschette, who resigned from the team to work with another project team. She was replaced by Dale Joseph. While modifying the team list, the team discovered that they had previously misspelled Ms. Brown's first name. Let's use this simple example to discuss what `diff` discovers and displays when it compares the original to the new Web site development team list, namely */abc/webteam.0999* and */abc/webteam.0900*. The two documents are illustrated in Figure 14.2, and results of the `diff` comparison appear in Example 14.11.

```
        ┌─────────────────────────┐  ┌─────────────────────────┐
        │      ABC Company        │  │      ABC Company        │
        │  Web Development Team   │  │  Web Development Team   │
        │       Sept. 1999        │  │       Sept. 2000        │
        ├─────────────────────────┤  ├─────────────────────────┤
        │  Brown, Jane            │  │  Brown, Janet           │
        │  Freschette, Marie      │  │  Jones, Pat             │
        │  Jones, Pat             │  │  Joseph, Dale           │
        │  Khoury, Nadia          │  │  Khoury, Nadia          │
        │  Smith, John            │  │  Smith, John            │
        │  Wong, Mark             │  │  Wong, Mark             │
        │  File: /abc/webteam.0999│  │  File: /abc/webteam.0900│
        └─────────────────────────┘  └─────────────────────────┘
```

Figure 14.2: The two documents used in Example 14.11.

Example 14.11 ▼ diff for Comparing Files

```
$ cd abc<Enter>
$ diff webteam.0999 webteam.0900<Enter>
3c3
< Sept. 1999
- - -
> Sept. 2000
6,7c6
< Brown, Jane
< Freschette, Marie
- - -
> Brown, Janet
8a8
> Joseph, Dale
13c13
< File: /abc/webteam.0999
- - -
> File: /abc/webteam.0900
```

In examining the `diff` output, we can see that four changes were made from */abc/webteam.0999* to */abc/webteam.0900*. There are four lines that include some sort of combination of number and letter codes: `3c3`; `6,7c6`; `8a8`; and `13c13`. Each of those lines denotes the beginning of a `diff` explanation of the respective change.

The first code, `3c3`, tells us that a change has been made to line 3 from the first file to that of the second file. Counting down from the top of each file, we see that line 3 indicates the date of the member list. Now, note that the line beginning with a left angle bracket (<) shows us line 3 as it appears in the first file (that is, *Sept. 1999*). Then there is a line with three dashes, which serves to separate line 3 of the first file from what is coming next. What comes next is a line that begins with a right angle bracket (>), which shows us line 3 as it appears in the second file (that is, *Sept. 2000*). It is easy to see that `diff` is telling us that the date has been changed from the first file to the second, and if we want one file to look identical to the other, we have to make some sort of change to line 3 in */abc/webteam.0999* or */abc/webteam.0900*. You have probably noticed that the first 3 in 3c3 means line 3 in the first file, and the second 3 means line 3 in the second file. The c code separates the first from the second.

Another way to paraphrase this is to say that lines appearing in the first file but not in the second file begin with a left angle bracket (<). Conversely, lines that appear in the second file but not in the first file begin with a right angle bracket (>). Any lines that have been modified between the first and second files are shown as < and >, but with three dashes on a line interjected between the two. We have focused on the third line, where `diff` notified us of changes in the dates for the respective team lists.

The second code, 6,7c6, is a little more complicated. The 6,7 is on the first file side, then a c, followed by a 6 on the second file side. What does it mean? Keep reading and you see < Brown, Jane on the next line and < Freschette, Marie on the following line. The `diff` command is telling us that these are lines 6 and 7 from the first file. Then we see the line with the three dashes, which indicates that references to the first file are complete, and we can anticipate seeing line 6 from the second file. Sure enough, > Brown, Janet appears on the next line and we see that a change has occurred: Jane has changed to Janet in line 6. But why did `diff` mention line 7 in the first file? Recall that we said in the last paragraph that the left angle bracket (<) indicated a line from the first file that did not appear in the second file. We know that Brown, Jane (line 6) did not appear in the second file because the line had been changed to Brown, Janet, so that explains the < before line 6. That must mean, then, that line 7 from the first file does not appear in the second file. In other words,

`Marie Freschette` is not mentioned in the second file. It also means that line 7 in the first file must be completely different from line 7 in the second file; it is likely that the previous line 8 (that is, `Jones, Pat`) has been moved up one position to line 7.

The third code, 8a8, appears to be a little more straightforward. The `diff` command provides no details about line 8 in the first file, but tells us that a line 8 has been added to the second file that says `Joseph, Dale`. Because the name is preceded by a right angle bracket (>), we know that this line does not appear in the first file. So we surmise that `Joseph, Dale` is interjected into line position 8 after `Jones, Pat` but before `Khoury, Nadia`, which remains unchanged (now) at line 9. Furthermore, `Smith, John` and `Wong, Mark` remain at lines 10 and 11, respectively, and a blank line remains at line 12.

The fourth and last code, 13c13, is similar to the first code. We can safely presume that there have been changes made to line 13. And `diff` spells them out: It shows us that the original line 13 said `File: /abc/webteam.0999` using the < designation, followed by a line with three dashes. Then it indicates, using >, that the second file now says `File:/abc/webteam.0900`. We can see that the file name has been changed to show the date of the new changes.

As shown in Table 14.2, `diff` provides codes in addition to supplying line numbers in its output. The `diff` command and its options and output codes may seem a bit complicated at first, but with practice, they are easy to grasp and make valuable analytical tools.

Table 14.2 diff Output Codes

Code	Description
a	Add or append lines to the first file to obtain the result shown in the second file.
c	Lines that have been changed between the first and second file.
d	Lines deleted from the second file. (Although Example 14.12 did not include a d, its meaning is reasonably straightforward.)

Two similar commands that may be of interest are `comm` and `diff3`. The `comm` command shows you which information is common to both files as well as the information that is unique to each file. It presents lines that are only in the first file in column one, lines that are only in the second file in column two, and lines that are found in both files in column three.

The `diff3` command compares three files. The output coding is a little different but the principles are the same as in `diff`. For further information, consult your information sources.

Comparing All Types of Files: cmp Command

In the preceding section, we discussed the `diff` command, which is used to compare text files line by line. The `cmp` (file compare) command differs from `diff` in several ways. First, `cmp` is used for text files and other types of files as well. Further, `cmp` compares byte by byte rather than line by line. On text files, `cmp` makes a character-by-character comparison.

Its syntax is

```
cmp [-options] file1 file2
```

When used with no options, `cmp` prints a message and stops as soon as it encounters the first difference between the files. The `cmp` response states the names of the files it has compared and then indicates exactly which byte is the first to differ between the two files. In the first part of Example 14.12, you can see that the first byte to differ between the two files being compared (the same team lists we compared in Example 14.11) is character 41 on line 3 (the 9 in the date in */abc/webteam.0999* versus the 0 in the date in */abc/webteam.0900*).

Example 14.12 ▼ cmp

To compare two files using `cmp` without options:

```
$ cmp /abc/webteam.0999 /abc/webteam.0900<Enter>
```
/abc/webteam.0999 /abc/webteam.0900 differ: char 41, line 3

To compare two files using `cmp` and an option:

```
$ cmp -l /abc/webteam.0999 /abc/webteam.0900<Enter>
```
41 7071

```
55 12164
56 10612
 .
 .
 .
1416012
cmp: EOF on /abc/webteam.0900
```

In the second part of Example 14.12, we ask for a more detailed comparison by typing the -l option after the cmp command. The command replies by listing all differing bytes between the two files. The output is in three columns: The first column contains the decimal value of the byte number; the second column, the corresponding octal value of the character found in that position in the first file examined; and the third, the corresponding octal value of the character found in that position in the second file examined.

There are no differences until byte number 41 is encountered. The first file, */abc/webteam.0999*, has a character in that position whose octal value is 70. The second file, */abc/webteam.0199*, has a character in that position whose octal value is 71. For all text files, these octal values refer to the values of the characters in the ASCII character set.

The cmp command is not the best comparison tool for text files, as you have undoubtedly surmised by now. It is more suitable for comparing data or program object files.

Compressing Files: gzip, gunzip, and zcat Commands

Data files, including text files, are generally compressed so they can be stored in less space or transmitted in a shorter period of time. Compression (or compaction) programs generally look for redundancies in files, and then use one representative token for all identical pieces of data. In this way, no data is lost.

Linux uses a command called gzip to compress data in specified files using an algorithm called Lempel-Ziv (LZ77) coding. The syntax is

```
gzip [-options] filename(s)
```

CHAPTER 14: ADVANCED LINUX UTILITIES

Other UNIX-like operating systems may use `gzip` or another program called `compress`, which uses a different version of the Lempel-Ziv coding and is generally used with the `tar` command for archiving data. The `gzip` command can compress (ASCII) files by as much as 80%.

By default, `gzip` names the compressed file with the original file name, but appends *.gz* to the end of the file name to indicate that it is a compressed file, as shown in Example 14.13. It then deletes the original file. Also by default, `gzip` transfers the original ownership and permission modes and access and modification times to the new *.gz* file.

Example 14.13 ▼ gzip

```
$ gzip -v phone3<Enter>
phone3:66.5% -- replaced with phone3.gz
```

You can use numerous options to enhance the use of `gzip` or to override the defaults. For a complete listing and description of options, consult your information sources. Three of the most handy are described Table 14.3.

Table 14.3 Selected gzip Options

Option	Description
-v	Verbose. Print the original name and the new compressed file name, along with the percent compression that the file has been subjected to.
-r	Recursive. When used with a directory name, execute `gzip` on all files in the directory and from that directory down through the file system.
n	Speed of compression; *n* is a number from 1 through 9. 1 executes compression at the fastest speed with the least compression. 9 executes compression at the slowest speed, resulting in the highest compression. The default value is 6.

The `gunzip` command uncompresses files that have been compressed with `gzip` or `compress`. Basically, `gunzip` reverses the gzip process, restoring the compressed file to its original uncompressed components. Its syntax is

```
gunzip [-options] filename(s)
```

This command uses most of the same options as `gzip` (see your information sources). For example, we use the `-v` option with `gunzip` in Example 14.14.

Example 14.14 ▼ gunzip

```
$ gunzip -v phone3<Enter>
phone3.gz:  66.5% -- replaced with phone3                    ▲
```

The next command, `zcat` is used for two reasons: to examine the contents of a compressed file without going through the process of uncompressing it; and to use a compressed file as input to one or more piped commands.

We use `zcat` for the first purpose in Example 14.15. The output from `zcat` is the same as the output of the uncompressed file, similar to what you would get with `cat`. You can see that `zcat` does the same thing for compressed files that its counterpart `cat` does for uncompressed files. However, like `cat`, `zcat` cannot go back and forth through the file output. For this purpose, you might want to use the `zless` command, which behaves just like the `less` program (see Chapter 5 to review the `less` command) except it requires compressed files as input arguments. The syntax is

```
zcat [-options] filename(s)
```

Example 14.15 ▼ zcat

```
$ zcat phone3.gz<Enter>                                      ▲
```

 NOTE: *The zip and unzip commands may also be available with your Linux distribution. You might prefer to use them instead to compress and uncompress files.*

Displaying Nonprintable Characters: cat Command Options

Here we discuss three options you can use with the old familiar `cat` command (refer to Chapter 5 for our original discussion of `cat`) to determine whether invisible or otherwise unprintable characters are in text files or file names (that is, directories) and to determine the nature of spaces in your text files. The latter may be important because of unexpected `diff` command output or problems with output from the `sort` command.

It may not be possible to resolve these issues or problems based on the typical viewing of directory or file contents. Using `cat` with the options discussed here may help you to determine how the file contents or names were created, and therefore to figure out how to manipulate them later. The syntax is

```
cat [-options] [file(s)]<Enter>
```

The options used in Example 14.16 are defined in Table 14.4.

Example 14.16 ▼ cat for Displaying Nonprintable Characters

```
$ cat testfile<Enter>
```
Thisfile   has   tabs andspaces
   andthisline   ends with   areturn
```
$ cat -etv testfile<Enter>
```
This^Ifile   ha^Gs   ^I tabs and^Ispaces $
   and^I^Gthis^Iline^G   ends with   a^Ireturn$ ▲

Table 14.4 Selected cat Options

Option	Description
-e	Display $ to indicated the end-of-line key, that is, <Enter> or <Return>
-t	Display ^I to indicate a <Tab> used as a space
-v	Display ^G to indicate the otherwise invisible <Ctrl>-g key sequence

When executing listings of directory contents, you may sometimes encounter file names containing a question mark (?). The creator of such a file name may have intentionally inserted the question mark, but this symbol may also indicate the presence of other characters that cannot be readily interpreted by the shell. When dealing with these odd file names in directories, you can use cat as the second process in a piped set of commands. For example, a typical ls<Enter> command might reveal the following:

```
testfile1
te?stfile2
```

Now we try cat:

```
$ ls | cat -vt<Enter>
```

The output might look something like

```
testfile1
te^Gstfile2
```

This example shows a <Ctrl>-g (that is, ^G) in the middle of what otherwise would have been called *testfile2*. How do you correct the file name? You could simply rename the file as follows:

```
$ mv te?stfile2 testfile2<Enter>
```

NOTE: *You cannot enter* te^Gstfile2 *at the command line. If you try, you will hear an error beep from Linux.*

CHAPTER 14: ADVANCED LINUX UTILITIES

If the correction strategy fails, you can try another technique. First, you need to obtain the inode number of the file with `ls -li`. (Remember that the file name displayed is probably *te?stfile2* because a simple `ls -li` does not display the hidden <Ctrl>-g characters.) Assume that the inode number for the file is 1311. Now enter:

```
$ find . -inum 1311 -exec mv {} testfile2 \;<Enter>
```

NOTE: *Artificially creating this situation is a bit difficult. But things like this do happen. We stuck to <Ctrl>-g (or ^G, if you prefer) as our chosen invisible character because it is the only one that Linux allows us to use.*

Assigning Unique File Names: Appending Information

Sometimes an application or a user or a programmer has to assign a unique name to a file. In this section, we discuss two methods of assigning unique names: automatically appending either the process number or the date as a suffix to the end of a file name. The syntax is

```
touch filename$$
```

By appending two dollar signs to the end of a file name, as shown in Example 4.17, the shell automatically appends a two- to five-digit process number to the end of that file name. This technique will likely produce a unique file name every time, but some people prefer the suffix to tell them a little more about the file. This is why the other method, appending a date as the suffix, is popular.

NOTE: *For both techniques, we are using the* `touch` *command to create example files. You, of course, can create files in many ways.*

Example 14.17 ▼ Appending a Process Number to a File Name

```
$ touch testfile$$<Enter>
$ ls testfile*<Enter>
testfile342
```
▲

305

Before we discuss the appending date suffix method, let's take a closer look at the possible output of the `date` command. The following is a typical shell response to the `date` command when used by itself:

```
$ date<Enter>
Wed Jul 14 12:48:32 CDT 2000
```

When creating file names, though, you probably do *not* want to include the text names of the day or month (such as Wed or July). Instead, you want to use their numerical equivalents (such as 07 for July). The numerical equivalent of the preceding date is generated as follows:

```
$ date +'%y%m%d%H%M%S'<Enter>
000714124832
```

Here we ask the shell for the date in the format of year (`y`), month (`m`), day (`d`), hour (`H`), minute (`M`), and second (`S`).

As seen in Example 14.18, the file name is formatted as a basic file name, followed by a dot as a separator, followed by the date as an extension in the month-day-hour format. If you will be generating more than one file name per hour, though, you should add more precise date fields (minute or even second) to the format to prevent files from being overwritten and, thus, the loss of information. The syntax is

```
touch filename.`date +'[options]'`
```

No matter what you decide, be aware of the command syntax. Note that two types of metacharacters are used: the single quotation mark ('), and the back quote (`).

Example 14.18 ▼ Appending the Date to a File Name

```
$ touch testfile.`date +'%m%d%H'`<Enter>
$ ls testfile.*<Enter>
testfile.071413
```

Exercises

1. Log in to the system and ensure that you are in your home directory. Create a new subdirectory called *newdir*. Change to this new subdirectory and create five zero-length files in it. Name the files *1, 2, 3, 4,* and *5.*

   ```
   $ mkdir newdir<Enter>
   $ cd newdir<Enter>
   $ touch 1 2 3 4 5<Enter>
   ```

2. List the contents of the *newdir* subdirectory. Then list the contents of the *newdir* subdirectory and pass the output to `xargs` to copy the files and rename them with the prefix *file*, so that the resulting copied file names are *file1, file2,* and so on. Finally, verify that the files were copied and that their names were assigned accordingly.

   ```
   $ ls<Enter>
   $ ls | xargs -t -i cp {} file{}<Enter>
   $ ls<Enter>
   ```

3. Copy the */etc/passwd* file into your *newdir* subdirectory so that you have one file in the directory containing text. All other files in the subdirectory will be zero length. Using `find`, `xargs`, and `grep`, `cat` the contents of the files that contain text.

   ```
   $ cp /etc/passwd .<Enter>
   $ find . -type f | xargs -t grep '.*' | cat<Enter>
   ```

4. Identify the directory in which the `find` command is located.

   ```
   $ whereis find<Enter>
   ```
   or
   ```
   $ which find<Enter>
   ```

   Determine the type of file (such as executable, ASCII, or directory) of the `find` command.

   ```
   $ file /usr/bin/find<Enter>
   ```

5. Using the `find` command, create a recursive listing of all files starting in your home directory, and redirect the output to a file namcd *myfiles*. Using the redirected *myfiles* file, determine the type of files located in the list.

   ```
   $ find /home/teamxx > myfiles ; file -f myfiles | less
       <Enter>
   ```

   or

   ```
   $ ls -R > myfiles<Enter>
   $ file -f myfiles | less<Enter>
   ```

   or

   ```
   $ find /home/teamxx | xargs file | less<Enter>
   ```

6. Create a file called *list1*. In *list1*, list the names of several people you know. Copy *list1* to a file called *list2*.

   ```
   $ vi list1<Enter>
   i
   Name 1
   Name 2
   Name 3
   .
   .
   .
   <Esc>
   :wq<Enter>
   $ cp list1 list2<Enter>
   ```

   Edit *list2* and make the following changes: Change the spelling of one of the names; remove one of the names; and add a new name.

   ```
   $ vi list2<Enter>
   i
   .
   .
   .
   <Esc>
   :wp<Enter>
   ```

7. Using `diff`, compare the contents of *list1* and *list2*.

   ```
   $ diff list1 list2<Enter>
   ```

   Did you notice anything?

8. Using `cmp`, compare the contents of *list1* and *list2*. Then invoke a complete or long comparison of the contents of both files.

   ```
   $ cmp list1 list2<Enter>
   $ cmp -l list1 list2<Enter>
   ```

9. Copy the */usr/share/magic* file to a file in your home directory named *mymagic*. Do a long listing of *mymagic* and record the number of bytes in the file.

   ```
   $ cp /usr/share/magic mymagic<Enter>
   $ ls -l mymagic<Enter>
   ```

10. Using the verbose option with `gzip`, compress *mymagic*. Record the percentage of compression and the name of the new compressed file.

    ```
    $ gzip -v mymagic<Enter>
    ```

    Do a long listing of the file and record the number of bytes. Compare this number to the number in the preceding instruction. Is there an approximate match on the percentage of compression?

    ```
    $ ls -l mymagic.gz<Enter>
    ```

11. Using `zcat` or `zless`, expand and view the contents of the file you compressed in the preceding exercise. (Use `zcat` if it's a small file, or `zless` if it's a large file.)

    ```
    $ zcat mymagic.gz | less<Enter>
    ```
    or
    ```
    $ zless mymagic.gz<Enter>
    ```

12. Using `gunzip` with its verbose option, restore the compressed file back to its original characteristics.

    ```
    $ gunzip -v mymagic.gz<Enter>
    ```

13. Invoke a long listing of the uncompressed file and record the number of bytes. Is the number the same as, greater than, or less than the number you recorded for Exercise 9?

    ```
    $ ls -l mymagic<Enter>
    ```

14. In your home directory, create a file named *invis* and type a few lines that include random <Tab>, <Spacebar>, and <Ctrl>-g keypresses between the words. (Feel free to replace the sample file contents with your own.) Then, display the file.

    ```
    $ vi invis<Enter>
    i
    <Tab> this<Tab>file has<Enter>
    several <Tab> mysterious spaces<Enter>
    and^G non-^Gprint<Tab>able<Enter>
    characters.<Tab>^G
    <Esc>
    :wq<Enter>

    $ cat invis<Enter>
    ```

15. Note in the preceding exercise that when you displayed the contents of *invis*, it didn't look quite right. Display and locate all the nonprintable characters to determine where you used tabs, spaces, and other nonprintables.

    ```
    $ cat -etv invis<Enter>
    ```

See Appendix B for answers.

Quiz

1. True or False: The most important characteristic of the `find` command is its capability to travel both ways through the tree-like hierarchy of a file system.

2. When you use quoting metacharacters with `find`, which of the following interprets the wildcards?

    ▲ `find` itself
    ▲ The shell
    ▲ Depends on the shell you are using at the time

3. Which of the following commands is used to determine the type of data in a file?

    ▲ `cmp`
    ▲ `diff`
    ▲ `find`
    ▲ `grep`
    ▲ `file`

4. True or False: The `gzip` command deletes the original file and replaces it with a compressed copy of the file, and then renames the copy with the original name but appends a *.z* extension to it.

5. To display nonprintable characters in a file, which of the following command lines would you use?

    ▲ `ls -la`
    ▲ `cat -etv`
    ▲ `find -inv`
    ▲ `grep -s`
    ▲ `file -v`

6. True or False: The `diff` command compares only text files.

See Appendix C for answers.

Chapter 15

The Linux X Window System

THUS FAR, WE HAVE CONCENTRATED on Linux at the command line—also called at the character cell prompt, at the console, or in the ASCII character environment, depending on the information source. After all, effective Linux usage, and especially administration, relies on your ability to use and understand command line concepts, commands, and utilities. However, Linux also has powerful and flexible graphical user interface (GUI) capabilities. This chapter provides an introduction to the GUI foundation, called the X Window System.

We wholeheartedly recommend installing the X Window System when you first install Linux on your system (our preference) or later after Linux has been installed. After you properly install and configure X, it will facilitate your productivity and enjoyment and will allow you to use many more Linux/UNIX programs.

WARNING: *For those planning to install X Window System, we echo the advice of all X installers: Pay special attention to your system's video card and monitor specifications! Failure to do so could result in system or monitor damage.*

A Brief History

The first X Window System was developed in 1984 by the Massachusetts Institute of Technology (MIT). The X Window System, which is often referred to as X or X11, provides a powerful network-based foundation for a Linux/UNIX GUI environment. X is a collection of programs, including servers, documentation, fonts, programming libraries, and utilities, but its foundation programs are as follows:

- ▲ Basic windowing program that provides windowing services
- ▲ The X Network Protocol, a protocol for network communication
- ▲ A low-level interface called `Xlib`, which sits between the higher-level programs (on top) and the network or base system (on the bottom)
- ▲ A window manager, an X application to control the type and appearances of the windows

The X Window System enhances UNIX in the same way that "other GUI operating system" enhances DOS, only more reliably. What do we mean by *enhance?* Some advantages and features of GUIs are listed next:

- ▲ An attractive and intuitive (that is, easy-to-use) human-to-machine interface
- ▲ Potentially easier ways of identifying, entering, and modifying data
- ▲ Several control devices that require no knowledge of programming or other commands (for example, buttons, icons, menus, and scrollbars)
- ▲ Consistency of look and utility, which leads to reduced training requirements for new applications
- ▲ Greater ease in managing multiple and simultaneous processes and applications

Now, all is not perfect in the world of GUIs. GUI programs by nature are generally large and rather inefficient because they tend to use a lot of resources. They have to write or call upon many controlling functions for window manipulation, graphics control, and data input from a keyboard and mouse. In short, GUIs require more resources than the command line but can also make complex programs easier to use.

Since the birth of X in 1984, commercial vendors—particularly the vendor- and researcher-based organization called the X Consortium, whose membership includes IBM, Digital Equipment, and MIT—have effectively made X the UNIX industry standard. X is installed on most UNIX systems around the world.

A free software conversion (port) of X for Linux and other UNIX variants, called XFree86, was developed by the XFree86 Project, now a member of the X Consortium. XFree86 is a version of MIT's X Window System v. 11, rel. 6 (that is, X11R6).

If XFree86 is installed on your system, you will see several X11R6 references as part of directory or file names. The original X version 11 was released in 1987, release 6 came out in 1994, and the latest version is X11R6.4. As of this writing, the latest release of XFree86 itself is 4.0.1. Your version of XFree86 probably has all the binary files, support files, libraries and tools you will need. If not, check the XFree86 Project Internet site at *http://www.XFree86.org*. You can also check that Web site for the latest version of XFree86.

X Window Networking

In Figure 15.1, we illustrate a simplified X Window System network consisting of various types of machines. In an environment like this one, an X application could run on one processor or even one type of processor. A user or administrator could sit at any other system in the network and run an X Window application. Thus, we can claim that X is platform independent. X allows a display and keyboard attached to one system to use programs (that is, clients) running on a completely different system, even a completely different type of system.

X Window System functions are split into terminal and application support. Typically, the application support runs on a Linux/UNIX system. The terminal support can run on the same Linux/UNIX system, on a remote Linux/UNIX system, or even on a non-Linux/UNIX system. An example of the last two systems is a one that may have a slow CPU of its own or may have no hard disk drive. The client applications would run on a remote, fast central server while only the terminal-supporting X Window server would run on the underpowered terminal. That's why we refer to the X Window System as a net-

INSTALLING AND ADMINISTERING LINUX

working window system. Any connections between the client and the server are TCP/IP protocol-based connections.

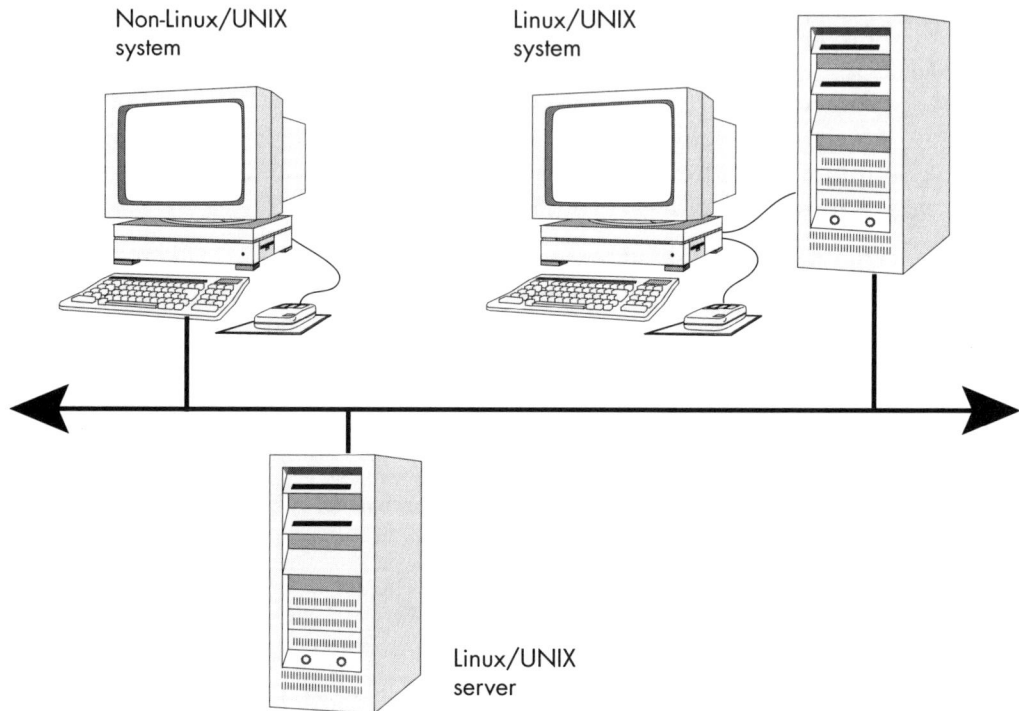

Figure 15.1: A simplified X Window System network.

Different Client/Server Environment Concepts

For those who do not customarily operate in UNIX environments, the concepts of client and server are generally understood to be the following: A server is a system that provides resources such as applications, hard drive storage, modems, printers, and so on to other systems across one or more networks; a client is a system that uses those resources, accessing them across one or more networks. In the Linux/UNIX environment, however, the client and server concepts are different.

In the world of Linux/UNIX, a *client* is defined as a device-independent program that runs on your local machine or on a remote machine and requires input from the user and the capability to display or otherwise provide output to the user. In other words, the client is the system or machine providing the application support. Common applications, such as `xcalc` and `xclock`, as well as the more complicated database or simulation applications, are clients to a Linux/UNIX system.

On the other hand, a *server* is a device-dependent program that runs on your local machine and controls the input devices (for example, keyboard and mouse) as well as the terminal display and other output devices. We say that the server is the system or machine providing the terminal support. In many cases—especially in a small network or home environment—the client and the server run on the same system. Even so, they still communicate with each other using the TCP/IP protocol.

X Client Features

A user interacts with X clients when he or she interacts with applications (such as `xclock`, `xcalc`, and `xterm`), which may be running on either a local machine or a remote machine. The applications themselves are the X clients that are invoked and run by the users in an X window system.

X clients can be started from the command line by special startup files or from other X clients. For example, you can start window managers manually or invoke them automatically when your machine boots up. To access remote machines, you may need special applications invoked on a local machine (for example, WRQ Inc.'s product, ReflectionX, allows Windows machines to access UNIX machines).

Most X clients share the same or similar options, such as foreground color, background color, display name, fonts, and window geometry. For example, invoke `xterm ?` on the command line. Examine the specifications and options. Then invoke `xclock ?` and compare those specifications and options. No doubt, `xterm` has more specifications and options, but some will be identical to `xclock`'s. Some standard options are listed in Table 15.1.

Table 15.1 Selected X Client Options

Option	Description
-bg color	Background color of the window
-fg color	Foreground color of the window
-bw number	Window border width in pixels
-fn font	Font set for the standard text size in the window
-geometry geom	Geometry of the window (such as 80x125+0+0)
-rv	Reverse the default image on the screen (that is, if the screen normally appears with black text on a white background, this option changes the appearance to white text on a black background)

X Server Features

XFree86 is the version of the X11R6 X Window System software that has been converted for use on Intel-based platforms. XFree86, then, is the basis for the X Server. XFree86 has to be configured for each system it runs on, which you can accomplish by specifying certain system attributes in a file called *XF86Config*, found in the */etc/X11* or */usr/X11R6/lib/X11* directories.

When you invoke XFree86 (either at the command line by typing the `startx` command or automatically upon system bootup), it reads the *XF86Config* file and follows the instructions found therein. Customarily, those instructions tell XFree86 how and when to

- ▲ Control and route keyboard, mouse, graphics pad stylus, or other such input to the correct clients
- ▲ Perform basic graphic operations on one or more screens
- ▲ Control video-related attributes such as colors, color depth, screen size, fonts, modelines, vertical sync ranges, horizontal sync, video chipsets, video RAM, and clockchips
- ▲ Allow simultaneous access by several clients
- ▲ Load special software modules

▲ Control special system actions (such as core dumps, video mode switching, and input device configuration)

The actual installation of the X Window System and the development of the *XF86Config* file are beyond the scope of this book. Consult your sources for this information.

Only after XFree86 has invoked the other server-style software can you say that the full combination of XFree86 and any other necessary software has become your X Server, ready to allow you to use the full features of the X Window System. You may occasionally hear others refer to video servers—such as Mach32, Mach64, or S3—as X servers. Such references occur probably because configuration of the video attributes is by far the most involved and occasionally perilous (for your monitor, if not done correctly) part of X Window System installation and configuration. But the full X server has to control much more than video output.

The X Window System provides the basis for your graphical interface. But the interface itself—the look, feel, and personality of X—is provided by a client application called a window manager.

X Window Managers

New users often believe that X and its various window managers are synonymous, but this is not the case. X is in charge of all communication between and among windows, applications, and input and output devices, whether those facilities are located on the local machine or are distributed across a local or wide area network. On the other hand, the window manager handles local operations such as the movement, resizing, or iconifying of windows. As stated previously, the window manager provides the look and feel of your X desktop.

Thus, a window manager is an X client, albeit a special one. It's the only one that has no windows itself, unless you count the window or menu that you summon when you left- click the empty desktop. But the window manager can move, resize, iconify (hide), deiconify (restore), map, and unmap windows. Your distribution or other version of Linux may provide several window managers (check your installation information or scout around your file system with `whereis` or a similar command). A user can switch from one to another in a given session but can use only one at a time.

Without a window manager, you can still invoke an X session and display windows, but you cannot move or resize them. In addition, if one window completely overlays another, you can access only the one on top. If part of a window is hidden by another window, you cannot access the hidden part of that window.

Several window managers are listed in Table 15.2. For more examples of window managers or for the latest ones, check the *http://www.plig.org* Web site.

Table 15.2 Window Managers

Window Manager	Description
`twm`	Tab window manager, the classic MIT window manager; included with the standard XFree86 distribution.
`olvwm`	Open Look Virtual Window Manager, a more advanced window manager; used by SunOS and Solaris UNIXes.
`fvwm`	Popular window manager; small, requires less than half the memory used by `twm`; greatly customizable.
`mwm`	Motif Window Manager; basis for CDE.
`Enlightenment`	Popular and well written; originally based on `fvwm`, but recent versions are written from scratch.
`AfterStep`	Descendant of `fvwm`; has floating window for application buttons, icons, and so on, and some animation.
`GNOME`	GNU Network Object Model Environment (pronounced "guh-nome") developed as part of the GNU project; complete user-friendly desktop comprised of utilities and applications. GNOME and related applications are free because of their availability under the GNU Public License (GPL). Described as the future of the graphical X desktop.

Continued

Table 15.2 Window Managers (Continued)

Window Manager	Description
CDE	Common Desktop Environment, a commercially developed standard desktop/window manager for most versions of UNIX.
KDE	K Desktop Environment, a freeware project designed to be similar to CDE but developed and released under GPL. KDE emphasizes international support and a standardized appearance and performance with many applications. KDE was formerly available only as a download from the Internet, but due to recent resolutions of copyright issues, some Linux distributions now include KDE. In fact, some now use KDE as the default window manager.

X Window Fundamentals

Start X Manually

No matter what distribution of Linux you purchased or downloaded from the Internet, you probably realized that, by default, it does not invoke X automatically when it boots up. You are probably left staring at the command line log-in prompt. In that case, you have to start it manually.

When you have completed the log-in procedure, you will be faced with your user or root prompt ($ or #, respectively). At the prompt, type `startx`. The screen goes blank briefly as your X session is initiated, and the window manager appears in front of you.

Exit X

You have two ways to exit X inside a window manager such as After-Step or fvwm. Using the first method, you need only move the cursor arrow to a blank area of your desktop (that is, an area without a window) and left-click. You are presented with a root menu. You then scroll down to a selection similar to *Exit* <window manager> and hold the mouse in that position or even left-click. A second part of the menu appears and, among other things, it asks you whether your intention is to *Really Quit* <window manager>?. If your intention is to quit, select the *Yes, Really Quit* option. After you have chosen to quit, you are returned to a command line prompt. Using this method, you will be able to gracefully exit X, which involves stopping all relevant applications and processes in order.

The second method simply involves entering the <Ctrl>-<Alt>-<Backspace> key sequence. Almost immediately, you are returned to a command line prompt. Alternatively, you could enter <Ctrl>-<Alt>-<F1>, followed by <Ctrl>-c. But, because the two key sequences achieve the same objective as the single-step sequence, you might as well use <Ctrl>-<Alt>-<Backspace>. The single-step method is pretty brutal, though. It stops the X server, but then all applications die ungracefully because they simply lose their connections. If you do not want the single-step sequence used on your machine, you can disable it in the */etc/X11/XF86Config* file.

Start X Automatically

Before you even think of instituting the following procedure for starting X automatically, you must ensure that your X configuration works properly. Otherwise, you may have trouble logging in to your system. To carry out this procedure, you have to be the root user.

Test xdm with the nodaemon Argument

The xdm program (X Display Manager) can control one or more X display sessions on one or more servers, local and remote. This is the application that presents you with what is called an xlogin widget (basically a graphical prompt for a user name and password) and then invokes the X Window System after you have been authenticated. You can customize xdm with the use of a configuration file, customarily called *xdm-config* (but that is beyond the scope of this book). All you have to do is ensure that xdm works correctly because it is used in the process of automatically starting X from bootup.

To test xdm, type the following at the command prompt:

```
# xdm -nodaemon<Enter>
```

The `nodaemon` option prevents `xdm` from following its normal procedure, which is to put its daemon beyond the control of the terminal. Thus, you are not preventing the daemon from being used by `xdm` but rather keeping it under some control.

If all goes well, `xdm` presents you with its xlogin widget. You type `root` as the log-in name, press <Enter>, type root's password, and press <Enter> again. The `xdm` program then creates the X Window environment with your chosen window manager. Although we have focused on `xdm`, it is not the only display manager. Other display managers such as the Gnome Display Manager and the KDE Manager are also available and have many features that can help you manage your environment.

If you got the results described, `xdm` works for you. It is safe now to move on to the next steps. But first, exit from the window manager using the root menu or start button. The `xdm` program takes you back to the xlogin widget. To get back to the command line, use the key sequence <Ctrl>-<Alt>-<F1>. That takes you back nearly to a command prompt, but you will not be at a prompt per se. You should see a cursor blinking on the line immediately below the `xdm -nodaemon` command. Now press <Ctrl>-c to terminate the `xdm` daemon and be left at the command prompt.

Edit the /etc/inittab File to Run Level 5

Using `vi` as your text editor, you'll modify the Linux initialization table found in the */etc/inittab* file, which controls, among other things, the run level (in other words, the number and type of services provided by Linux when it boots up). Be very careful. Browse down through */etc/inittab* until you see the line `id:3:initdefault`, and change the 3 to a 5. Do not change anything else! Save and exit */etc/inittab*. To Linux, run level 5 means that it should no longer boot to full multiuser mode, as it did with run level 3. It should now boot to X11 mode.

Reboot the System

At this juncture, all you have to do is reboot the machine. When Linux boots again, the command line log-in prompt does not appear. Instead, you are presented with the graphical xlogin widget.

Basic Components

Display

Figure 15.2 illustrates what your X Window System *display* might look like when using one of the less complex window managers. All window managers do not look like this; some have more or fewer applications showing different backgrounds and so on, depending on the preferences of the system administrator or the person who installed X. Moreover, ordinary users will have some ability to add or delete applications or other information.

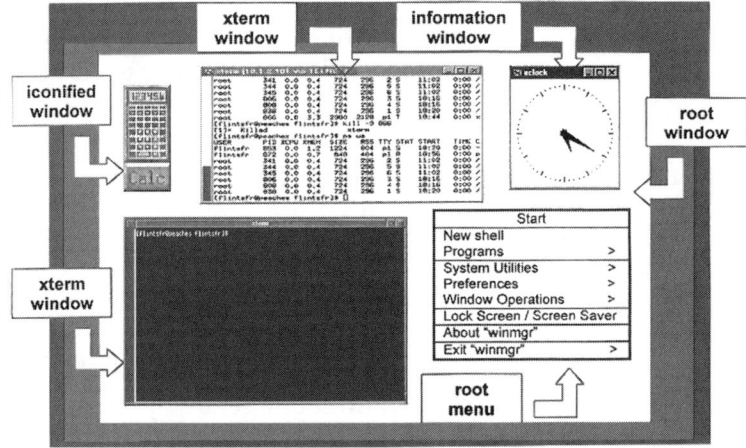

Figure 15.2: An example of an X Window display.

The basic components of the display are described next:

▲ **Root window.** Also called the *desktop,* this is the area that fills the entire screen. You can move your mouse to an open part of this area (that is, an area not covered by other windows or other displays), and then left-click to access the root menu, a menu that helps you start other windows or otherwise customize your environment. A sample root menu appears in the bottom-right corner of Figure 15.2. Note that we have chosen a generic name (*winmgr*) for the window manager. Now, if you right-click an open area of the root window, you automatically invoke the Programs menu, which is the same menu you would get if you accessed a root menu and then clicked *Programs* (owing to space constraints, we did not show the Programs menu in Figure 15.2). Thus, right-clicking to invoke the Programs menu is just a shortcut.

▲ *Information window.* The `xclock` window is an example of an application window that displays information for the user's benefit.

▲ ***xterm** window.* An xterm window is a terminal emulation window that has been opened for any number of purposes. Figure 15.2 shows two terminal windows open, one for each process.

▲ *Iconified window.* In Figure 15.2, the calculator symbol (with *Calc* across the bottom) is not a window but a representation of a window. The represented process has not been terminated.

root Menu

As we mentioned, when you move the mouse pointer to an open area of the root window and left-click, the *root menu* appears. The menu options are described in Table 15.3. You can Either move the mouse pointer over one or more options or left-click to select a specific option.

Table 15.3 root Menu Options

Option	Description
New shell	Create another `xterm` window.
Programs	Types of programs available, as well as some specific programs.
System Utilities	Types of utilities available.

Continued

Table 15.3 root Menu Options (Continued)

Option	Description
Preferences	Types of changes you can make to your environment.
Window Operations	Types of available window operations.
Lock Screen / Screen Saver	Invoke the `xlock` program.
About "winmgr"	Invoke a menu with information about your host machine, the window manager you are using, and your X environment.
Exit "winmgr"	Restart your X session; switch from your present window manager to another; cancel the quit/exit from X; or verify your quit/exit from X.

Mouse Pointers, Input Focus, and Location Cursors

Linux can work with either a two-button or three-button mouse, but the documentation with most distributions recommends that you use a three-button mouse or invoke three-button mouse emulation (using both buttons at once simulates the use of the middle button) during Linux installation. Meanwhile, moving the mouse causes the movement of a small icon, commonly called a *pointer* or a *cursor*, on the terminal screen. There are several types of pointers.

When used on an X display, the mouse and its pointer can be used to select whatever window you would like to *activate* (making the window capable of receiving input). Note that when you activate a window, its frame changes color (it becomes highlighted). Further, when you direct some input information or data to that highlighted active window, you are *focusing*. There are two types of focus: explicit focusing, where you move the pointer to a window and left-click the mouse to activate the window, and pointer focusing, where you only have to move the pointer to a window to activate it. Most window managers use explicit focusing.

When you place the pointer in or on windows or other objects, pressing the left button activates the window or object. Pressing the right button or pressing the middle button—or, on a two-button mouse, pressing both the left and right buttons simultaneously—will also cause certain actions to take place, such as the appearance of a menu from which you can select further actions.

In X, the *location cursor* is similar to the cursor on the command line of your character-based screen. Its location determines where to insert your keyboard input on a terminal emulation screen. However, the location cursor isn't activated until you activate the terminal window first.

Window Frame

The frame around a window is often taken for granted. Although we generally think of the window contents and frame as one and the same, they are not. Strictly speaking, the *frame* is provided by the window manager application and allows a certain amount of window manipulation without affecting the operation of the application running in the window itself. However, that window manipulation requires the proper placement and operation of the mouse. The basic components of the window frame may vary slightly from one window manager application to another (for example, one may have an exit button at the far right end of the title bar, but another may not).

The first component of the window frame is the *title bar,* which runs across the top of the window between the window operations button on the left and the minimize and maximize buttons on the right. Predictably, the title bar contains the title of the window. For instance, the window emulating a terminal screen would be titled *xterm.* You can use the title bar to move the window from place to place on the root menu by the drag-and-drop method.

NOTE: *The term* drag and drop *refers to the following actions: Position the mouse cursor over something (such as a title bar or menu option) and press but do not release the left mouse button; then move the mouse cursor to another location (drag) and release the left mouse button (drop).*

You can reduce the window to its icon representation (its minimum size) by left-clicking the *minimize button,* which is immediately to the right of the title bar. If the window is smaller than its maximum size, you can maximize it by left-clicking the *maximize button,* next to the minimize button (maximum size usually means that the window will fill the entire root window). Some window managers also provide an exit or *close button,* which usually looks like a square with an X in its center, in the upper-right corner of the window frame. Left-clicking that button will close the window, the same as left-clicking the window operations button and selecting the *close/exit* option.

Speaking of resizing the window, there are several ways of making the window larger or smaller. All require proper placement of the mouse pointer. Note that if you place the pointer exactly in the corners of the window frame, the pointer changes to resemble something like an arrow pushing against the corner. By dragging and dropping at that point, you can alter the window's dimensions in two directions (height and width) simultaneously, if you want.

If you just place the mouse on any of the four borders (top, bottom, left, or right) of the window frame at any one time, the pointer again changes, but this time to something resembling an arrow pushing against that border only. Now you can drag and drop again, but you can change only one window dimension at a time.

If you move the mouse pointer to the upper-left corner of the window frame and left-click on what is called the *window operations button,* you will activate a drop-down menu containing several commands. You can move the pointer down the menu and select the operations of your choice.

Icons

You probably already know about the benefits of icons on your desktop. They are a handy way of multitasking without repeatedly having to invoke applications, and they are a handy way to manage your root window (that is, desktop) space. When an application window has been changed to an *icon,* the process remains invoked and ready, but the screen clutter is reduced.

You can create an icon from an active application in two ways. One is by left-clicking the window operations button in the top-left corner of the application window, and then scrolling down the resulting drop-down menu to select the minimize (or hide/restore or similar instruction) option. The benefit of using this method stems mainly from having a choice of options presented to you. The result is the same as the second and simpler method, namely, left-clicking the minimize button on the window frame.

Depending on the window manager used, the resulting icons for identical applications may be different in appearance. For example, minimizing the calculator window in fvwm95 results in an icon that looks like a button bar. Minimizing the same window in lesstif results in an icon that looks like a reduced-scale calculator. No matter which window manager you use, the resulting icons are actually bitmap images.

xterm Fundamentals

An *xterm window* is an X client application that simulates a common video terminal such as a DEC vt100. By now, you have undoubtedly noticed that you can create and use `xterm` windows (commonly called `nxterm`, `AIXterm`, or something similar, depending on the version of UNIX) while in X, to enter Linux/UNIX commands in the same manner you entered them at the command line when X was not invoked.

Create an xterm Window

You can create additional windows in X in two ways. First, from an already opened `xterm` window, you can type `xterm &`. Alternatively, you can move the mouse pointer to an open area of the desktop (that is, the area not already occupied by a window), and left-click the mouse. Then, from the resulting root menu, left-click *New shell,* the first selection under *Start* at the top of the root menu.

Copy Text

The `xterm` window allows you to copy and paste text to another part of the window or to another window. Place the mouse pointer at the first letter of the text you want to copy and then left-click and drag over all the text you want to copy. The text is highlighted. When you release the mouse button, the highlighted text is copied into a buffer. Then you move the mouse pointer to a position in the same window or in another `xterm` window. If you are using a three-button mouse, press the center button to copy the text. If you are using a two-button mouse, push both buttons at once.

Create a Scrollbar

If you want to create a window with a scrollbar in it, first create another preliminary window. In that preliminary window, type one of the following command sequences:

    $ xterm -sb leftbar<Enter>

or

    $ xterm -sb rightbar <Enter>

Each of these sequences creates a new window with a scrollbar on the side you specify.

If you want to create a scrollbar in an existing window, place the mouse pointer inside that window, hold down the <Ctrl> key and press the center button on the mouse (on a three-button mouse) or press both mouse buttons at once (on a two-button mouse). The VT Options menu is displayed on the screen. The first, or one of the first, selections on the menu is *Enable scrollbar*. Click that selection, and a scrollbar appears in your window.

To use the scrollbar, place the mouse pointer in the scrollbar itself and then press the left mouse button to move up or press the right mouse button to move down. If you want to remove the scrollbar, redo the instruction and left-click *Enable scrollbar* to remove the check mark next to that selection.

Use the `man` pages, the help options, and other information sources to see what else you can do with the `xterm` command.

Close an xterm Window

To close an `xterm` window, you have several alternatives: At the prompt in the window, press <Ctrl>-d or type `exit` and press <Enter>; double-click the Window-Ops button in the upper-left corner of the window; or left-click that same Window-Ops button and then left-click *Close* on the resulting drop-down menu.

Customize xterm

We have already discussed a couple of `xterm` options: running the second `xterm` window in the background, so that you can move back and forth from window to window (the & option); and adding a scrollbar to the new `xterm` window (using the `-sb` option with either the `-leftbar` or `-rightbar` option).

In this section, we present a few more of the dozens of options available to you with the `xterm` command. Combining these options gives you perhaps thousands of possibilities for new `xterm` windows. Take a look at Example 15.1 and Table 15.4 to see how `xterm` can work for you.

Example 15.1 ▼ create an xterm window

On host machine *SYSTEMB*, create an `xterm` window for X server 0. Allow this process to run in the background:

```
$ xterm -display SYSTEMB:0 &<Enter>
```

On this host machine, create an `xterm` window with a red background and white foreground with Times Roman 10 normal font, 80 pixels wide and 40 pixels long, and positioned in the top-left corner (0,0 position). Allow the window to run in the background.

```
$ xterm -bg red -fg white -fn rom10 \<Enter>
> -geometry 80x40+0+0 &<Enter>
```

▲

Table 15.4 Selected xterm Options

Option	Explanation
`-bg color`	Background color of the window.
`-cr color`	Cursor color. The default color is the foreground color.
`-display Name:Number`	Host server name and X server display number where the command will run. If not specified, the client program gets the *hostname* and displays the number from the `DISPLAY` environment variable.

Continued

Table 15.4 Selected xterm Options (continued)

Option	Explanation
`-e command`	Command to be executed in the window. This flag executes a command; it does *not* start a shell. The command and its arguments (if any) must appear last on the `xterm` command line.
`-fg color`	Foreground color of the window.
`-fn font`	Font to be used for all normal-sized text.
`-fullcursor`	Full height (not the underscore style) text cursor.
`-geometry Geometry`	Location and dimensions of the window. The default is 80x25+0+0, that is, 80 pixels wide, 25 pixels long, located in the top-left corner (that is, at the 0,0 position) of the screen.
`-help`	Available option flags.
`-i`	Display a newly-created window as an icon, not a window.
`-keywords`	List the `xdefaults` keywords.
`-l`	Append output from the `xterm` command to the login.
`-lf file`	Location where output is saved. The default file is *xterm.logxxxxx*, where *xxxxx* is the PID of the `xterm` command.
`-n icon name`	Icon name used by the `xterm` command.
`-name application`	Application name to use for *.Xdefaults*.
`-sb`	Scrollbar. `-leftbar` places the scrollbar on the left.
`-sl`	Maximum number of lines to save that are scrolled off the top of a window. The default is 64.
`-T title`	Name of the window in the title bar. If `-n` is not specified or a name for the icon has not been specified in *.Xdefaults*, this name is displayed also on the icon of the window.
`-W`	Move the cursor to the middle of the `xterm` window when it is created.
`-xrm string`	Resource string to be used.

> **NOTE:** *You can apply the options in Table 15.4 to other X applications such as* `xcalc` *and* `xclock`. *For further information regarding those applications and their options, check the* man *pages and other information sources.*

Now that you have had a look at `xterm` windows in general, it's time to look at a special way of using them: to create a special window for the root user.

Additional Basic X Window Commands

Become the root User

When using `xterm` windows in an X session, you can become the root user in two ways. First, if you are operating in an ordinary `xterm` window, you can simply enter su - <Enter>. You are prompted immediately with the root `Password:` prompt, at which point you type the root password. Then you are prompted with the root prompt, #, and you can conduct root business.

Alternatively, left-click an open desktop area, scroll down the root menu, and select *System Utilities*. Another drop-down menu, called System Utilities Button Bar, appears. Scroll down that menu and select *Root Shell*. An `xterm` window appears. At the top is the title Root Window and within the window is the root `Password:` prompt. Type the proper password and press <Enter>, and you are given the root # prompt.

Let Another User Run a Client on Your System

As we discussed earlier, the X Window System uses the client/server model. Remember, the client is an application (such as `xterm` or `xcalc`), and the server is the program that supports the application by controlling input and output. In many cases, the client and server both run on the same system. The last topic in this chapter is `xhost`, which you must invoke before any of the clients will connect and work.

With X, however, you can run a client on your own system in the network, yet display the application on another (presumably remote) terminal screen. This arrangement gives others access to software programs running on your system. Others can therefore enter commands in the window and use their mouse, despite the fact that the actual process is running on your system.

Assume that you are trying to run a client application on the *sys1* machine, but you want to display the output on the *sys2* server. The application is simply `xterm` (that is, you want to open an `xterm` window), but it could be any X Windows application begun through the character cell. Example 15.2 shows three possible ways to invoke `xterm`.

To run the client remotely and display its results locally, you must tell the client process where to display its window. X applications use the value of the `DISPLAY` environment variable to indicate the TCP/IP host name of the server (that is, the name of the system on which the client should display its output).

If the `DISPLAY` value has not been set, you must include the `-display` option in the command to invoke the client application. If the `DISPLAY` value is set, you can override it by using the `-display` option and the specified server name when starting the client. Typically, the display value is set to something like `:0.0` for the local server or `sys2:0.0` to tell the client to display its output on the remote server called *sys2*. The part before the colon specifies the server's TCP/IP host name or IP address. The part after the colon specifies the server number and display number, but the display number is optional. Unless you run multiple servers on one machine or have multiple displays controlled by a single server, set these values to 0. The TCP/IP protocol must be installed and configured on the network.

Example 15.2 ▼ Invoke xterm

Option 1: In an `xterm` window on *sys1*, redefine the `DISPLAY` variable as *sys2:0.0*. You can then invoke the application, and the shell automatically sends the output wherever that environment variable tells it to go.

```
$ DISPLAY=sys2:0.0<Enter>
$ xterm &<Enter>
```

Option 2: In an xterm window on *sys1*, enter

```
$ export DISPLAY=sys2:0.0; xterm &<Enter>
```

Option 3: In an xterm window on *sys1*, enter

```
$ xterm -display sys2:0.0 &<Enter>
```

The export command is a TCP/IP command that sends another command to a specified remote system for execution.   ▲

Run a Client on Someone Else's System

Suppose you want to be able to use applications on someone else's system. To do that, open an xterm window, activate it, and enter the following on the command line:

```
$ rlogin -l username remote_hostname<Enter>
```

You must use a user name that has already been created on the remote host. rlogin is one of the remote-host execute commands, commonly called r commands. The -l (that's the letter *l*) option basically clears the way for you to specify the user name. The remote host name is the TCP/IP name of the system you are trying to log in to. (The r commands, which we do not cover in this book, are introduced here only to illustrate how to accomplish this simplified client/server application execution.)

The shell responds with a password prompt. Simply fill it in and press <Enter>, and you are authenticated to the remote system. Now use one of the two following command sequences to invoke an application on the remote host and display it on your system:

```
$ xterm -display sys1:0.0 &<Enter>
```

or

```
$ export DISPLAY=sys1:0.0; xterm &<Enter>
```

To accomplish the procedures described in this section and the preceding one, you have to give the systems the capability to allow, restrict, or limit other remote hosts from accessing their displays or applications. To do so, the `xhost` command must be executed on the server(s).

xhost Command

As mentioned, the X Window System allows users at one host system to run a client on another system. But there may be times, for security or other reasons, when it is not desirable to allow a particular user or system to connect to another. One way to deny access to a user or a system is to use the `xhost` command on the system to which access is sought.

At the target machine, the user invokes a terminal emulation screen and enters

```
$ xhost [ + | - ] [name]<Enter>
```

The square brackets indicate that the plus and minus signs are optional, as are the user or host names. The examples in Table 15.5 should help to clarify these concepts. If you need further information, consult your information sources. Note that using only `xhost +` will open up the machine in question to everyone on the network and, if applicable, possibly to everyone on the Internet! Consequently, if your machine is exposed to a large network or to the Internet, you should install security on the machine. Although `xhost` may not be a comprehensive answer, it can be a first step.

Table 15.5 xhost Syntax Options

Syntax	Explanation
xhost	Ask for message: Is access control enabled or not?
xhost +	Turn off access control; grant access to everyone.
xhost -	Turn on access control; grant access only to those on the list.
xhost + name	Add *name* to the list of users/hosts allowed to connect to this X server (the + sign is optional here).
xhost - name	Delete *name* from the list of users/hosts allowed to connect to this X server.

After you use `xhost` to invoke access control to an X server machine, a file similar to *X*.hosts* is created in the */etc* directory. That file contains the names of the host machines and users who are allowed to access the X server machine in question.

Exercises

1. Start the X Windows environment with the `startx` command.

   ```
   $ startx<Enter>
   ```

   What window manager is invoked by default? Are any windows displayed by default? If so, what are they called?

2. If an `xterm` window appears, verify that it is activated, or activate it if it is not. If there is no `xterm` window, create one.

   If an `xterm` window has been created already, check to see whether the window's title bar is highlighted in blue. If it is not, move your mouse pointer to the `xterm` window and left-click. The window frame changes color to indicate that the window is now activated.

   If there is no `xterm` window yet, you may have to left-click an open space in the root window or press an equivalent start button and then select *New shell, xterm,* or a similar item from a root menu. Each distribution of Linux, and each window manager within each distribution, has a different but similar way of conjuring up these `xterm`-like windows.

3. Using the `xterm` window, try some commands such as `ls` (with or without other arguments), `date`, `cal`, and `whoami`.

4. Resize the width of the window.

   Move your mouse pointer to the right edge of the window frame. Note how the pointer changes shape (for example, from a single-headed arrow or I-beam to a double-headed arrow, or from a single-headed arrow to an arrow pushing against a perpendicular line), indicating that the mouse can now be used to change one dimension of the window (the width or the height, depending on which edge the cursor is on). Press and hold the left mouse button and move the mouse to alter the window's dimensions. An outline might appear, indicating the new window size. Also, a small feedback indicator might appear, which tells you the new dimensions in pixels or lines and columns. An indication of the location of the upper-left corner of the window may also appear. As we stated previously, each window manager has its own idiosyn-

CHAPTER 15: THE LINUX X WINDOW SYSTEM

crasies. When the window is the desired size, simply release the left mouse button.

If you saw the small feedback indicator, note that it contains the same kind of information you might use if you were to create a new `xterm` window from the command line of an existing `xterm` window, using the `xterm` command with `-geometry` as an argument, followed by the dimensions and location.

5. Change the height and width of the window simultaneously.

   Move your mouse pointer to a corner of the window frame. Note how this time the pointer again changes shape (for example, to an arrow pushing against a corner), indicating that the mouse can now be used to change both window dimensions (width and height) at once. Press and hold the left mouse button and move the mouse to alter the window dimensions. You will get the same kind of response feedback you received in Exercise 4. Again, when the window is the desired size, simply release the left mouse button.

6. Drag and drop the `xterm` window from one side of the root window to the other.

   Move your mouse pointer to the title bar of the window frame. Note how this time the pointer again changes shape (for example, to a large dot), indicating that you can now use the mouse to move the window. Press and hold the left mouse button and move the mouse to alter the window's location. You get the same type of response feedback you received in Exercises 4 and 5, except you will not be altering the window size. When the window reaches the desired location, release the left mouse button.

7. Now use the options in the window operations (button) menu to move and resize the window.

   In the `xterm` window, left-click the window operations button (that is, the button to the left of the title bar) on the window frame. The window operations menu appears. Left-click the *Move* command, and you will notice a similar feedback to the response in Exercise 6, except that you do not have to hold down the left button as you move the window around. When the window is in the desired position, simply press the left button and the window will stay put.

Now left-click the window operations button. From the window operations menu, left-click the *Resize* command. You will notice the same type of feedback as in Exercises 4 and 5, except that you do not have to hold down the left button as you alter the window's dimensions. When the window is the desired size, simply press the left button and the window remains that size.

NOTE: *Instead of left-clicking to hold the window in the desired position or to maintain the new dimensions, depending on which function you are exercising, you can also press <Enter>.*

8. Take a close look at the window operations menu again. Are there any items on it that appear grayed, or dimmed? If so, why?

   On the `xterm` window, left-click the window operations button (that is, the button to the left of the title bar) on the window frame again. The window operations menu appears.

9. Here's something you may not have tried. On the window operations menu, type the letter m instead of clicking *Move*, and then use the arrow keys. This is another way to move your window. Now try the underlined letters for some of the other functions.

   On the `xterm` window, left-click the window operations button and the window operations menu appears. This time, instead of left-clicking the *Move* command, just type m on the keyboard. You will notice a similar feedback to the response in Exercise 7, and you will not have to hold the left button down as you move the window around. When the window is in the desired position, simply press the left mouse button or press <Enter>, and the window stays put.

10. With the window operations menu closed, try some of the underlined letters. Do they work?

    Activate the `xterm` window. Then, without activating the window operations menu, try using the underlined letters you noted when that menu was open.

11. Iconify (that is, minimize) the `xterm` window. After it is an icon, restore it back to the root window.

    Activate the `xterm` window. Three buttons appear to the right of the title bar. Left-click the iconify, or minimize, button, which is immediately to the right of the title bar. The `xterm` window apparently disappears, but an icon remains. The icon indicates that the process is still available for use; you need only reactivate it.

    Left-click the `xterm` icon. The icon disappears and the full-fledged `xterm` window reappears.

12. Now maximize the `xterm` window. What happens?

    Look again at the three buttons to the right of the `xterm` window's title bar. Left-click the middle button, called the maximize button.

13. After you maximize the `xterm` window, resize it to a smaller size.

    Note that three buttons appear to the right of maximized `xterm` window's title bar. Left-click the middle button again.

14. Use the root menu to open another `xterm` window.

    Move the mouse pointer to an open area of the root window (desktop) and click the left mouse button. The root menu appears. Left-click *New shell* or a similar command.

15. Start another different type of clock using the root menu.

    Move the mouse pointer again to an open area of the desktop and click the right mouse button. The Programs menu appears. Move the mouse pointer down to *System* and left-click. The System submenu appears. Left-click *Time Tool*. A different type of clock appears.

16. The `xterm` command has many command line options. Try viewing these options using the `xterm -help` command. You need to pipe the output from the command to `more` or `less`. Note that some distributions of Linux/UNIX do not allow the use of the pipe with the `xterm` command.

If an `xterm` window appears on the desktop, activate it. Otherwise, create an `xterm` window by left-clicking an open area of the desktop and selecting *New shell* or a similar command from the resulting root menu.

At the command line, enter:

```
$ xterm -help | less<Enter>
```

17. Start another `xterm` window from the command line within an `xterm` window. Give the new window the following characteristics:

    ▲ Background color: sky blue
    ▲ Foreground color: green
    ▲ Title: My New Window
    ▲ Scrollbar: left side

    ```
    $ xterm -bg skyblue -fg green -T "My New Window" -sb
      -leftbar<Enter>
    ```

18. Now start an `xclock` from the command line within one of the windows. Have it run in the background. Give the clock the following characteristics:

    ▲ Background color: white
    ▲ Foreground color: red
    ▲ Hands on the dial: blue
    ▲ Second hand update: every second

    ```
    $ xclock -bg white -fg red -hd blue -update 1 &<Enter>
    ```

19. For the next few exercises, make sure that you have created at least two `xterm` windows. (If you create an `xterm` window from another `xterm` window, make sure you add the & argument to the `xterm` command so that the second window runs in the background of the first and you can move easily from one window to the other.) In one `xterm` window, use the `vi` editor to create a file called *ex15file*. Add a few lines of text to this file, but do not exit from it.

    ```
    $ vi ex15file<Enter>
    i
    ```

Chapter 15: The Linux X Window System

```
Hi, how are you?
I am fine.
Today is not Friday.
I will transplant this line to ex15file.new.
I'll copy this line to ex15file.new, too.
<Esc>
:wq<Enter>
```

20. In the second `xterm` window, use the `vi` editor to create another file called *ex15file.new*. Go into Insert mode, but do not add any text to the file yet.

```
$ vi ex15file.new<Enter>
i
```

21. Copy a few lines of text from the *ex15file* in the first `xterm` window to the *ex15file.new* in the second window. Then exit `vi` in both windows.

- ▲ Move the mouse pointer back to the window in which you entered text in the *file ex15file*.
- ▲ Place the mouse pointer at the beginning of the lines you want to move to *ex15file.new*.
- ▲ Press the left mouse button and hold it while you move the mouse pointer across the lines you want to copy.
- ▲ When you reach the end of the text you want to copy, release the left button.
- ▲ Move the mouse pointer to the window with *ex15file.new* already begun, and then point in the file where you want to insert the lines you are copying from *ex15file*.
- ▲ If you have a three-button mouse, press the middle button to insert the text lines. If you have a two-button mouse, press both buttons at once to insert the lines.
- ▲ Exit vi in both windows.

22. You have now completed the single-machine part of this exercise. Your choices now are to try the optional network-based exercises (proceed to Exercise 23) or to end your X Windows session. If you choose to end your session, take the following actions:

- ▲ Go to an open area of the desktop and left-click.

INSTALLING AND ADMINISTERING LINUX

- ▲ Select *Exit winmgr*.
- ▲ From the resulting Really Quit winmgr submenu, select *Yes, Really Quit*.

23. As the root user, create a user named *remote1* on your client system and give that user the *remote1* password. Revert to your normal user identity and enter xhost +<Enter> in an xterm window to enable all other users access to your X server. The shell should reply with a message such as *access control disabled, clients can connect from any host*.

    ```
    # useradd remote1<Enter>
    # passwd remote1<Enter>
    Changing password for user remote1
    New UNIX password: remote1
    Re-type new UNIX password: remote1<Enter>
    # logout<Enter>

    login: teamxx<Enter>
    Password: teamxx<Enter>
    $ startx<Enter>
    ```

    If an xterm window is created by default, activate it by left-clicking the mouse pointer on it. Then, at the command line, enter

    ```
    $ xhost +<Enter>
    ```

24. Check to see whether the DISPLAY variable has been set.

    ```
    $ echo $DISPLAY<Enter>
    ```

    You have probably noticed that before you can set a value for DISPLAY, you need to know the TCP/IP name of your computer. This can be obtained by typing the command hostname, with no options or arguments.

    ```
    $ hostname<Enter>
    ```

    If the value for DISPLAY is already set to hostname:0.0, proceed directly to Exercise 25. If the DISPLAY value is not hostname:0.0, set it by entering the following:

    ```
    $ DISPLAY=hostname:0.0<Enter>
    ```

Chapter 15: The Linux X Window System

25. After you have ensured that your `DISPLAY` variable is set correctly, stay at your own system but start an `xterm` session on someone else's computer and have it appear on your system. First, you need to know the other system's host name. When specifying a log-in ID, use `remote1`.

    ```
    $ rlogin -l remote1 other_client_hostname<Enter>
    Password: remote1<Enter>
    $ export DISPLAY=your_client_hostname:0.0; xterm &
      <Enter>
    ```

    Voila! A new window appears.

26. In the window you just started on the other system, use `hostname` to verify that the window is running on the remote system. Check the value of the `DISPLAY` variable on that system. It should indicate the name of your (remote) client/host system.

    ```
    $ hostname<Enter>
    $ echo $DISPLAY<Enter>
    ```

27. From the remote system's window, execute `xcalc &`.

    ```
    $ xcalc &<Enter>
    ```

    From which system is the calculator being executed?

    You can verify your answer with the `ps` command. When you have completed this exercise, close the remote system's window.

    ```
    $ ps<Enter>
    $ exit<Enter>
    ```

28. Exit from your X Windows environment.

    ▲ Go to an open area of the desktop and left-click.
    ▲ Select *Exit winmgr*.
    ▲ From the resulting Really Quit winmgr submenu, select *Yes, Really Quit*.

See Appendix B for answers.

Quiz

1. Which of the following statements are true?

   ▲ Connections between clients and servers in a Linux/UNIX environment can be based on any networking protocol.
   ▲ A window manager is one of the basic components of an X Window System.
   ▲ In a Linux/UNIX environment, a server provides resources such as hard disk drives and printers.
   ▲ You can use only one window manager at a time.
   ▲ You can quit an X session with the <Ctrl>-<Alt>-<Backspace> key sequence, but it's not graceful.

2. Provide a brief definition of an X Server.

3. Which of the following commands is used to run a client on a different system?

   ▲ xhost
   ▲ export
   ▲ xterm
   ▲ telnet
   ▲ fvwm

4. What do the following xterm options mean?

   ▲ -bg red
   ▲ -fg black
   ▲ -T ledger
   ▲ -geometry 80x125+0+0
   ▲ -n lgr

5. When you are in X, how many ways are there to become a root user? Briefly, what are they?

See Appendix C for answers.

Chapter 16

Installing Linux

IN THIS CHAPTER, AFTER DISCUSSING some Linux installation myths and how to avoid incurring major installation headaches yourself, we look at the reasons why a boot disk is necessary. We also briefly review swap space and hard disk partitioning strategy. Then we show you how to install Linux from the local CD-ROM drive.

The bulk of this final chapter consists of two exercises. In the first, we chronicle the system equipment—a type of paper-plus-investigation routine. In the second, we proceed screen by screen through a typical Linux installation. The demo installation is on a system that uses integrated drive electronics (IDE) technology, the more common PC architecture.

Doing Your Homework

Be aware that the horror stories you may have heard about Linux installation are myths. Linux installation is not a horror story; it's simply a bit different. The myth makers either did not investigate or chronicle their equipment for quick and easy reference before beginning their Linux installation or perhaps their equipment was too new. Their versions of the Linux kernel may not have had the necessary drivers for new hard disks, video cards, or other pieces of equipment.

To prevent disagreeable and frustrating experiences during your installation, you simply have to do your homework. You must identify and chronicle the equipment on your system because you need this information during the installation.

Homework help is available. Check out the Red Hat Web site, which has an extensive list of all compatible hardware:

```
http://www.redhat.com/support/hardware/
```

Where Are You Starting From?

You may be building a brand-new system or trying to install Linux on an older system. If you plan to purchase new equipment, take the time to do some research on the Internet to learn which systems are supported by Linux. In other words, check out the interface and adapter cards, hard drives, controllers, modems, network cards, sound cards, ports, memory, video chips, and monitors. Be meticulous.

Be vigilant about receiving all technical booklets on all parts of the system from the vendors, including detailed information on the hard drives, controllers, modems, network cards, sound cards, ports, memory, video chips, and monitor. We cannot overemphasize the importance of knowing the exact details of video and monitor technical specifications. If your system is being assembled by a dealer, make sure—before you leave the premises—that they have given you all the booklets and utility disks that shipped with every card and accessory inside your system.

You should try to deal with a company that is willing to give you copies of any new drivers or utilities that they had to acquire to correctly set up your system. Drivers and utilities shipped with interfaces are often obsolete, so technicians must acquire and use their own. Dealers and technicians that share this information are worth their weight in gold.

Regarding installation on older or existing equipment: Generally the more established and better supported the system, the better off you'll be. However, there are some exceptions. We recommend that you perform the same checks on hardware, drivers, and utilities that you'd make on any new system. You may end up replacing unsupported hardware. As a result of the new interest in Linux, valuable Web sites have emerged that specialize in assisting you with acquiring documentation on systems, interfaces, and adapters.

You will probably have to start by taking the cover off the system and identifying the various adapters and video cards, sometimes right down to chipsets. Meanwhile, information on monitors can be tough to come by. You may find yourself having to rely on the autoprobe functions of installation programs. At other times, you may have to find other sources of information, including those chronicled in Chapter 3. It's handy to contact or join the local Linux or UNIX user group (some regions are large enough to have one of each).

Linux runs on a 386 or 486 with 16MB of memory. But do not expect to get a decent X Window System desktop such as KDE to perform unless you have at least 32MB of memory. Having said that, these systems will work very well at the command line, if that is sufficient for your needs.

Discovering and Chronicling System Equipment

Many good tools are available that can help you discover what is inside your system. The trick is to find a utility that does not require the installation of another operating system to begin with. It would be ideal to find a utility that functions on a system that has been booted by, say, just one operating system diskette (you may have experienced similar situations where a single DOS diskette has rescued you; I know I have). It seems silly and unproductive to have to load another different operating system, but it still happens.

A component list based on an example system appears in Table 16-1. The components we want to identify are listed in the first column. The corresponding names, specifications, and settings of our example system appear in the second column. You can use this list as a sort of template, or you can create your own customized list. The list will likely change a little depending on the exact system you have and what you use to discover the system attributes. We have provided a similar template in the first exercise to help you list the required system information.

Incidentally, we gathered the information about the example system using the `winmsd` utility, which no doubt indicates to you that Microsoft Windows was installed on the system before the installation of Linux. We could also have used Windows 95's own Device Manager found in the Control Panel under System. As you can see, this system is hardly brand new, but it has proven to be a very good Linux system nonetheless.

Table 16.1 Components in the Example System

Component	Name/specifications/settings
System BIOS/bus	Award Modular BIOS v4.51PG, AT/AT-compatible EISA/ISA HAL
HDD capacity and controller type	3.2 GB/SCSI
CPU	x86 Family 5 Model 4 Stepping 3, Genuine Intel 200 MHz
Driver that Windows used for reference	SiSV.sys v4.00
Monitor	TTX CPS-1760, Multi-frequency
RAM size/type	64MB/SDRAM
Display type	4MB Video Memory, Shared Memory BIOS v1.04e, 10-01-97
CD-ROM type/speed	SCSI/24x
Video adapter type	SiSV compatible display adapter
Keyboard type	US-102
Video adapter settings	Settings: 640x480 16bpp Horizontal: 30-65 kHz Vertical: 50-90 Hz
HDD/peripheral interface type/controller	SCSI Adaptec 1522B; I/O Port 340; IRQ 11; BIOS address CC000h
Video chip type /video memory	SiS 5597/5598/4MB
Networking details	Standalone IP 192.168.6.35 Mask 255.255.255.0
Digital to analog converter (DAC)	SiS
Printer	HP LaserJet 6
Sound card	None
Modem	None
Mouse type/number of buttons	Microsoft Serial/2

Investigating and Preparing

Identify System Attributes

Your system may already be set up such that you can quickly discover its attributes. On the other hand, you may have to shut down your system to get inside its box, so that you can see the adapters and other accessories inside.

Table 16.2 is a table of system attributes that you can use to check the equipment on your system. The component names and their corresponding specifications and settings may differ from system to system. If you do not have a probing utility program, you should get one before undertaking this exercise.

Table 16.2 Components in Your System

Component	Names/specifications/settings
System BIOS/bus	
CPU	
Monitor (is the manual available?)	
Display type	
Video adapter type	
Video adapter settings/specs	
Video chip type/video memory	
Digital to analog converter	
Sound card	
Mouse type/number of buttons	
HDD capacity/controller type	
Driver OS uses for reference	
RAM size/type	
CD-ROM type/speed	

Continued

Installing and Administering Linux

Table 16.2 Components in Your System (continued)

Component	Names/specifications/settings
Keyboard type	
HDD/peripheral interface type; IRQ; port address; memory addresses	
Networking details (interface card name/specs; addresses; mask; host names; domain name; name servers; default gateway)	
Printer name/model number/specs	
Modem type/specs	

Create a Linux Install Boot Disk

Technically, all Linux CDs are bootable. Whether your Linux CD will boot from your system depends on whether this option is available on your PC. If your system doesn't accommodate booting from a CD-ROM, you will have to create the necessary boot and supplemental diskettes. During the installation, the Linux installation program prompts you for these diskettes.

Creating an install boot disk depends on the type of operating system you have to begin with, and whether you want to use that operating system to create the boot disk. Two methods are addressed here. The first is creation from a DOS/Windows operating system, that is, creating the Linux boot disk when the system on which you are installing Linux is already a DOS/Windows system. The second method is creation from a UNIX system, that is, when your target system's OS is already one of the several available versions of UNIX.

Creating a Boot Disk from DOS/Windows

To create an install boot disk in the DOS/Windows environment, you need to invoke the `rawrite` program, which resides on the Linux installation CD. To find and invoke it, insert the Linux CD into the CD-ROM drive and then go to a Command Prompt window. Assuming that the CD is in the F: drive, first change to that drive. Second,

Chapter 16: Installing Linux

from within the CD's root directory, change to the *F:\images* directory. Now invoke `dir` on the *F:\images* directory, like this:

```
F:\>dir<Enter>
Volume in drive F is xxxxx
Volume Serial Number is aaaa-bbbb

 Directory of F:\images

05/02/99  06:50p    <DIR>             .
05/06/99  10:06p    <DIR>             ..
05/06/99  11:40p              280 <translation table>
04/19/99  07:24p        1,474,560 boot.img
04/19/99  07:25p        1,474,560 bootnet.img
04/29/99  04:10a              399 ls-lR
04/29/99  04:10a              156 ls-lR.gz
04/19/99  01:29a        1,474,560 pcmcia.img
04/19/99  03:26p        1,474,560 rescue.img
         9 File(s)     5,899,075 bytes
                              0 bytes free
```

Next, invoke the `rawrite` program. Although you haven't seen `rawrite` or the directory it resides in, feel free to introduce its DOS command sequence, as follows:

```
F:\images>\dosutils\rawrite
Enter disk image source file name: boot.img
Enter target diskette drive: a:
Please insert a formatted diskette into drive A: and
   press -ENTER- :
F:\images>
```

Run the `rawrite` program for each image file needed from this directory. Then you boot the system with the diskette. The installation screens are quickly reviewed here so that you will know how to respond to them.

Creating a Boot Disk from UNIX

In a UNIX environment, you could use the `dd` utility to create a set of boot and related image diskettes. Before we get to `dd`, though, we'll show you how to mount the CD as a UNIX file system, check for the appropriate image files on the CD, and then create the boot diskette.

First we mount the CD:

`[root@Linda /root]#` mount /dev/cdrom

Now we check to see whether the mount procedure succeeded:

```
[root@Linda /root]# mount
/dev/hda1 on   / type ext2 (rw)
none on /proc type proc (rw)
none on /dev/pts type devpts (rw,mode=0622)
/dev/fd0 on /mnt/floppy type msdos (rw)
/dev/cdrom on /mnt/cdrom type iso9660 (ro)
```

Now we change to the CD-ROM's directory:

`[root@Linda /root]#` cd /mnt/cdrom

And now we list the files on the CD-ROM:

```
[root@Linda /root]# ls -l
total 5779
-r--r--r--  1 root  root        280 May  6 21:40 TRANS.TBL
-r--r--r--  1 root  root    1474560 Apr 19 17:24 boot.img
-r--r--r--  1 root  root    1474560 Apr 19 17:25 bootnet.img
-r--r--r--  1 root  root        399 Apr 29 02:10 ls-lR
-r--r--r--  1 root  root        156 Apr 29 02:10 ls-lR.gz
-r--r--r--  1 root  root    1474560 Apr 18 23:29 pcmcia.img
-r--r--r--  1 root  root    1474560 Apr 19 13:26 rescue.img
```

At this point, we invoke dd to copy the necessary images on to the floppy disk. We begin with *boot.img*:

```
[root@Linda /root]# dd if=boot.img of=/dev/fd0 bs= 1440k
1+0 records in
1+0 records out
```

You would invoke the dd program for each of the image files needed from this directory.

Swap Space Options

Two very important and interdependent functions of the Linux kernel are memory management and process management. Process management will fail if there is insufficient memory.

Swap space is also sometimes referred to as *disk paging* or *virtual memory*. We prefer the term disk paging because Linux temporarily writes pages of memory to the hard disk when RAM is full. You should try to avoid this entirely because system performance suffers. Swap space is never a fix for a lack of physical RAM.

That said, swap space can be in the form of a dedicated swap partition or a swap file. The partitioning can be simple or complex. There are pros and cons in the use of each option. The two issues are: Which option do you need or want and how large should you make the partitions or files?

We recommend a dedicated swap partition because you will get better performance. Swap partitioning must be planned before installation so that you can create the necessary partition types and sizes during installation. The three types of partitions are primary, extended, and logical (these are discussed later in the chapter).

Our swap partition is an extended partition within the (primary and extended) Linux operating system partition. Refer to Figure 16.1 for a simple conceptual illustration of a hard disk with a physical partition *(hda7)* dedicated to memory swapping. The swap partition's file system is type 82, which is why it appears in a partition table as Linux swap and not Linux native, like other Linux partitions.

You should not entirely rule out the use of swap files, however. You can create swap files after the installation for use in emergencies. They will work with the rest of your computer memory configuration(s).

Suppose that you want to create a 20MB swap file named *linswap*. You've examined your partitions and found that your *tmp* partition has the room for it.

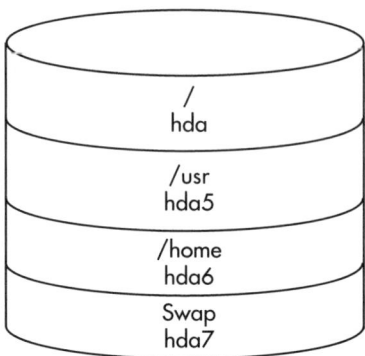

Figure 16.1: A simple swap partition.

First, tell Linux that you want to create the *linswap* swap file:

```
# dd if=/dev/zero of=/tmp/linswap bs=1024 count=20480
  <Enter>
```

Now, prepare the file as swap space:

```
# mkswap /tmp/linswap 20480<Enter>
```

Ensure that the file is written to the disk:

```
# /etc/sync<Enter>
```

Now turn on the swap file:

```
# swapon /tmp/linswap<Enter>
```

Swap files such as */tmp/linswap* should be deactivated and removed as soon as possible after the emergencies are over. To do so, first turn off the swap file:

```
# swapoff /tmp/linswap<Enter>
```

Be careful using this `swapoff` command, though. Make sure that the system load is such that the swap file is not being used. Otherwise, you could get unpredictable and potentially disastrous results. After turning off the swap file, you can delete it.

If longer term solutions are needed, consider adding RAM or repartitioning the hard disk (that is, after you do a proper system backup).

CHAPTER 16: INSTALLING LINUX

Please do not count on using the rather inefficient and potentially volatile swap file for anything besides the short term because if something corrupts your swap file, it might corrupt your whole file system.

If your system has only 16MB of RAM or less, a swap partition is mandatory. In such cases, the swap partition has to be at least 16MB. Note that the performance of X Window System is unacceptable with only 16MB of RAM.

The amount of swap space you choose to create depends on the system and on the version of Linux you're installing (later versions require more memory, which might affect your virtual memory requirements). A reasonable, albeit rough, estimate is a size equal to twice the amount of physical RAM. For example, if you have 32MB of RAM in the system and the system will be running two or three applications, you are well advised to configure 64MB of swap space. You can start with this amount and then monitor your system and application performance and make adjustments later as necessary. For systems with 64MB of RAM or more, a swap partition equal to the RAM installed is a good starting point. We consider a swap partition greater than 200MB wasteful.

The issue of swap space size is worth thinking about before proceeding with your installation. Any adjustments to increase the size of the swap partition after installation involve backing up and restoring file systems and applications, repartitioning, and reformatting

Hard Disk Partitioning

Partitioning can be as simple or as complex as you deem necessary. In the following, we illustrate a somewhat complex approach to partitioning. We plan to separate the following file systems by assigning each one to its own partition. We decided to use this configuration for several reasons:

▲ To keep the / (root) partition inside the 1023 cylinder range (that is, to observe the "1023 cylinder rule") and thus facilitate system booting. The root partition needs to be between 80MB and 100MB. It need contain only the files necessary to boot the system as well as some configuration files. You should not keep applications and data here.

▲ To give */usr* its own logical file system partition so that, if more applications are installed than you had originally expected, you can easily back up and restore this file system partition and then increase its size without having to touch the / (root) file system partition. This is where you should keep most of the application software, so be generous. Some system planners will also further separate */usr/local* to keep their own scripts and customized software separate from, say, Red Hat's RPM package software. Further, they may separate */usr/src* to isolate the Linux kernel sources and RPM software sources.

▲ To give */home* its own logical file system partition to protect the / (root) file system from being accidentally filled to 100% capacity, which could halt the system.

▲ To use a separate logical swap partition for performance and maintenance reasons.

/usr/local/ and */tmp* may also be good candidates for separate partitions. Using the preceding configuration, the files and directories are divided and placed according to the following listing. Assuming this hard disk is IDE technology, the hard disk is generally called *hda*, and its partitions are called *hda1* for the root (/), *hda5* for */usr*, *hda6* for */home*, and *hda7* for the swap partition. The boot process shows *hda: <hda1 <hda5 hda6 hda7>>*, respectively.

The following directories are in / (root):

```
drwxr-xr-x   2 root   root     2048 Sep 13 06:56 bin
drwxr-xr-x   2 root   root     1024 Sep 13 07:09 boot
drwxr-xr-x   5 root   root    34816 Sep 17 16:36 dev
drwxr-xr-x  29 root   root     3072 Sep 19 08:25 etc
drwxr-xr-x   4 root   root     3072 Sep 13 06:48 lib
drwxr-xr-x   2 root   root    12288 Sep 13 06:22 lost+found
drwxr-xr-x   4 root   root     1024 Sep 13 06:23 mnt
dr-xr-xr-x  73 root   root        0 Sep 17 10:36 proc
drwxr-x---  18 root   root     1024 Sep 19 12:12 root
drwxr-xr-x   3 root   root     2048 Sep 13 07:00 sbin
```

Chapter 16: Installing Linux

```
drwxrwxrwt 14 root  root  1024 Sep 19 12:22 tmp
drwxr-xr-x 16 root  root  1024 Sep 13 07:00 var
```

The next directory ends up in /usr:

```
drwxr-xr-x 20 root  root  1024 Jun 13 06:41 usr
```

And the following directory ends up in /home:

```
drwxr-xr-x  5 root  root  1024 Jun 17 09:05 home
```

Installing Linux on an IDE System

The installation exercise is reasonably straightforward, and we walk through the installation with you, screen by screen. Before we do so, however, we discuss invoking the installation program and the techniques used for responding to the installation program and entering the necessary information.

NOTE: *Throughout this installation, when you are asked by the installation program for descriptions of components in your system, the text refers to some presumed attributes, based on what we had available when writing this book. For example, Step 4 asks for keyboard information; Step 12, hard disk partitions; Step 20, mouse; Step 21, network; Step 22, remote printer/host; Step 29, video adapter/hardware; and Step 30, monitor specifications. At those points in the exercise, make sure that you enter the attributes pertaining to the system on which you are installing Linux.*

Invoke the Linux Installation Program

The Linux installation program consists of a series of *dialog boxes*, sometimes called *screens* or *windows*. These dialog boxes present you with information and request information and decisions.

Following are the two most common methods for invoking the installation program:

▲ Inserting the Linux CD-ROM into the CD drive and booting the system (provided that the system's CMOS is configured to allow booting from the CD-ROM drive).

Installing and Administering Linux

▲ Inserting a Linux-bootable floppy disk into the floppy disk drive and booting the system (provided that the system's CMOS is configured to allow booting from the floppy disk drive).

Giving Information to the Installation Program

As you install Linux, you will notice several different ways of inputting information. A quick summary follows:

▲ *Text input.* In some dialog boxes, you will be asked to type information, usually on a dashed line. This insertion method is often used with others, such as buttons and toggles.

▲ *Check boxes.* These are spaces defined by brackets or boxes that you toggle to select or deselect by pressing the <Spacebar>.

▲ *Buttons.* These are generally square boxes that you access with the <Tab> key and then select by pressing the <Enter> key.

▲ *Scroll and select.* Some dialog boxes contain lists, such as components, packages, or default services, from which you have to choose by scrolling up or down and then selecting. Use combinations of the <Tab> and <Spacebar> keys, followed by pressing <Enter>.

Step 1. Welcome!

If we were to walk away from the first screen without making a selection, the installation program would proceed to boot the system on its own.

```
                  Welcome to Red Hat Linux!

    •    To install or upgrade a system running
         Red Hat Linux 2.0 or later, press the <Enter> key.

    •    To enable expert mode, type: expert <Enter>.
         Press <F3> for more information about expert mode.

    •    This disk can no longer be used as a rescue disk.
         Press <F4> for information on the new rescue disks.

    •    Use the function keys listed below for more information

 [F1-Main] [F2 - General] [F3 - Expert] [F4 - Rescue] [F5 - Kickstart] [F6 - Kernel]
```

Let's summarize what the options in the preceding dialog box mean.

- ▲ ***Install or upgrade a system running Red Hat Linux 2.0 or later.*** This is your best choice if you know that your system as assembled contains supported adapters and cards. This mode tries to autodetect all the cards and their settings for you.

- ▲ ***Enable expert mode.*** Select this mode if autoprobing does not appear to be finding the cards with their correct settings. You will have to supply the necessary information on all settings, such as IRQ, I/O, and DMA. This selection is *not* for the non-expert.

- ▲ ***Enable rescue mode.*** This is a recent feature to the installation startup that allows you to boot your system if the LILO or boot sectors get trashed. There is also a procedure here that allows you to create a rescue disk after the fact if circumstances dictate. However, you do not have to use this install menu to create a rescue disk. If your system boots normally, you can create a rescue disk at any time by going back to the *images* directory on the Linux CD and using the following command:

   ```
   dd if=rescue.img of=/dev/fd0 bs=72k
   ```

The <F5> function key invokes what is known as kickstart mode, which provides a method of implementing unattended installations. This is a nice feature for cloning system installations.

The next screen presumes that you have chosen the first option, which is considered the normal mode of installation.

Step 2. If You Need Help

The following dialog box informs you that when you register the product, you will receive 90 days of support.

```
                       Red Hat Linux
      Welcome to Red Hat Linux!

      This installation process is outlined in detail in the
      Official Red Hat Linux Installation Guide available from
      Red Hat Software. If you have access to this manual,
      you should read the installation section before continuing.

      If you have purchased Official Red Hat Linux, be sure to
      register your purchase through our website,
      http://www.redhat.com.
                              OK
```

Step 3. Select Language

This screen asks what language you want to use to perform the installation. You will be asked later about the language you want to use for the system itself. Do not confuse the two.

```
                     Choose a Language
      What language should be used during the installation process?
                       English     _
                       French      #
                       German      ¬
                       Hungarian   ¬
                       Icelandic   ¬
                       Italian     ¬
                       Norwegian   ¬
                       Romanian    ↓
                              OK
```

Step 4. Specify Keyboard

You cannot afford to get creative on the Specify Keyboard screen. This is a technical question about keyboard drivers. If you answer this question incorrectly, all types of issues may arise when you try to enable and remap the keys. Not all keyboards are created equal. You can, however, choose the closest one here and adjust it later when the system is up and running.

Chapter 16: Installing Linux

```
                        Keyboard Type

               What type of keyboard do you have?

                         slovene         ↑
                         tr_f-latin5     ¬
                         tr_q-latin5     ¬
                         tralt           ¬
                         trf             ¬
                         trq             ¬
                         uk              ¬
                         us              ↓

                             OK
```

Step 5. Specify Installation Method

Because you are going to install Linux from the CD-ROM drive, you should select *Local CDROM*.

```
                      Installation Method

        What type of media contains the packages to be installed?

                         Local CDROM
                         NFS Image
                         Hard drive
                         FTP
                         SMB image

                             OK
```

Now insert the Linux CD-ROM.

```
                            Note
            Insert your Red Hat CD into your CD drive now

                    OK              Back
```

Step 6. Specify Initial or Upgrade Installation

In this exercise, you are dealing with a new installation, so choose *Install*. Remember, *Install* will not preserve any information. *Upgrade*

363

preserves existing configuration files by renaming them and giving them a specific file name extension (such as *filename.rpmsave*).

```
                        Installation Path

        Would you like to install a new system or upgrade a
        system which already contains Red Hat Linux 2.0 or later?


                Install                     Upgrade
```

Step 7. Choose Installation Class

Choose *Custom*. If you were to choose *Workstation* or *Server*, the only differences would be in component selection (that is, the ultimate decisions on which packages will be installed). Remember, any of these can be reconfigured at any time by accessing one of the RPM package installers later.

```
                        Installation Class

    What type of machine are you installing? For maximum flexibility,
    choose "Custom".
                            Workstation
                            Server
                           √Custom

                OK                          Back
```

Step 8. Configure for an IDE System Screen

The object of this exercise is to install Linux on an IDE system. So choose *No* and continue with an IDE installation.

```
                        SCSI Configuration

                Do you have any SCSI adapters?

            √No             Yes             Back
```

Step 9. Use Disk Druid for Disk Partition

You are going to use Disk Druid. Remember that both Disk Druid and `fdisk` are destructive to existing partitions.

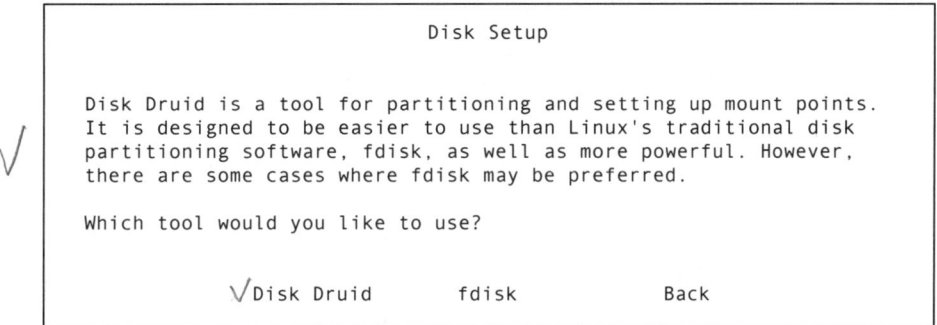

Step 10. View Hard Disk Attributes

The following screen indicates that you have an 8.2 GB IDE hard disk that it calls drive *hda*, which is the correct designation for any IDE hard disk. You will now proceed to create your file system partitions. At this point, select *Add*.

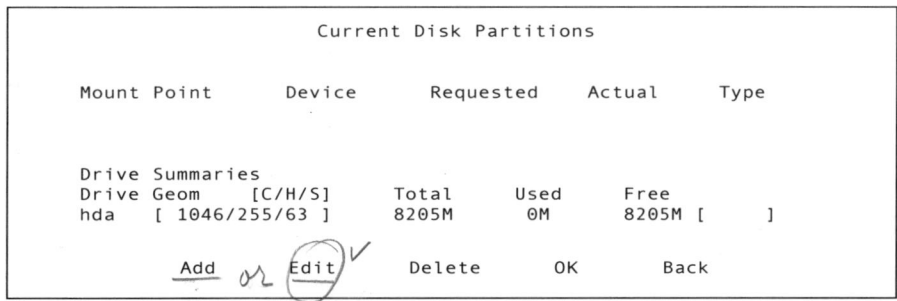

Step 11. Add or Edit Partitions

Every time you add a partition, the following dialog box appears after you select *Add* or *Edit* in the Current Disk Partitions box. Thus, if you add more than one partition—and you will in this exercise—you will see this dialog box more than once. Clicking *OK* will take you back to

INSTALLING AND ADMINISTERING LINUX

the Current Disk Partitions menu, which will be updated to show the partition and mount point you have just added.

If you are editing existing partitions, the dialog box is slightly different. For example, the *Type* will already be specified. Also, there will be an *Allocation Status* (which will read *Successful* or *Unsuccessful*) instead of the *Allowable Drive* specification. Again, clicking *OK* will return you to the (updated) Current Disk Partition menu.

```
                        Edit New Partition
        Mount Point: /_ _ _ _ _ _ _ _ _ _ _ _ _ _ _ _ _
        Size (Megs): _ _ _ _ _ _ _ _         Type: Linux Swap
                                                   Linux Native
        Grow to fill disk?  [   ]                  DOS 16 bit <32M
                                                   DOS 16 bit >=32M
        Allowable Drive:    [   ] hda

                    OK                          Cancel
```

Step 12. Create New Hard Disk Partitions

This screen shows the configuration we used when preparing this exercise. Create partitions that reflect the system on which you are installing Linux. Every time you add, delete, or edit partitions, this dialog box will appear, showing you how you are progressing with new or different partitions or other specifications. Note that *none* of the changes take effect until you press *OK* at the very end of the partitioning process.

After you have the configuration you want, select *OK* to save these changes to your partition tables.

```
                    Current Disk Partitions
  Mount      Point      Device        Requested      Actual     Type

  /          hda1       800M          3631M          Linux      Native
  /usr       hda5       700M          3200M          Linux      Native
  /home      hda6       268M          1239M          Linux      Native
             hda7       128M          133M           Linux      Swap

  Drive Summaries
  Drive      Geom [C/H/S]   Total       Used        Free
  hda        [3067/64/32]   8205M       8204M       0M [              ]

         Add           Edit         Delete          OK         Back
```

Step 13. Format Swap Space

The following dialog box advises you that the installation program will format the swap space. Again, if this will be a production system, we recommend selecting the *Check for bad blocks* option.

```
                         Active Swap Space

    What partitions would you like to use for swap space?
    This will destroy any information already on the partition.

              Device          Size (k)
     [ * ]    /dev/hda7       136521

     [ * ]  Check for bad blocks during format

                       OK                      Back
```

Step 14. Format New System Partitions

For this installation, you will format all the file system partitions so that you can be confident they will start out clean. You should also check for bad blocks.

All newly created partitions should be formatted. Old partitions, containing information that you do not mind removing, should also be newly formatted. Existing partitions containing files or data that you want to preserve should not be formatted. Such preservation efforts would likely apply only if you were upgrading your Linux operating system.

```
                        Partitions to Format
    What partitions would you like to format? We strongly suggest
    formatting all of the system partitions, including / , /usr,
    and /var. There is no need to format /home or /usr/local if they
    have already been configured during a previous install.

    [ * ]  /dev/hda1    /
    [ * ]  /dev/hda6    /home
    [ * ]  /dev/hda5    /usr

           [ * ]   Check for bad blocks during format
                         OK                            Back
```

Step 15. Choose Components to Install

Components are groups of software packages that provide an overall service or feature to the system. The components listed in the next screen are not the complete list, but rather the ones we suggest installing for this exercise. You may notice that the dialog box on your screen is a little smaller than the one shown here, but by following the arrows, you will eventually reveal all the components.

[handwritten: Linear mode / Mouse selection]

CHAPTER 16: INSTALLING LINUX

```
        Components to Install

        ents to install:
            inter Support           ↑
            Window System           ¬
            JOMEt                   ¬
            )E                      ¬
            ail/WWW/News Tools      ¬
            OS/Windows Connectivity ¬
            ile Managers            ¬
            raphics Manipulation    ¬
            onsole Multimedia       ¬
            multimedia support      ¬
            Networked Workstation   ¬
         √[ * ] Dialup Workstation  ¬
         √[ * ] NFS Server          ¬
         √[ * ] SMB (Samba) Connectivity ¬
         √[ * ] Anonymous FTP Server ¬
         √[ * ] Web Server          ¬
         √[ * ] DNS Name Server     ¬
           [ * ] Kernel Development ¬
           [ * ] Extra Documentation ↓

        [ * ]   Select individual packages

        OK                          Back
```

Only the components are listed here, not the individual packages. To see the packages that comprise the components, you have to choose *Select individual packages.* But before you do so, be prepared: You will slow down the installation process. You also run the risk of getting confused and mistakenly installing parts of components or packages that will not install because other requisite packages they depend on may not have been installed.

If you are performance-minded, you may want to be selective at this stage. On the other hand, you may want to choose all components and, thus, all packages. As you scroll down through this dialog box, you will eventually see the *Everything* choice at the bottom of the component list.

 WARNING: *The installation program will tell you if you have inadequate disk space. In the meantime, do not forget your planning and do not make disk space too tight in the root (/) and /usr file system partitions.*

Try to resolve all dependencies (*package dependency* means that one package or component may not work unless its companion packages are also installed) before continuing. If any dependencies are inadvertently missed, the installation program warns you of that as well. You can still add them any time after installation.

Step 16. Create Install Log

Select *OK* here. As careful as you may be, you can never tell when the *install.log* file might be needed to bail you out of unforeseen trouble.

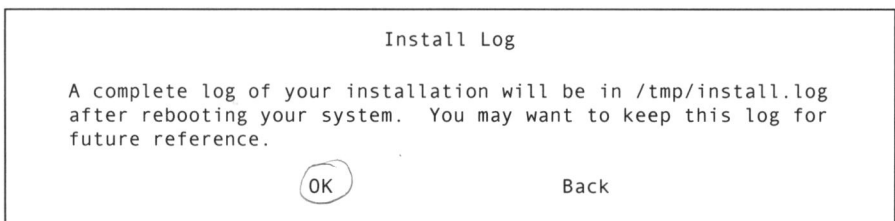

Step 17. Installation Progress: Search for Overlapping Files

Here the installation program looks for any overlapping files—that is, those files that would be duplicated during this new installation process. This screen appears only when preservation, to some extent or another, has been chosen.

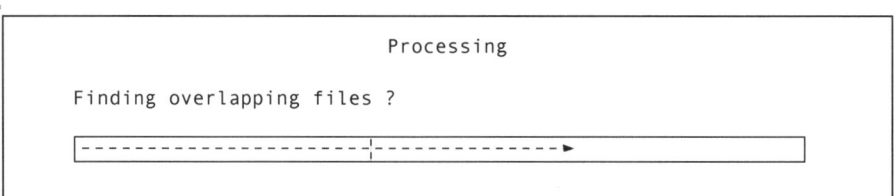

Step 18. Install Status

Throughout the installation process, you will see the Install Status box, which shows you the progress of the installation of individual packages and programs (top half), as well as the overall progress of

Chapter 16: Installing Linux

the total Linux installation (bottom half). Note that as the individual packages are installed, the installation program provides the package name, the size of the package, and a brief description of the package.

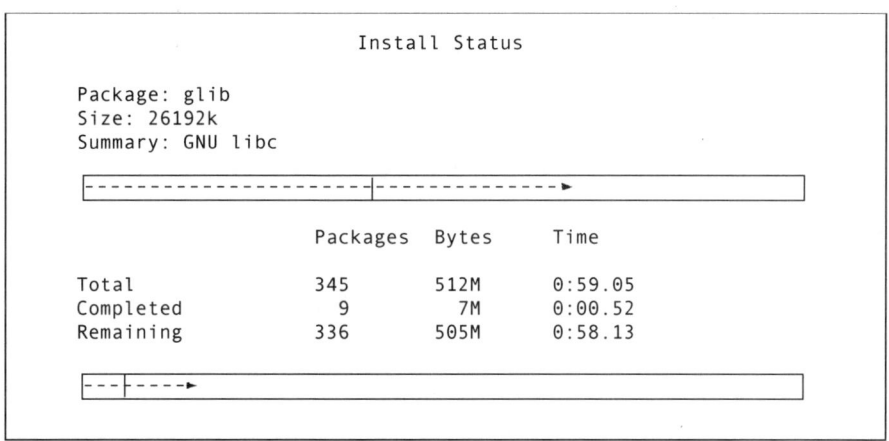

On the bottom, the installation program keeps track of the space used by the installed packages, as well as the remaining space required. Moreover, it tracks the total, elapsed, and remaining installation time. This might be a good time for you to take a break while the installation proceeds.

Step 19. Probe to Identify Mouse

At this point, the installation program probes to identify your mouse. Here it found the PS/2 mouse we used to develop this exercise.

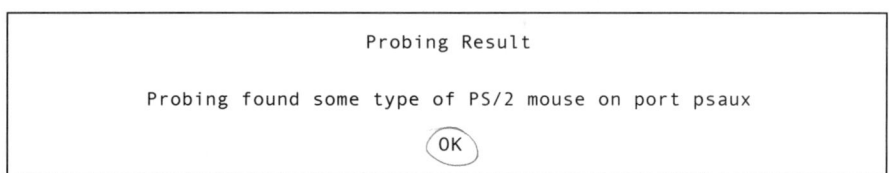

Step 20. Configure Mouse

The program immediately asks you to configure the mouse it found. If you have a three-button mouse, you will be better equipped to take

Installing and Administering Linux

advantage of X Window System. However, if your mouse has only two buttons, you should select *Emulate 3 Buttons.* If you ever want to change the mouse configuration, you can use the */usr/sbin/* `mouseconfig` or `linuxconf` command.

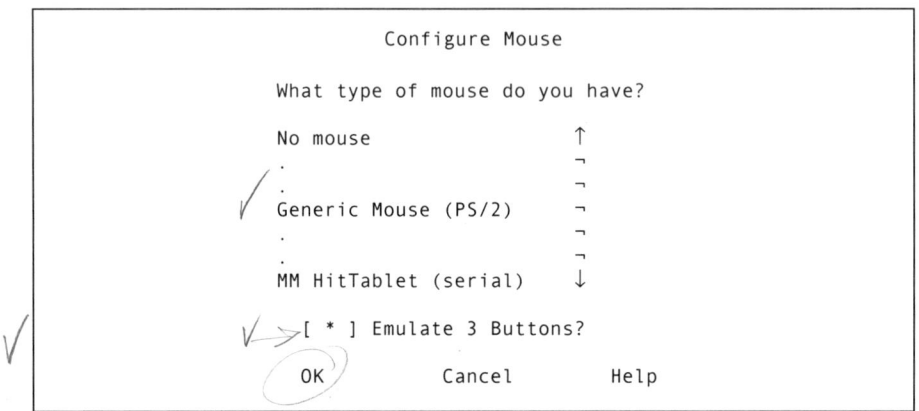

This screen is fairly straightforward. Select *Yes.*

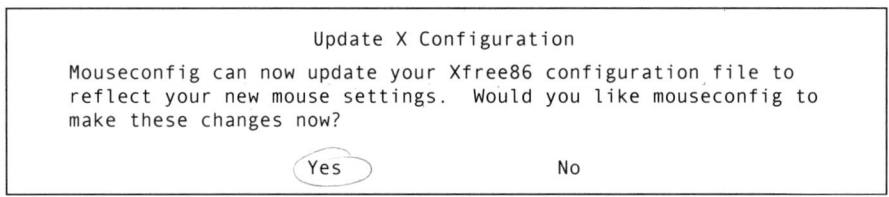

Step 21. Configure Network

In the following screen, select *Yes* because you will be connecting to a local area network.

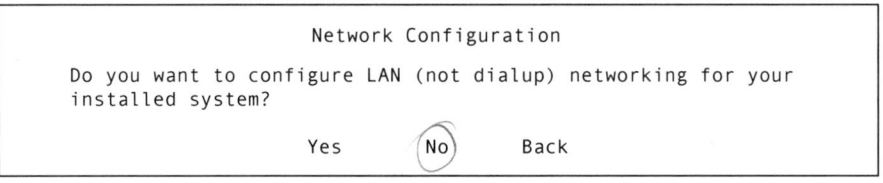

Our installation program found the network interface card shown in the next screen. We hope it will find the one in your system too and will load the appropriate drivers.

CHAPTER 16: INSTALLING LINUX

```
                        Probe
      A NE2000 PCI card has been found on your system.
                         OK
```

You will be connecting to a network, so select the *Static IP Address* option.

```
                      Boot Protocol

   How should the IP information be set?  If your system
   administrator gave you an IP address, choose static IP.

                Static IP address
                BOOTP
                DHCP

                OK                      Back
```

The only two mandatory entries are *IP address* and *Netmask*. The *default gateway* and *nameserver* entries are optional.

```
                      Configure TCP/IP

   Please enter the IP configuration for the machine.
   Each item should be entered as an IP address in dotted-decimal
   notation (for example, 1.2.3.4)

   IP address:              192.168.6.35
   Netmask:                 255.255.255.0
   Default gateway (IP):    192.168.6.254
   Primary nameserver:      192.168.6.1

                OK                      Back
```

The only mandatory entry here is *Host name*; the other entries are optional. For this exercise, enter only the minimum amount of information necessary. You can use `linuxconf` to modify this information later, if you want.

373

Installing and Administering Linux

```
                      Configure Network

     Please enter your domain name, host name, and the IP addresses
     of any additional nameservers. Your host name should be a
     fully-qualified host name, such as mybox.mylab.myco.com.
     If you don't have any additional nameservers, leave the
     nameserver entries blank.

     Domain Name:
     Host name:                     SIM_SHOP
     Secondary nameserver (IP):
     Tertiary nameserver (IP):

                   OK                          Back
```

Step 22. Configure Time Zone

During the development of this exercise, we chose *Canada/Mountain*. Choose whatever is appropriate to your location. If you ever want to change the time/clock configuration, you can use the */usr/sbin/timeconfig* command.

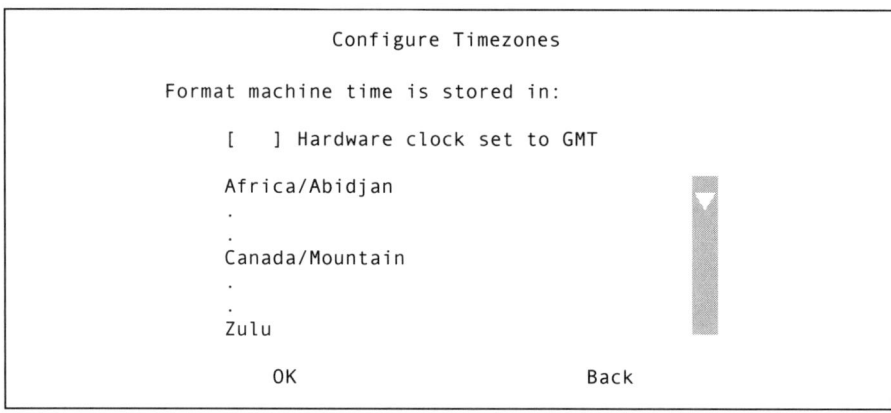

```
                     Configure Timezones

          Format machine time is stored in:

                 [  ] Hardware clock set to GMT

                 Africa/Abidjan
                 .
                 .
                 Canada/Mountain
                 .
                 .
                 Zulu

                 OK                          Back
```

Step 23. Select Default Services

The services you select in the following screen should correspond to the components you chose to install at Step 15. The question to ask here is, which ones should be *automatically* started at boot time? These will be entered in the startup *init* file. You can run */usr/sbin/ntsysv*

Chapter 16: Installing Linux

or /usr/sbin/ `chkconfig` any time after installation to change the services that automatically start on reboot. If you are not sure what each acronym means or what each service is, just highlight the name and press <F1> to view its description.

[handwritten: N/A Cheap + Bytes disks]

```
                          Services
           What services should be automatically started?

                       [ * ] apmd
                       [ * ] atd
                       [ * ] crond
                       [ * ] gpm
                       [ * ] httpd
                       [ * ] inet
                       [ * ] keytable
                       [ * ] linuxconf
                       [ * ] lpd
                       [ * ] named
                       [ * ] netfs
                       [ * ] network
                       [ * ] nfs
                       [ * ] pcmcia
                       [ * ] portmap
                       [ * ] random
                       [ * ] smb
                       [ * ] sound
                       [ * ] syslog

                           OK         Back
```

[handwritten: skip]

Step 24. Configure Remote Printer

Answer *Yes* to this question. Your printer will be attached not to the local system, but rather to the local area network.

```
                      Configure Printer
              Would you like to configure a printer?
                   Yes          No          Back
```

In the following, we chose to install an HP LaserJet 6 printer on the network.

```
          Select Printer Connection
     How is this printer connected?
              Local
              Remote lpd
              SMB/Windows 95/NT
              NetWare

         OK                    Back
```

Some system administrators might change only the print queue name and leave the spool directory path alone. Of course, they would have to change the last entry of that spool path to match the name of the chosen queue. For example, if the name of the queue is *lpacct*, the name of the spool directory would be *var/spool/lpd/lpacct*.

```
              Standard Printer Options
   Every print queue (which print jobs are directed to) needs a
   name (often lp) and a spool directory associated with it.
   What name and directory should be used for this queue?

        Name of queue:      lp
        Spool directory:    /var/spool/lpd/lp

         OK                                    Back
```

Because you are going to be using a network printer, you have to tell the installation program the name of the host system to which the printer is attached. We named that host *SIM_SHOP* for this exercise.

```
              Remote lpd Printer Options
   To use a remote lpd print queue, you need to supply the hostname
   of the printer server and the queue name on that server which jobs
   should be placed in.
        Remote hostname:    SIM_SHOP
        Remote queue:       /var/spool/lpd/lp

         OK                                    Back
```

The printer we connected to is an HP LaserJet 6, so the *4/5/6 series* selection was adequate.

Chapter 16: Installing Linux

```
                    Configure Printer
            What type of printer do you have?
            Apple Dot Matrix                      ↑
                .                                 ┐
                .                                 ┐
            HP LaserJet 4.5.6 series              ┐
                .                                 ┐
                .                                 ┐
            Xerox XES printers                    ↓

                   OK                 Back
```

We suggest that you use the *Fix stair-stepping of text* option to accommodate the carriage return and carriage return/linefeed expectations of different systems. In other words, if you do not think your printer will perform an automatic carriage return after each line, you should select the *Fix stair-stepping* option.

```
                      HP LaserJet 4.5.6 series
    You may now configure the paper size and resolution for the printer.

                      Paper Size        Resolution
                      letter            300 x 300
                      legal             600 x 600
                      a3
                      a4

              [ * ] Fix stair-stepping of text?

                   OK                 Back
```

The next screen provides a quick summary of the information you have provided to the installation program, and what it did with it. If everything is accurate, press *OK* to continue. If you need to correct something, choose *Back*.

```
            Verify Printer Configuration

   Please verify that this printer information is correct.

      Printer type:      REMOTE
      Queue:             lp
      Spool directory:   /var/spool/lpd/lp
      Remote host:       SIM_SHOP
      Remote queue:      /var/spool/lpd/lp
      Printer driver:    HP LaserJet 4/5/6 series
      Paper size:        letter
      Resolution:        300 x 300
      Bits per pixel:    Default

                OK                        Back
```

Step 25. Set Root Password

Remember to choose a good password, and then make sure you remember it. Linux has rules and guidelines for proper passwords. Reviewing them would be worthwhile.

```
                         Root Password

   Pick a root password.  You must type it twice to ensure you
   know what it is and didn't make a mistake in typing.
   Remember that the root password is a critical part of system
   security!

         Password:
         Password (again):

                    OK             Back
```

Step 26. Configure Authentication

Choose to configure NIS now and also use shadow passwords and MD5 encryption.

Chapter 16: Installing Linux

```
                     Authentication Configuration
          [ * ] Enable NIS

          NIS Domain:       _____
          NIS Server: [ * ] Request via Broadcast
                 or use:    _____

          [ * ] Use Shadow Passwords
          [ * ] Enable MD5 Passwords

                          OK              Back
```

Step 27. Create Bootdisk

We mentioned the boot disk previously in the chapter. Creating a boot disk is definitely a good idea! Select *Yes*. However, you can always create a boot disk after you have installed Linux as well, by using the `mkbootdisk` command.

```
                               Bootdisk

     A custom boot disk provides a way of booting into your Linux
     system without depending on the normal bootloader.  This is
     useful if you don't want to install lilo on your system,
     another operating system removes lilo, or lilo doesn't work
     with your hardware configuration.  A custom boot disk can
     also be used with the Red Hat rescue image, making it much
     easier to recover from severe system failures.

     Would you like to create a boot disk for your system?

                    Yes           No            Back
```

Now insert a blank floppy disk and press *OK*.

```
                               Bootdisk

          Insert a blank floppy in the first drive /dev/fd0.

                                  OK
```

Installing and Administering Linux

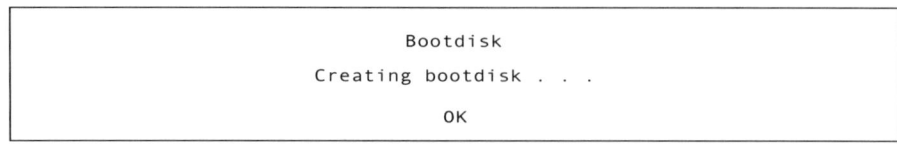

Step 28. Configure LILO

Although LILO is beyond the scope of this book, assume that you are planning to use it to manage the booting of multiple operating systems on your hard disk(s). Therefore, select the *Master Boot Record* option.

Select *OK* in the next screen and keep going. You will not need linear mode this time because it is a feature used for SCSI installations, and this is an IDE installation.

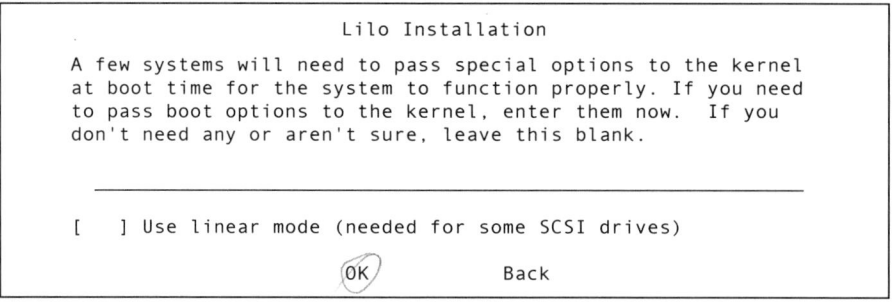

Step 29. Video Adapter: Use PCI Probe

The installation program will probe to find your video adapter. If it has correctly identified your monitor, select *OK*. An Install status box appears briefly while the installation program loads the appropriate video adapter server.

CHAPTER 16: INSTALLING LINUX

```
                    PCI Probe
         PCI probing found a:

         PCI Entry: Mach64 CD (Range Pro)
         X Server: Mach64

                      OK
```

Step 30. Set Up Monitor

Although scores of monitor names appear in the following screen, our monitor was not listed. Consequently, we selected *Custom* here. By choosing *Custom*, we had to fill in more information.

```
                    Monitor Setup

  What type of monitor do you have? If you would rather specify
  the sync frequencies of your monitor, choose "Custom" from
  the list.

                Custom                    ↑
                ADI DMC-2304              ¬
                  .                       ¬
                  .                       ¬
                  .                       ¬
                ViewSonic VPA 150         ↓

                Ok                      Back
```

We hope your monitor appears in the list. But if it doesn't, *Custom* is the way to go for you, too. Read the next message carefully. After you have been properly warned, select *OK* to continue.

```
            Custom Monitor Setup

Now we want to set the specifications of the monitor. The two
critical parameters are the vertical refresh rate, which is
the rate at which the whole screen is refreshed, and most
importantly the horizontal sync rate, which is the rate at
which scan lines are displayed.

The valid range for horizontal sync and vertical sync
should be documented in the manual of your monitor. If in
doubt, check the monitor database /usr/X11R6/lib/X11/doc/Monitors
to see if your monitor is there.

              OK                      Back
```

Our monitor was capable of up to 60 Hz, so we selected the generic *Super VGA @ 56 Hz* to be safe. This can also be adjusted later using the *Xconfigurator* program.

```
         Custom Monitor Setup (Continued)

You must indicate the horizontal sync range of your monitor.
You can either select one of the predefined ranges below that
correspond to industry-standard monitor types, or give a
specific range.  It is VERY IMPORTANT that you do not specify
a monitor type with a horizontal sync range that is beyond the
capabilities of your monitor.

         Standard VGA, 640 x 480 @ 60 Hz
         Super VGA, 800 x 600 @ 56 Hz
             .
             .
             .
         Monitor that can do 1600 x 1200 @ 76 Hz

              OK                      Back
```

We chose *50–90 Hz* because our monitor operates in this range.

CHAPTER 16: INSTALLING LINUX

```
            Custom Monitor Setup (Continued)

You must indicate the vertical sync range of your monitor. You
can either select one of the predefined ranges below that
correspond to industry-standard monitor types, or give a
specific range. For interlaced modes the number that counts is
the high one (e.g., 87 Hz rather than 43 Hz).

                        → 50 - 70
                          50 - 90
                          50 - 100
                          40 - 150

           OK                              Back
```

The installation program now invokes the *Xconfigurator* program.

```
                       Probing to begin

Xconfigurator will now run the X server you selected to probe
various information about your video card. It is normal for
the screen to blink several times.

                            ( OK )
```

Step 31. Start X

For this exercise, just select *Skip*. If something were to go wrong now, it would be inconvenient and not very educational. On the other hand, if you have the time and necessary perseverance, select *OK*. The worst that can happen is that you will have to endure another detailed *Xconfigurator* session to configure your X Window session server(s).

```
                         Starting X

Xconfigurator will now start X to test your configuration.

             ( OK )                          Skip
```

383

Step 32. Installation Complete

Yes, congratulations! Installing Linux can make for a long exercise. Having made it to this point, you need not be afraid of installing Linux at your home or office.

```
                              Done

      Congratulations, installation is complete.

      Remove the boot media and press return to reboot.  For
      information on fixes which are available for this release of
      Red Hat Linux, consult the Errata available from
      http://www.redhat.com.

      Information on configuring your system is available in the
      post install chapter of the Official Red Hat Linux User's Guide.

                               OK
```

Appendix A

Command Summary

Logging Off and Shutting Down

Command	Description
`<Ctrl>-d`	Log off the Linux system (or the current shell)
`exit`	Log off the Linux system (or the current shell)
`logout`	Log off the Linux system (or the current shell)
`shutdown`	Shut down the system by disabling all processes; requires user to be root Use `-h` in single-user mode for total shutdown `-r`, with `now` or the time in minutes, reboots the system

Directories

Command	Description
`mkdir`	Make directory
`cd`	Change directory; the default is $HOME directory
`rmdir`	Remove a directory (beware of files starting with dot)
`rm`	Remove file `-r` option removes the directory and all files and subdirectories recursively
`pwd`	Print working directory (that is, tell users what directory they are in)

Continued

Directories (continued)

Command	Description
`ls`	List files
`-a`	All
`-l`	Long
`-d`	Directory information
`-r`	Reverse alphabetic
`-t`	Sort by time changed
`-C`	Multicolumn format
`-R`	Recursive listing
`-F`	Place / (backslash) after each directory name and * (asterisk) after each executable file

Basic File Management

Command	Description
`cat`	List file contents (concatenate) Open a new file with redirection (for example, `cat> newfile`) Use <Ctrl>-d to end input
`chmod`	Change permission mode for files or directories Use `r,w,x` symbolic permissions for read, write, and execute Use + (plus), - (hyphen), or = (equal) to grant, revoke, or specify exact permissions Use `u,g,o,a` to give permissions to user, group, others, and all Can also use numerics: 4 = read, 2 = write, 1 = execute **NOTE:** Linux sums permissions: first is user, next is group, last is other. For example, `chmod 746 file1` gives user `r, w`; group `r`; others `r, w`
`chown`	Change the owner of a file (for example, `chown owner file`)
`cp`	Copy file
`del`	Delete files with prompting; `rm` for no prompting
`mv`	Move and rename file
`.`	Current directory

Continued

Basic File Management (continued)

Command	Description
`..`	Parent directory
`/string`	Find string forward
`?string`	Find string backward
`- -`	Move backward - pages
`- ?`	Move forward - pages
`rm`	Remove (delete) files `-r` option removes directory and all files and subdirectories
`head`	Print first several lines of a file
`tail`	Print last several lines of a file

`wc`	Report the number of elements in a file, as specified:
	  `-l` lines
	  `-w` words
	  `-c` characters
	No options displays lines, words, and characters

`su`	Switch user
`id`	Display user ID environment and how it is currently set
`tty`	Display the active device Useful in X Window System because you can create several `pts` devices and it is handy to know which one is active. The `whoami` command provides the same function.

Advanced File Management

Command	Description
`banner`	Display banner Also redirect banner to another terminal, *nn*, by specifying `>/dev/ttynn`
`cal`	Calendar command (`cal [month] year`)
`diff`	Show differences between two files
`find`	Find files anywhere on disk; specify location by path (searches all subdirectories under specified directory)

Continued

Advanced File Management (continued)

Command	Description	

`find` (continued)	`find` (find *path expression action*)
	 Examples:
	 `find / -name "*.txt" -print`
	 `find / -name "*.txt" -exec li -1 {} \;`
	 Executes `li -1` where names found are substituted for {}. The ; (semicolon) indicates end-of-command to be executed. The \ (backslash) removes its usual interpretation as a command continuation character.	

	`-name` *f1*	File names matching *f1* criteria
	-user *u/*	Files owned by user *u/*
	`-size` +*n* (or -*n*)	Files larger or smaller than *n* block
	`-perm` *num*	Files whose access permissions match *num*
	`-exec`	Execute a command with results of the `find` command
	`-ok`	Execute a command interactively with results of the `find` command
	`-o`	Logical OR
	`-print`	Display results; this is usually included
`grep`	Search for pattern (for example, `grep pattern files`); pattern can include regular expressions	
	`-c`	Count lines with matches but do not list
	`-l`	List files with matches but do not list
	`-n`	List line numbers with lines
	`-v`	Find files without pattern
	Expression metacharacters	
	[ ]	Match any one character from set or range inside
	^	Match beginning of line when ^ begins the pattern
	$	Match end of line when $ ends the pattern
	.	Match any single character (same as ? in shell)
	*	Match 0 or more occurrences of preceding character
	NOTE: .* (dot asterisk) is the same as * (asterisk) in the shell.	

Continued

Advanced File Management (continued)

Command	Description
sed	Stream (text) editor; used with editing flat files

sort	Sort and merge files
	  -r Reverse order
	  -u Keep only unique lines

Editors

Command	Description
vi	Screen editor
emacs	Screen editor +

Shells, Redirection, and Piping

Command	Description
< (read)	Redirect standard input *Example:* `command < file` reads input for command from a file
> (write)	Redirect standard output *Example:* `command > file` writes output for command to a file, overwriting the file's contents
> > (append)	Redirect standard output *Example:* `command > > file` appends output for command to the end of a file
2>	Redirect standard error *Example:* `command 2 > > file` appends standard error to a file *Redirection examples:* command < infile > outfile 2> errfile command > > appendfile 2> > errfile < infile

Continued

Shells, Redirection, and Piping (continued)

Command	Description
`;`	Command terminator used to string commands on single line
`	`	Pipe information from one command to the next command *Example:* `ls	cpio -o > /dev/fd0` passes the results of the `ls` command to the `cpio` command
`\`	Continuation character to continue command on a new line; will be prompted with > for command continuation
`tee`	Reads standard input and sends standard output to both standard output and a file *Example:* `ls	tee ls.save	sort` `ls` output goes to *ls.save* and is also piped to the `sort` command

Metacharacters

Command	Description
`?`	Match any single character
`[abc]`	Match any character from the list
`[a-c]`	Match any character from the list range
`!`	Not any of the following characters *Example:* `$echo [!tn]*` echoes all file names that do not begin with *t* or *n*
`;`	Command terminator used to string commands on a single line
`&`	Command preceding ampersand to be run in background mode
`#`	Comment character
`\`	Remove special meaning (no interpretation) of the following character
`"`	Interpret only $, ' (backquote), and \ characters between the quotes
`` ` ``	Set variable to results of a command *Example:* `` now = `date` `` sets the value of `now` to the current results of the `date` command
`$`	Preceding variable name indicates the value of the variable

Variables

Command	Description

=	Set a variable
	Example:
	`d = "day"`
	sets the value of `d` to the day specified
	
	Set the variable to the results of a command
	Example:
	`now = 'date'`
	sets the value of `now` to the current result of the `date` command

HOME	Home directory
PATH	Path to be checked
SHELL	Shell to be used
TERM	Terminal being used
PS1	Primary prompt character, usually $ or #
PS2	Secondary prompt character, usually >
$?	Return code of last command executed
set	Display current local variable settings
export	Export variables so that they are inherited by child processes
env	Display inherited variables
echo	Echo a message *Examples:* `echo HI` or `echo $d`
\c	Turn off carriage returns (by placing \c at the end of the message)
\n	Print a blank line (by placing \n at the end of the message)

Tapes and Floppy Diskettes

Command	Description
fdformat	Format a floppy diskette
backup	Back up individual files

Continued

Tapes and Diskettes (continued)

Command	Description

`backup` (continued)	`-i` Read file names from standard input
	`-v` List files as they are backed up
	Example:
	`backup -iv -f/dev/rmt0 file1, file2`
	
	`-u` Back up file system at the specified level
	Example:
	`backup -level -u filesystem`
	
	`|` Pipe list of files to be backed up into command
	Example:
	`find . -print
		backup -ivf/dev/rmt0`
		where you are in the directory to be backed up

`restore`	Restore commands from backup
	
	`-x` Restore files created with `backup -i`
	`-v` List files as they are restored
	`-T` List files stored on tape or floppy diskette
	`-r` Restore file system created with `backup -level -u`
	Example:
	`restore -xv -f/dev/rmt0`

`cpio`	Copy to and from an I/O device. Destroy all data previously on tape or floppy diskette. For input, must be able to place files in the same relative (or absolute) path name as when copied (can determine path names with `-it` option). For input, if file exists, compare last modification date and keep most recent (can override with `-u` option). `-o` Output `-i` Input `-t` Table of contents `-v` Verbose `-d` Create needed directory for relative path names `-u` Unconditional to override last modification date

Continued

Tapes and Diskettes (continued)

Command	Description

`cpio` (continued)	*Example:*
	 `cpio -o > /dev/fd0`
	 `file1`
	 `file2`
	 `<Ctrl>-d`
	
	 or `cpio -iv file1 < /dev/fd0`

`tar`	Alternative utility to back up and restore files

Transmitting

Command	Description
`mail`	Send and receive mail. With userid, send mail to that user ID. Without userid, display your mail. When processing your mail, at the ? prompt for each mail item, you can: `d` — Delete `s` — Append `q` — Quit `<Enter>` — Skip `m` — Forward
`uucp`	Copy file to other UNIX system (UNIX-to-UNIX copy)
`uux`	Execute on a remote system (UNIX-to-UNIX execute)

System Administration

Command	Description
`kill` *PID*	Kill the batch process with the specified PID number `kill-9` *PID* is an unconditional kill
`mount`	Associate logical volume to a directory *Example:* `mount` *device directory*
`ps -ef`	Show process status
`umount`	Disassociate file system from directory

Miscellaneous

Command	Description
banner	Display banner
date	Display current date and time
nice	Assign lower priority to following command *Example:* `nice 'ps -f`
passwd	Modify current password
sleep n	Sleep for *n* seconds
stty	Show and/or set terminal settings
touch	Create zero length file; update modification time
startx	Initiate X Window System
wall	Send message to all logged-in users
who	List users currently logged in (`whoami` identifies this user)
man	Display manual pages for the specified command

System Files

Command	Description
/etc/group	List groups
/etc/motd	Message of the day; usually displayed at log in
/etc/passwd	List of users and sign-on information; password shown as ! Can prevent password hacking by editing to remove !
/etc/profile	System-wide user profile executed at log in Can override variables by resetting in the user's profile file

Shell Programming Summary

Shell Variables

Command	Description
`Var=string`	Set variable to *string*, with no spaces between the variable, equal sign, and the designated string Enclose spaces with double quotes Special characters in the string must be enclosed by single quotes to prevent substitution Piping (|), redirection (<, >, >>), and & symbols are not interpreted
`$var`	Give value of `var` in a compound
`echo`	Display value of `var` *Example:* `echo $var`
`HOME`	Home directory of user
`MAIL`	Mail file name
`PS1`	Primary prompt character, usually $ or #
`PS2`	Secondary prompt character, usually >
`PATH`	Search path
`TERM`	Terminal type being used
`export`	Export variables to the environment
`env`	Display environment variables settings
`${var:-string}`	Give value of `var` in a command; if `var` is null, use `string` instead
`$1 $2 $3...`	Positional parameters for variable passed into the shell script
`$*`	Used for all arguments passed into the shell script
`$#`	Number of arguments passed into the shell script
`$0`	Name of the shell script
`$$`	Process ID (PID)
`$?`	Last return code from a command

Continued

Shell Commands

Command	Description
`#`	Comment designator
`&&`	Logical AND. Means run the command following the && only if the command preceding the && succeeds (return code = 0).
`||`	logical OR. Means run the command following the || only if the command preceding the || fails (return code < > 0).

`for loop`	Specify a command or a series of commands to be carried out as long as a variable or a file name meets certain value specifications.
	Example:
	`# Comment - Begin the loop`
	`for variable/file range`
	`do`
	`    cp $a textdir/$a`
	`done`
	`#Comment - the loop is ended`
	Example:
	`# Comment - Begin the loop`
	`for a in *.doc`
	`do`
	`    command(s)`
	`done`
	`#Comment - The loop is ended`

`if-then-else`	User is allowed to select from alternatives based on the result of the execution of a command. The `else` portion is optional.
	`# Comment - Begin the loop`
	`if`
	`    command`
	`then`
	`    command (alternative 1)`
	`else`
	`    command (alternative 2)`
	`fi`
	`# Comment - The loop is ended`

`read`	Read from standard input
`shift`	Shift arguments 1–9 one position to the left and decrement number of arguments

Continued

Shell Commands (continued)

Command	Description

`test`	Used for conditional test; has two formats:
	`if test expression`
	Example:
	`if test $- -eq2`
	`If [expression]`
	Example:
	`if [ $# -eq 2 ]`
	Note that spaces are required
	
	Operators:
	
	-eq =
	-lt <
	-le =<
	-ne <>
	-gt >
	-ge =>
	
	String operators:
	
	= Equal
	! = Not equal
	`-z` Zero length
	
	File status (for example, `-opt file 1`)
	
	`-f` Ordinary file
	`-r` Readable by this process
	`-w` Writable by this process
	`-x` Executable by this process
	`-s` Nonzero length

`while loop`	Allow the user to execute (or not) a command depending on the exit status (or results) of another command.
	`#Comment - Begin the loop`
	`while command(2)`
	`do`
	    `command(s)`
	`done`
	`#Comment - The Loop is ended`

vi Editor

Entering vi

Command	Description
`vi file`	Edit the specified file
`vi file file2`	Edit files consecutively (via `:n`)
`.exrc`	File that contains the `vi` profile
`wm=nn`	Set wrap margin to *nn*
	Enter a file other than at the first line by adding: + (last line) + *n* (line *n*) + `/pattern` (at the first occurrence of *pattern*)
`:n`	Next file in stack
`:set all`	Show all options
`:set nu`	Display line numbers (off when `set nonu`)
`:set list`	Display control characters in file
`:set wm=n`	Set wrap margin to *n*
`:set showmode`	Set display of the word INPUT when in input mode

Reading in, Writing in, Exiting vi

Command	Description
`:w`	Write buffer contents
`:w file2`	Write buffer contents to *file2*
`:w >> file2`	Write buffer contents to end of *file2*
`:q`	Quit editing session
`:q!`	Quit editing session and discard any changes
`:r file2`	Read *file2* contents into buffer following current cursor
`:r! com`	Read results of `com` shell command following current cursor
`:!`	Exit shell command (filter through command)
`:wq` or `ZZ`	Write and quit editing session

Appendix A: Command Summary

Navigating in vi

Command	Description
`h`, `l`	Character left, character right
`k` or `<Ctrl>-p`	Move cursor to the character above cursor
`j` or `<Ctrl>-n`	Move cursor to the character below cursor
`^`, `$`	Beginning of current line, end of current line
`w`, `b`	Word right, word left
`<Enter>` or `+`	Beginning of the next line
`-`	Beginning of the previous line
`G`	Last line of buffer

Cursor Movement in vi

Can precede cursor movement commands (including the cursor arrow) with the number of times to repeat. For example: 9 <right arrow> moves right 9 characters.

Command	Description
`0`	Move to first character in the line
`$`	Move to last character in the line
`^`	Move to first nonblank character in line
`fx`	Move right to character *x*
`Fx`	Move left to character *x*
`tx`	Move right to character preceding *x*
`Tx`	Move left to character preceding *x*
`w`	Tab word (nw = n tab word) (punctuation is read as words)
`W`	Tab word (nw = n tab word) (ignores punctuation)
`b`	Backtab word (punctuation is read as words)
`B`	Backtab word (ignore punctuation)
`e`	Tab to ending character of next word (punctuation is read as words)
`E`	Tab to ending character of next word (ignore punctuation)
`(`	Move to beginning of current sentence

Continued

Cursor Movement in vi (continued)

Command	Description
`)`	Move to beginning of next sentence
`{`	Move to beginning of current paragraph
`}`	Move to beginning of next paragraph
`H`	Move to first line on screen
`M`	Move to middle line on screen
`L`	Move to last line on screen
`<Ctrl>-f`	Scroll forward one screen
`<Ctrl>-d`	Scroll forward half screen
`<Ctrl>-b`	Scroll backward one screen
`<Ctrl>-u`	Scroll backward half screen
`G`	Go to last line in file
`nG`	Go to line *n*
`<Ctrl>-g`	Display current line number

Searching and Replacing in vi

Command	Description
`/pattern`	Search forward for *pattern*
`?pattern`	Search backward for *pattern*
`n`	Repeat find in the same direction
`N`	Repeat find in the opposite direction

Adding Text in vi

Command	Description
`a`	Add text after cursor (end with <Esc>)
`A`	Add text at end of current line (end with <Esc>)
`i`	Add text before cursor (end with <Esc>)
`I`	Add text before first nonblank character in the current line

Continued

Adding Text in vi (continued)

Command	Description
o	Add a line following the current line
O	Add a line before the current line
<Esc>	Return to command mode

Deleting Text in vi

Command	Description
<Ctrl>-w	Undo entry of current word
@	Kill the insert on this line
x	Delete current character
dw	Delete to end of current word (observe punctuation)
dW	Delete to end of current word (ignore punctuation)
dd	Delete current line
D	Erase to end of line (same as d$)
d)	Delete current sentence
d}	Delete current paragraph
dG	Delete current line through end of buffer
d^	Delete to beginning of line
u	Undo last change command
U	Restore current line to original state before modification

Replacing Text in vi

Command	Description
ra	Replace current character with *a*
R	Replace all characters overtyped until <Esc>
s	Delete current character and append text until <Esc>
s/s1/s2	Replace *s1* with *s2* (in the same line only)
S	Delete all characters in the line and append text

Continued

Replacing Text in vi (continued)

Command	Description
`cc`	Replace all characters in the line (same as `S`)
`ncx`	Delete *n* text objects of type *x*: w, b words) sentences } paragraphs $ end of line ^ beginning of line <Enter> append mode
`C`	Replace all characters from cursor to end of line

Moving Text in vi

Command	Description
`p`	Paste last text deleted after cursor (`xp` transposes two characters)
`P`	Paste last text deleted before cursor
`nYx`	Yank *n* text objects of type *x*
`"ayy`	Use named registers for moving, copying, cut and paste with `"ayy` command for register a (use registers a-z) Then paste with `"ap` command

Appendix B

Exercise Answers

Chapter 2

7. We hope you noticed something peculiar about September. The shortening of September 1752 was decreed by Pope Gregory to bring the calendar back into sync with Earth's rotation. The Pope's decision caused turmoil at the time because many people believed he was trying to take away 11 days of their lives.

8. August 1999 and August 99 are not the same. The year 99 is taken literally as the second-to-last year of the first century A.D., not a two-digit form of the year 1999. Remember to be specific about the century when asking about the calendar.

Chapter 3

2. The name of the command is `date`, and the command is found in */usr/bin*.

4. At the top of the `date` command's first page, you read that the information has been taken from the *sh-utils.info* file and that the node name is date invocation. The name of the next node is uname invocation.

5. Yes. The name of this node is uname invocation, which is the same as what appeared adjacent to Next in the `date` page.

6. The name of the most-previous node is date invocation, which, coincidentally, is the first `date` page you encountered.

10. Linux's shell responds with a usage message, specifying options and other arguments for `mount`.

11. This time, Linux's shell responds with an invalid option diagnosis, followed by the same usage message that appeared for Exercise 10 when you invoked `mount` with its `help` argument.

12. According to the Web site, Torvalds released version 1.0 in 1994. The answer to the second question depends on when you access the Web site but will likely appear in the sentence following the version 1.0 statement.

13. The first answer is promptly displayed on the Web site; the answer to the second question is displayed on the page accessed by clicking the *here* hyperlink on the Web site. The answer depends on the date you access the Web site.

14. The magazine's slogan is "The Premiere Linux Magazine."

15. The names of those items depend on when the Web site is accessed; they change every day. The first software package is named and described immediately after the *freshmeat.net* banner; the editorials are accessed by left-clicking the editorials hyperlink to the right of the same banner.

16. Again, the dates and titles of the most recent message depend on when you access the newsgroup or discussion. They are updated frequently, though typically not on a daily basis.

Chapter 4

4. Using the `-a` option results in a listing of all files in the directory, including the hidden files that are not normally displayed when using the `ls` command alone. Using the `-R` option results in a recursive listing of all nonhidden files in the directory structure, from the current working directory to the bottom.

6. Because the two are fairly new directories and have had little or no activity, both are sized at 1024 bytes (that is, two times the size of the basic 512-byte directory building block).

APPENDIX B: EXERCISE ANSWERS

8. Because the two are new zero-length files, both are sized at 0 bytes.

   Regarding inode numbers, because both were created at nearly the same time in the same part of the directory structure, their numbers should be similar and close, but still different. Despite their zero-byte size, they are still given inode numbers. Meanwhile, your answer may vary according to the workstation or terminal.

9. `$ cd<Enter>`

   `$ ls -R<Enter>`

10. `$ stat mydir<Enter>`

11. The rmdir command does not work, and returns the following: *mdir: mydir: Directory not empty.*

Chapter 5

16. The file is difficult to read because it is longer than one screen and scrolls past the screen very quickly. When you use the `more` or `less` commands, the file is then listed one screen at a time and you can move ahead (with `less`, ahead and back) at your own pace. Therefore, it is a lot easier to read.

19. You cannot remove the directory because it is not empty. After you remove the files from *goodstuff*, you can remove the directory. Note that if a directory contains only the .. and . special files, it is considered empty, so removal is not impeded.

Chapter 6

3. Creating zero-length files.

4. There is no difference in the file information. Both are the same physical file, with two different file names. You can check this by executing `ls -li` to get the inode number on each file name. You will see that each file name has the same inode number.

An ordinary file has a link count of 1. A file with a single link to it has a link count of 2. Both the original *mycal* file and its link have link counts of 2.

5. The output is identical to the output of `mycal`, which is a display of the calendar of the current month.

   You can't execute the `mycal` command. You will get a reply from Linux of *bash: myscripts/mycal: Permission denied.* Changing the permissions to read-only on the linked file name is the same as changing permissions on the file to the (original) file itself.

6. No, removing the linked file name does not remove the original file to which it is linked. Removing *home_mycal* simply removes the directory entry in the *myscripts* directory that refers to *homemycal* and changes the link count from 2 to 1. The *./myscripts/mycal* file remains intact. However, if you execute an `ls -l` on the original file, you will see that the link count is reduced.

9. You cannot execute `mycat` against the *.bash_profile* file because you have removed the user's x permission. Linux responds: *bash: ./mycat: Permission denied.*

13. The simple `$ ls myscripts` works because the user still has read permission on the *myscripts* directory, and that's all `ls` needs. However, `$ ls -l myscripts`, which requires both read and execute to work, does not work in this case because the x permission has been removed from that directory. Instead, you get:

    ```
    ls: myscripts/mycat: Permission denied
    ls: myscripts/mycat: Permission denied
    ```

14. `mycal` will not execute because the x permission is needed to access any files, including executables, in a directory.

15. Both x and w permissions are needed to remove something from a directory.

Chapter 8

1. The output of `ls` gives the names of the nonhidden files and subdirectories in only the current working directory. The output of

APPENDIX B: EXERCISE ANSWERS

ls * gives the names of the files and subdirectories in the current working directory and all subdirectories recursively down the directory tree from the current working directory. ls * does not display hidden files but ls -a does. ls -a does not display the contents of subdirectories but ls * does.

5. You might have because the command is case sensitive. If you have files or directories beginning with uppercase letters from *C* through *T*, they are listed, as well as all files and subdirectories recursively below them, no matter what they begin with and no matter whether they are uppercase or lowercase.

12. No. The word count, which is essentially the number of files found in the directory, is higher in Exercise 12 by 1 because by the time the count is taken in Exercise 12, the file created in Exercise 11 (*temp*) is included.

13. Yes, the answer is what you expect and is identical to the file count in Exercise 10. The file created in Exercise 11, *temp*, was removed before Exercise 13, so the word count and file count numbers should be the same.

14. Yes, the number is displayed on the screen and is the same number as found in Exercises 13 and 10. And yes, *junk2* has the right file name listing.

17. No, they do not. The output from one does not have to be pipelined to any other. A minor relation might be drawn between the output of pwd and ls because the files and directories listed by ls depend on the current working directory. But regardless of where in the structure you find yourself, there will be some output from ls. Consequently, it is considered a minor relationship.

Chapter 9

7. You must use double quotes here because of the space between the words.

8. You have to use the quotes around the right angle bracket. Otherwise, the shell interprets the symbol as a redirection.

10. Your home directory will have reverted to the default */home/username* directory. Why? Changing the variable from the command line sets the value for only the length of the Linux session, which ends when you log out. And after you log out, the changed variable is removed from your shell variables. When you log back in, the shell adopts the home directory defined in your profile.

14. All three methods work because the shell always disables wildcards, no matter what quoting method is used.

17. The output of `echo '* $n `ls`'` is **`* $n `ls`** because single quotes disable everything between them.

    The output of `echo "* $n `ls`"` is **`* hello filea`** because double quotes disable only variable and command substitution variables.

    The output of `echo \* \$n \`ls\`` is **`* $n `ls`** because a backslash disables the character following it. Note that we used a backslash in front of each backquote.

    The output of `echo * $n `ls`` is **`filea hello filea`**.

    The output of `echo * $n "ls"` is **`filea hello ls`**.

Chapter 11

2. The PID of the subshell is different from the PID of the log-in shell because a child PID is always different from its parent PID. Check this by comparing a child PID with its PPID. They should be different, and the child's PPID should be identical to the parent's PID.

4. You will be logging out of the system. It's handy to check where you are from time to time so that you can avoid accidental logouts.

7. In the subshell, the value of x is null and is not shown in the `set` command listing.

Appendix B: Exercise Answers

10. No, because the subshell has its own environment and its variable values are not passed back to its parent process.

12. You find yourself back in the directory in which you started. When `sc1` is invoked, it is invoked in a subshell, which has its own environment. In the subshell, then, you as the user are moved into the *root* directory. But then the command finishes, the subshell closes (thus ending the visit to the *root* directory) and you are returned to the log-in shell process, which is in your original directory (*/home/username*).

14. The values of both `var1` and `var2` are null (that is, they have no value). Script *sc2* runs in a subshell. When it finishes, control is passed back to the parent process. But variables and values set in the subshell are not passed back to the parent process. The exporting performed in the subshell benefits child processes to that subshell but not the parent of the subshell.

15. This time the value for `var1` is `hello` and the value for `var2` is your log-in name. Because the values for the variables were set in the current shell and therefore in the current process environment, they remain current and verifiable by the `echo` command. Setting them with `sc2` is just like setting them at the command line by typing them in manually.

Chapter 12

2. All the answers are "yes." The message displays at log-in (using the dot does not require logging in, so you would not have seen the message), the primary prompt reflects whatever directory you were in, and `dir` returns the same information as `ls -l`.

3. This time, the answers are "no" to all the questions. The subshell, which is a child process to the log-in shell, does not inherit the variables, aliases, and other functions. In fact, you get a *command not found* error message to your attempt at invoking `dir`. That's why we move along to Exercise 4, to set up some additional functions so that child processes are as customized as the log-in shell.

5. Now the variables, functions, and aliases also apply to the subshell. The answers to the questions are "yes."

Chapter 13

6. We anticipated that you listed more entries that began with *l* than files. That's because the `ls` also includes subdirectories (which, in turn, includes all their contents, not just those that begin with *l*).

Chapter 14

7. You probably noticed that the number of coded messages displayed by `diff` coincides with the number of changes you were asked to make to *file2*. That's not always exactly the case, especially if you combine some changes, or press <Enter> once or twice in addition to the typed changes.

9. All the answers should be approximately, if not exactly, the same and should be in the 155 KB range.

10. Again, unless the speed of compression is changed in individual cases, all the answers should be approximately, if not exactly, the same. Based on default parameters, the percentage of compression should be about 72%. The name of the file is *mymagic.gz* unless the original file name was modified beforehand. The size of the newly compressed file—again, if no changes have been made to the speed of compression—should be approximately 45 KB. Finally, there should be agreement on the percentage of compression: The size of the compressed file, compared with the size of the original uncompressed file, should reflect approximately 72% compression by `gzip`.

13. Again, even if default speed of compression settings have been changed for whatever reason, the size of the newly uncompressed *mymagic* file should be the same as the original *mymagic* file.

Chapter 15

1. The answers to these questions vary with each Linux distribution; in fact, they vary from version to version of any single Linux distribution. Some distributions use fvwm or fvwm95. Some use KDE or GNOME. Typically, the window manager automatically displays an `xterm` window of some sort, and the window is usually called something similar to xterm.

8. Generally, no items appear grayed (meaning, unavailable for the particular window) because this is, after all, a window operations menu. Occasionally, though, you may notice that some items are unavailable in a window, depending on the state of the window or the commands that have already been invoked in or on the window.

10. No, they don't work unless the window operations menu is displayed. Otherwise, they appear as characters typed on a command line.

12. The `xterm` window expands to cover the entire root window, covering any other windows that might have been displayed, with the exception of any `xclocks`, which stay on top of the `xterms`.

27. You are still operating on the remote client/host, so `xcalc` is executing on that system.

Appendix C

Quiz Answers

Chapter 2

1. `mail -f newmail`

    Remember, the correct syntax is

    `command -option argument`

2. `$ mail username`

3. `talk`, `write`, or `wall`

4. The calendar for the year A.D. 8.

5. `who` or `finger username`. Both provide the last log-in time.

Chapter 3

1. Two ways. The first is deliberately, by specifying the `--help` option after the command name you want to investigate. The second is accidentally, the result of using a command incorrectly. Linux returns with a preliminary diagnosis of your problem, followed by a quick summary of the command's proper usage.

2. The basic Linux Web site is *http://www.linux.org*. The basic X Window System Web site is *http://www.xFree86.org*.

3. This is a type of trick question. We didn't mention it in the text, but we did mention a few Internet sites where you might have learned his name. His name is Tux.

4. `locate`. The other three commands use the same basic man database. With `locate`, you search the file system or a database path that you can specify.

5. `$ man commandname | lpr<Enter>`. Although this may seem like a trivial question, someday you may find yourself on another system, wanting to print some man information. Remembering basic command sequences like this may prove to be handy.

6. K Desktop Environment: `"Help"`
ASCII/command line: `info`
Fvwm95: `xman`
We disguised the `KDE Help` command a bit. Including its full name would have been a giveaway.

7. The Usenet newsgroups are a worldwide system of computers that store, update, and exchange collections of discussion text files.

Chapter 4

1. Relative path name: *slatemr/pgms/suba*; absolute path name: */home/slatemr/pgms/suba*.

2. The single dot (.) specifies "with respect to the current directory," and the double dot (..) specifies "with respect to the parent directory."

3. Moves you up two directories in the directory tree structure. It's as if you instructed the system to "go to the parent directory of the current directory; now go to the parent directory of the parent directory."

4. The directory to be removed must be empty, and your current working directory must be at least one directory level higher than the directory to be removed.

5. `-l`   Provides a long listing of files
   `-a`   Lists hidden files
   `-R`   Lists subdirectories and their contents

APPENDIX C: QUIZ ANSWERS

`-i`	Displays the inode number
`-d`	Displays information about a directory

6.
   - ▼ !
   - ▼ aBcDe
   - ▼ my_file
   - ▼ my.file
   - ▼ .myfile

7. The following message appears: *mkdir: cannot make directory 'test' : File exists.* The system has seen that a directory named *test* already exists, and reports that back to the user. No further action is taken by the system.

8. The first command creates a subdirectory named */dir1* in */home/rubbleba* and then, in */dir1*, a subdirectory named */dir2*. After that, a subdirectory named */dir3* is created in the */dir2* subdirectory.

   The second command creates three subdirectories named */dir1*, */dir2*, and */dir3* all in */home/rubbleba*, but they are not within one another.

Chapter 5

1. The first command makes */home/flintsfr* the current directory.

   The second command tells Linux to copy the *file1* file and name the copy *file2*. Thus, each copy of the file has a unique name and inode number. Changes made to one copy of the file will not affect the other copy.

2. The first command makes */home/flintsfr* the current directory.

   The second command tells Linux to rename the file, originally called *file1*, to *newfile*. The newly named file has the attributes of the original file.

3. The first command makes */home/flintsfr* the current directory.

INSTALLING AND ADMINISTERING LINUX

The second command tells Linux to allow the file called *newfile* to be known also as *myfile*. An `ls -l` on the */home/flintsfr* directory shows two files, one by each name, although only one file is physically on the disk. An `ls -li` on that directory substantiates that, by showing that both files have the same inode number. Any changes made to *newfile* also show up if you use or access *myfile*.

4. The commands are `cat`, which scrolls continuously until the entire file has been displayed on the screen; `more`, which displays continuous text one screen at a time; and `less`, which is the same as `more` but allows the flexibility of moving both forward and backward in the file while it is displayed on the terminal screen.

5. The command that the `man` pages automatically invoke is `less`. You know this because you are given the ability to move forward and backward to examine the contents of a `man` page.

Chapter 6

1. 755

2. `$ chmod go-x reporta<Enter>`

3. `$ chmod 744 reporta<Enter>`

4. Yes. He is a member of the same group as Judy (that is, finance). That group has execute permission on the *jobs* directory as well as write permission on the *joblog* file.

5. No. Although his group, finance, has write permission on the *joblog* file, they do not have execute permission on the *work* directory. As a member of others, Fred may have execute permission on the *work* directory, but he does not have execute permission on the *joblog* file.

6. Yes. The finance group and others have execute permission on the two directories, *jobs* and *work*. The group also has read permission on the *joblog* file. Fred presumably has write and execute permissions on his own home directory.

APPENDIX C: QUIZ ANSWERS

Chapter 7

1. Command mode and Insert mode.

2. Press the <Esc> key. Remember, however, that <Esc> does not toggle Command mode on and off. If you press the <Esc> key repeatedly, you remain in Command mode and eventually hear an annoying beep.

3. a and i. The other two commands delete text.

4. False. The u command will undo only the last command. The undo buffer contains only one entry.

5. True. Adding a single g at the beginning of a search and replace command allows you to do that.

6. Watch out, this is a trick question! You can't quit vi while in Insert mode! Thus, the answer is none of the above. To exit vi, you first have to get into Command mode by pressing <Esc>. Then you can use :x, :wq, <Shift>-zz, or :q!.

Chapter 8

1. This command lists all the files beginning with any three characters. The fourth character must not be in the range *a* to *z*. Then any number of characters can follow, after which the second-to-last character must be from 0 through 9. The final character must be *t*.

2. Standard input (0) is the keyboard; standard output (1) is the screen; standard error (2) is the screen.

3. Standard input (0) is a file named *letter*; standard output (1) is handled by the mail program; standard error (2) is the screen.

4. Standard input (0) is the keyboard; standard output (1) is a file named *newprofile*; standard error (2) is a file named *l*.

5. `$ cat filea > fileb 2> filec`

6. `$ cat filea > fileb 2>&1`

417

7. `$ cat filea > fileb 2> /dev/null`

8. Output the text string *hello* on the screen of terminal `tty1` (provided `tty1` has not set mesg *n*).

Chapter 9

1. The home directory is /home/*flintsfr*.

2. The home directory is *$HOME*. Note that this question used single quotes!

3. The current directory is /home/*flintsfr/docs*. Note that `pwd` is enclosed in backquotes.

4. The files in this directory are *.

5. *aa bb cc /home/flintsfr*

6. *

7. False. A listing of shell variables would contain all terminal environment variables, not vice versa.

8. False. You do not create built-in variables. Moreover, uppercase versus lowercase is only a convention.

9. Variable substitution and command substitution.

10. Redirection, command/variable substitution, wildcard expansion, command execution.

Chapter 10

1. Whenever you are trying to change variable values in your current environment and you're using the bash shell.

2. You use the `export` command.

3. The answer is 5, the value of the original log-in shell. Changing the value in the child process (in this case, the subshell) has no effect on the value of the same variable in the parent process.

APPENDIX C: QUIZ ANSWERS

4. Strictly speaking, this is false. Each command returns an exit (or return) code after any attempt at completion. That is, a return code is given back to the parent process even if the command has failed.

5. $ `echo $$<Enter>` and $ `ps ef<Enter>`

   The `ps` command provides more information, but one of the parameters it displays is the process ID (PID) number for the various processes that are currently running.

6. The variable and its value become part of the current process environment. The variable and its value are available for any child process but cannot be passed back to the parent process.

7. The answers are the second (`r` but not necessarily `w` or `x`); fourth (755); and fifth (`-rw-r-xr-x`). These show the file needs only the read permission. The first answer (`drwsxrwxrwx`) might seem right at first, but it refers to a directory. The third answer (`x` and `r`) is incorrect because of the word *and*. The last two answers are red herrings.

Chapter 11

1. Use the `ps f` command. The `f` option (or flag) shows the family tree of each running process.

2. True. Only the root user or superuser can control the jobs of other users.

3. Signal `-9` (also known as `KILL` in the tcsh shell or `SIGKILL` in the bash shell) cannot be caught or ignored, so it terminates a process at the point of execution, not allowing for a graceful shutdown of the process. Use `-9` with caution.

4. (1) The job will not lock up the user's terminal while it is running. (2) If the user wants to or has to log out of the system, the job continues running. Upon the user's return, the status of the job can be checked.

5. They are called daemons. They are usually started when the system is started and stop only when the system shuts down.

6. False. The user is always in the original directory, if the command was started in the normal fashion (that is, without using the dot [.] command). Because the command executes in a subshell, any environment changes made in the subshell are not passed back to the parent process.

Chapter 12

1. Although both files are read at log in, only the *.bashrc* file is read every time a child process (such as a subshell) is invoked. The *.bash_profile* generally contains environment variables, and *.bashrc* contains aliases and other functions.

2. False. You are not obligated to have a *.bashrc* file. But you will get some unexpected, and probably undesirable, results if you put all your variables, aliases, and functions in only your *.bash_profile* file.

3. True. All Linux processes are spawned from the `init` process, which originates during system bootup.

4. The */etc/profile* file is called the global profile because it contains all the variables that will apply to all users on the system. If users want to override the */etc/profile* variables or create variables of their own, they must modify their respective *.bash_profile* files.

5. All three are environment variables. `HISTSIZE` defines the maximum number of previous commands that the bash shell displays when you enter the `history` or `fc` commands. If you do not specify a `HISTSIZE`, the default value is 17 (other sources say 16; try this for yourself). `HISTFILE` is the name of the file in which you want the text of all your previous commands to be deposited after you log out. The default file name is *$HOME/.bash_history*. `HISTFILESIZE` is used to specify the maximum number of previous commands that you can add to `HISTFILE` before the earliest commands are discarded. If you do not specify a `HISTFILESIZE`, the default size is 500.

APPENDIX C: QUIZ ANSWERS

6. You can undo any alias temporarily with `unalias`. However, if the alias has been defined in your *$HOME/.bashrc* file, it will be read and invoked every time a child process is spawned and every time you log in. Consequently, if you only want to knock out an alias in your current shell for your current session, use `unalias`. If you want to permanently knock out an alias, you must modify the appropriate files.

7. If you are going to properly customize your environment, keeping these files straight is important. The sentence goes like this: "In the bash shell, */etc/bashrc* is to */etc/profile* as *$HOME/.bashrc* is to *$HOME/.bash_profile*."

Chapter 13

1. `$ find / -name 'mis*' -type f<Enter>`

2. List all processes that begin with the */sbin* string in their respective command paths and that belong to the root user. The -w option is a bit of a red herring; it simply ensures that searches are performed on the whole word so that user names or processes that contain the respective strings but which form only part of longer strings are *not* included in the output.

3. A recursive long listing is carried out from the */home/username* directory downward through the file system. We will be looking for listings of lines that end in *um* or *isc* or that contain *ync*. (We are using `egrep` because we need to an OR `grep`. Moreover, because we are using `ls -l`, this is the same as asking for file names that end in *um* or *isc* or that contain *ync*.). Then we take those long listed file entries (as lines) and pipe them to the `sort` command. The `sort` command sorts the lines in reverse order based on the eighth field (that is, the file names themselves). Some but not all results are presented. The display begins with the second line, and only seven lines are displayed.

As you can surmise, this complex command may require you to continue the command from the first command line with the primary prompt to the second command line with its secondary

421

prompt. (Refer to Chapter 8, where this technique is first discussed.)

Chapter 14

1. False. Unfortunately, `find` travels only recursively down through a file system structure.

2. `find` itself. This time, the quoting metacharacters are used to keep the interpretation away from the shell.

3. `file` is the command that reports to you on the type of files you choose to examine.

4. False. Everything is true except that the extension is *.gz*, not just *.z*.

5. Use `cat -etv` to display all possible nonprintable characters, including end-of-line indicators, tabs, spaces, and other invisible characters.

6. True. `diff` compares text files only, and it's really the best choice for doing so. Use `cmp` to compare all types of files except text files.

Chapter 15

1. The second, fourth, and fifth statements are true. Regarding the first, connections are based on TCP/IP. The third is the definition of a server in non-Linux/UNIX environments.

2. The XFree86 program (as configured using the *XF86Config* file) with other software that helps XFree86 to control other functions and attributes of the X environment, is the X Server for your system(s).

3. `export`, along with another command and other options and arguments. A case could be made for including `telnet` as well because it too can be used to connect to other machines. Then, once connected, a user can execute clients on the remote system.

4. `-bg red`: the background color of the new `xterm` window is red; `-fg black`: the foreground characters are white; `-T ledger`:

the title of the window is *ledger*, `-geometry 80x125+0+0`: make the window 80 pixels wide and 125 pixels long and place it in the upper-left corner of the root window; `-n lgr`: when the window is minimized, the title of its representative icon is *lgr*.

5. Two ways. (1) You can open another `xterm` window, and at the prompt, type `su` and then supply the password. (2) You can left-click an open desktop area, and then scroll down the resulting root menu and select *System Utilities*. On the drop-down menu called System Utilities Button Bar, scroll down and select *Root Shell*. An `xterm` window appears, titled Root_Window. Within this window is the root `Password:` prompt. Fill in the proper password and you are given the `root # _` prompt.

Index

Symbols
* (asterisk), wildcard 156–158
` (backquote), setting variables 187
\ (backslash), continuation character 172–173, 189
! (bang) command 138, 249–250
{ } (curly brackets), preserving variable names 186
$ (dollar sign) prompt 14
. (dot), current directory indicator 68
! (exclamation point), wildcard 159
" (double quote marks), setting variables 186
- (hyphen)
   in command syntax 17
   metacharacter 156
| (pipe) command 169–170
? (question mark), wildcard 158–159
; (semicolon), grouping commands 172
[ ] (square list brackets) 159–160
[–] (square range brackets) 160

A
About winmgr menu option 326
adduser command 16
AfterStep manager 320
AIX 4
alias command 244–246
antitrust consent decree 3
arguments, definition 18
ash shell 155
ash.static 155
asterisk (*), wildcard 156–158
AT&T/Bell
   antitrust consent decree 3
   purchase of SUN Microsystems 5
authentication, configuring 378

B
backquote (`), setting variables 187
backslash (\), continuation character 172, 189

Baehr, Martin 9
bang (!) command 138, 24–250
banner command 30–31
bash shell
   definition 155
   initialization file 238–241
   kill signals 220
   setting variables 184
bg command 224
-bg option (xterm) 331
binary notation 112–114
bit bucket, directing output to 166
books about Linux 51, 53–54
boot disk, creating 352, 379
Bourne shell 154
BSD Unix 4
built-in shell variables 181

C
-c option (wc command) 32
C shell 154
cal command 18–20
calendars 18
cat command 98, 164–165, 303–305
cd command 69
CDE manager 321
change permission 116
chmod command 109–114
clear command 29
client/server environment 316–317
cmp command 299–300
comm command 298
command aliases
   creating 244–246
   file containing 241, 243–244
   removing 246–247
   using 246–247
command history
   definition 248

displaying 248–249
setting size of 240
command line parsing 189–190
command reference summary
   directories 385
   diskettes 391–393
   editors 389, 398–402
   file management 386–389
   logoff 385
   metacharacters 390
   miscellaneous 394
   piping 389
   redirection 389
   shell programming 395–397
   shells 389
   system administration 393
   system files 394
   tapes 391-393
   transmitting commands 393
   variables 391
   vi editor 398–402
commands
   ! (bang) 138, 249–250
   | (pipe) 169–170
   adduser 16
   alias 244–246
   arguments 18
   banner 30–31
   bg 224
   cal 18
   cat 98, 164–165, 303–305
   cd 69
   chmod 109–114
   clear 29
   cmp 299–300
   combining 283
   comm 298
   connecting with pipes 169–170
   cp 93–96
   date 18–19
   diff 294–298
   echo 30, 184
   egrep 272–273
   exit 14
   export 183, 203–205
   fc 248–249
   fg 223
   fgrep 272–273
   file 293
   filters 170

find 255–262, 287–288
finger 21
general syntax 17
grep 265–268, 287–288
grouping 172
gunzip 302
gzip 301–302
head 276–277
history 248
info 45–47
jobs 222–223, 225
kill 216–220
less 99–100
line continuation 172–173
ln 97
locate 47–48
logout 14
lpq 102
lpr 101
lprm 96, 102
ls 73–76
mail 22, 23, 25
man 41–45
mesg 28
mkdir 69, 72, 118
more 99–100
mount 80–82
mtools 85
mv 95–96
nohup 220–221
options 17
ps 213–214
pwd 68–69
rm 100–101, 159
rmdir 70, 72
set 182–183
setenv 183
slocate 47–49
sort 273–276
splitting output of 171
stat 77
tail 277–278
talk 27–28
tee 171
touch 86
ulimit 240
umask 114–115, 117, 240
umount 81
unalias 246–247
unset 185

useradd 16
vi 129
wall 27–28
whatis 263–264
whereis 264
who 20
who am I 21
whoami 21
write 25, 28
xargs 283–288
xhost 336–337
zcat 302
commands, finding with
  whatis command 263–264
  whereis command 264
  which command 265
compressing files 300, 302
cp command 93–96
-cr option (xterm) 331
curly brackets ({}), preserving variable names 186

D

daemons 226
data compression 300, 302
date command 18–19
dates, appending to file names 306
default services, selecting 374
desktop (X Windows) 324
destructive redirection 163, 167
diff command 294–298
directories
  changing 69
  command reference summary 385
  creating 69, 71–72
  displaying contents of 73–76
  displaying information about 76
  exercises 88–89, 103–106
  long listings 75, 107–108
  permissions, specifying 70
  quizzes 90, 106
  removing 70, 72, 100–101
directory permissions
  change permission 116
  changing 109–114, 116–117
  creating personal directories 117
  defaults, checking 115
  definition 109
  execute permission 111
  file owners 108

read permission 111
  summary table of 120
  write permission 111, 118
directory trees 66
diskettes, command reference summary 391–393
-display option 331
distributions
  definition 10
  mixing and matching 11
  number of 10, 40
  online sources for 11
distributors of Linux 40
documentation
  books 51, 53–54
  exercises 58–61
  HOWTOs 51
  Linux Documentation Project 50–53
  magazines 53–54
  official Linux distributions 38–39
  quiz 62
  unofficial Linux distributions 39–40
dot (.), current directory indicator 68
double quote marks ("), setting variables 186

E

-e option (xterm) 332
echo command 30, 184
echoing text to terminals 30
ed editor 143
egrep command 272–273
Emacs editor 143
Enlightenment manager 320
/etc/bashrc file 241
/etc/profile file 238–241
ex editor 143
exclamation point (!), wildcards 159
exercise answers
  Chapter 2 403
  Chapter 3 403
  Chapter 4 404
  Chapter 5 405
  Chapter 6 405
  Chapter 8 406
  Chapter 9 407
  Chapter 11 408
  Chapter 12 409
  Chapter 13 410
  Chapter 14 411
  Chapter 15 412

427

exercises
    customizing user environment 251–253
    documentation 58–61
    files and directories 88–89, 103–106
    getting started with Linux 33–35, 58–60
    permissions 121–124
    processes 227–232, 251–253
    shell variables 191–194
    shells 174–177
    text editors 144–151
    utilities 279–281, 307–310
    X Window System 338–345
exit codes 210
exit command 14
Exit winmgr menu option 326
export command 183, 204–205
exporting shell variables 183

F

FAQs, Web site 52
fc command 248–249
fg command 223
-fg option (xterm) 332
fgrep command 272–273
file command 292–293
file contents
    counting characters, words, and lines 32
    displaying nonprintable characters 303–305
    displaying parts of 276–278
file contents, searching with grep
    examples 270–272
    extracting data 266
    grep options 269
    grep syntax 266, 269
    metacharacters 268–269
    regular expressions 266–269
file descriptors 161
file management, command reference
        summary 386–389
file names
    appending dates 306
    appending process numbers 305–306
    forcing uniqueness 305–306
    naming conventions 77–79
    pattern matching with wildcards 156–160
file owners 108
file permissions
    changing 109–114, 116–117
    defaults, checking 115
    definition 109

execute permission 111
file owners 108
read permission 111
summary table of 120
write permission 111, 118
file systems, DOS
    accessing floppy disks 84
    creating 80
    mounting 80
    mtools utilities 84
    unmounting 81
file systems, floppy disks
    creating 79–80
    mounting 80–82
    unmounting 81
file systems, hard disk
    current directory, determining 68
    directories, changing 69
    directory trees 66
    hierarchical structure 65–68
    home directory, returning to 68
    path names 67
    root directory 65
file types
    determining 292–293
    directories 64
    ordinary files 63
    special files 64
files
    access and modification dates, updating 87
    accessing on networks 65
    classifying 292–293
    comparing (all file types) 299–300
    comparing (text files) 294–298
    compressing 300, 302
    copying 93–96
    creating 164
    directory contents 64
    displaying information about 76
    exercises 88–89, 103–106
    inode (index node), 64–65
    linking 97
    long listings 75, 107–108
    moving 95–96
    multiple names for 97
    printing 101–102
    quizzes 90, 106
    removing 100–101
    renaming 95–96
    standard error, redirecting 165

INDEX

standard input, redirecting 162–167
standard output, redirecting 163, 167
uncompressing 301
viewing contents of 98
zero length, creating 86
files, finding
  linked files 290–291
  locate command 47–48
  shell functions 288–290
  slocate command 47–49
files, finding with find command
  aliases for 291–292
  combined with a noninteractive action 258–259
  combined with an interactive action 259–260
  command options 261–262
  -links option 291
  search conditions 256–257
  syntax 255
  versus shell functions 288–290
files, hidden
  and wildcards 158
  naming conventions 77, 79
filters 170
find command
  aliases for 291–292
  combining with xargs and grep 287–288
  -links option 291
  searching for files 255–262
  versus shell functions 288–290
find options 261
finger command 21
floppy disks
  command reference summary 391–393
  DOS 84
-fn option (xterm) 332
free software 10
Free Software Foundation, Web site 11
-fullcursor option (xterm) 332
functions
  system, file containing 241
  user-defined, file containing 243–244
fvwm manager 320

G

-geometry option (xterm) 332
global profile 238–239
GNOME manager 320
GNOME Web site 56

GNU General Public License 10
grep command
  combining with xargs and find 287–288
  searching file contents 265–266
grouping commands 172
gunzip command 301–302
gzip command 301–302

H

hard disk attributes, displaying 365
hard disk partitions
  adding and editing 365
  creating 357–359, 365–366
  formatting system partitions 367
hardware compatibility 11
head command 276–277
-help option (xterm) 332
HISTFILESIZE, shell variable 241
history command 248
HISTSIZE, shell variable 241
$HOME/.bash_profile file 242–243
$HOME/.bashrc file 243–244
host name, specifying 240
HOSTNAME, shell variable 240
HOWTOs 51
HOWTOs, Web site 51
HP-UX 4
hyphen (-)
  in command syntax 17
  metacharacter 156

I

-i option (xterm) 332
IBM versions of UNIX 4
iconified windows 325
icons 328–329
IDE configuration 364
In Canada, Web site 55
info command 45–47
info pages 45–47
information window 325
inheriting shell variables 203
input focus 326
install log, creating 370
install program, invoking 359–360
installation class, selecting 364
installation method, specifying 363
installation progress indicator 370
installing Linux, on an IDE system
  authentication, configuring 378

429

boot disk, creating 379
components, selecting 368
default services, selecting 374
disk partitioning 365
hard disk attributes, displaying 365
hard disk partitions, adding and editing 365
hard disk partitions, creating 366
IDE configuration 364
install log, creating 370
install program, invoking 359–360
installation class, selecting 364
installation method, specifying 363
installation progress indicator 370
keyboard, specifying 362
language, selecting 362
LILO, configuring 380
monitor set up 381–383
mouse, configuring 371
mouse, detecting 371
network, configuring 372
new install vs. upgrade 363
overlapping files 370
password, setting 378
remote printer, configuring 375–377
swap space, formatting 367
system partitions, formatting 367
time zone, configuring 374
video adapter, detecting 380
Welcome! dialog box 360–361
installing Linux, preparation for
   boot disk, creating 352
   current system, researching 348
   disk paging 355
   hard disk partitioning 357–359
   sample component list 349
   swap space options 355
   system attributes, identifying 351

J

jobs command 222–223, 225

K

KDE Desktop Environment Web site 56
KDE manager 321
Kernighan, Brian 2
keyboard, specifying 362
-keywords option (xterm) 332
kill command 216–220
kill signals
   ignoring 220
   sending 218–220

Korn shell 155
ksh shell, initialization file 238–241

L

-l option (wc command) 18, 32
-l option (xterm) 332
language, selecting 362
Lempel-Ziv (LZ77) coding 300
less command 99–100
-lf option (xterm) 332
LILO, configuring 380
Linux distributions, Web site 11
Linux Documentation Project 50–53
Linux kernel versions, time line of 9
Linux Online, Web site 55
Linux software sources, Web site 55
Linux, history of
   Baehr, Martin 9
   MINIX, copyright on 8
   Torvald, Linus 8
   Version 1.0 released 8
ln command 97
locate command 47–48
location cursors 327
Lock Screen/Screen Saver menu option 326
logging in 14
log-in names 240
log-in process 199
LOGNAME, shell variable 240
logoff, command reference summary 385
logout command 14
lpq command 102
lpr command 101
lprm command 96, 102
ls command 73–76

M

-m option (who command) 21
magazines about Linux 53–54
mail
   receiving 23, 25
   sending 22–23
mail directory, specifying 240
MAIL, shell variable 240
man command 41–45
man pages
   accessing 41
   contents of 42–43
   exiting 44
   navigating 44
   printing 44

mc shell 155
McIlroy, Douglas 1
mesg command 29
messages
   banners 30–31
   blocking receipt of 26–28
   clearing from the screen 29
   conversational 27
   to all users 27
   to one user 25
metacharacters
   and wildcards 156–160
   as literal characters 188
   command reference summary 390
   quoting 188–189
MINIX
   birth of 6
   copyright on 8
   Web site about 54
mkdir command 69, 72, 118
monitors
   clearing the screen 29
   echoing text to 30
   potential damage 313
   setting up 381–383
more command 99–100
mount command 80–82
mouse
   configuring 371
   detecting 371
mouse pointers 326
-mtime option (find) 261
mtools utilities, Web site 57, 84
mtoools commands 85
mtools utilities Web site 57
Multics 1–2, 7–8
mv command 95–96
mwm manager 320

N

-n option (xterm) 332
-name option (xterm) 332
Network File System
networks, configuring at installation 372
New shell menu option 325
-newer option (find) 261
newsgroups about Linux 56
nohup command 220–221
nondestructive redirection 163, 167

Novell buys Unix System Laboratories 6
numeric notation 112–114

O

-o option (find) 261
olvwm manager 320
online resources
   books 56
   Current Projects 52
   FAQs 52
   Free Software Foundation 11
   GNOME 56
   HOWTOs 51
   In Canada 55
   KDE Desktop Environment 56
   Linux distributions 11
   Linux Documentation Project 50
   Linux kernel versions, time line of 9
   Linux Online 55
   Linux software sources 55
   magazines 54
   MINIX 54
   mtools 57
   mtools utilities 84
   newsgroups 56
   Stallman, Richard 10
   Torvalds, Linus 9
   X Windows sources 56
open architecture standards 4
Open Software Foundation (OSF) 5
open source software 10
options
   combining 17
   definition 17
OSF (Open Software Foundation) 5
OSF/1 5
Ossanna, Joseph 1
overlapping files 370

P

parent-child relationships 199–202
password, setting 378
PATH, shell variable 239
pattern matching
   file names, with wildcards 156–160
   mtools utilities 85
pdksh shell
   definition 155
   setting variables, 183

-perm option (find) 261
permissions
    exercises 121–124
    quiz 124
    setting 240
    specifying for directories 70
PID, checking 199
pipe (|) command 169–170
piping, command reference summary 389
.plan file 22
POSIX 6
powering down to kill a process 216
Preferences menu option 326
printer, configuring 375–377
printing commands 102
printing files 101
process ID, checking 199
process numbers, appending to file names 305–306
processes
    definition 197
    exercises 227–232, 251–253
    invoking 215
    log-in 199
    monitoring 213, 214
    parent-child relationships 199–202
    quizzes 211, 233–254
    required environment 198
processes, background
    definition 215
    invoking 215
    resuming 223
    suspending 223
processes, foreground
    definition 215
    invoking 215
    resuming 223
    suspending 222–223
processes, terminating
    kill command 216–220
    kill signals, ignoring 220
    kill signals, sending 218–220
    powering down 216
    reasons for 215
    zombies 220
Programs menu option 325
.project file 22
ps command 213–214
PS1, shell variable 240
pwd command 68–69

Q

question mark (?), wildcard 158–159
quiz answers
    Chapter 2 413
    Chapter 3 413
    Chapter 4 414
    Chapter 5 415
    Chapter 6 416
    Chapter 7 417
    Chapter 8 417
    Chapter 9 418
    Chapter 10 418
    Chapter 11 419
    Chapter 12 420
    Chapter 13 421
    Chapter 14 422
    Chapter 15 422
quizzes 346
    documentation 62
    files and directories 90, 106
    getting started with Linux 35
    permissions 124
    processes 211, 233, 254
    shell variables 195
    shells 178
    text editors 151
    utilities 282, 311
quoting metacharacters 188–189

R

read permission 111
redirection
    appending to a file 163, 166
    combined 167
    command reference summary 389
    destructive 163, 167
    nondestructive 163, 167
    to the bit bucket 166
reexecuting commands
    Linux 249–250
    vi editor 142
resizing windows 327–328
return codes 210
Ritchie, Dennis 1
rm command 100–101, 159
rmdir command 70, 72
root menu 325–326
root window 324
rsh shell 155

S

sash shell 155
-sb option (xterm) 332
security
   authentication, configuring 378
   permissions and 119
   user names 13
security, passwords
   at log-in 13
   encryption 16
   guidelines for 17
   naming conventions 17
   setting 16
semicolon (172
set command 182–183
setenv command 183
sh shell, initialization file 238–241
shareware 10
shell programming, command reference summary 395–397
shell prompt, customizing 240
shell scripts
   creating 206
   definition 206
   invoking 207–210
shell variables
   built-in 181
   case sensitivity 181
   checking settings 185
   command reference summary 391
   default, setting 235–244
   definition 179
   exercises 191–194
   exporting across shells 183
   HISTFILESIZE 241
   HISTSIZE 241
   HOSTNAME 240
   inheritance 203
   listing 180, 182
   LOGNAME 240
   MAIL 240
   PATH 239
   PS1 240
   quiz 195
   resetting 185
   setting by command substitution 187–188, 203–207
   setting by variable substitution 183
   terminal environment 179, 181
   USER 240
   user-defined 181, 203
shells
   ash 155
   ash.static 155
   bash
      definition 155
      kill signals 220
      setting variables 184
   Bourne 154
   C 154
   command reference summary 389
   current, determining 14
   default, determining 156
   definition 153–154
   exercises 174–177
   Korn 155
   mc 155
   pdksh 155
   pdksh, setting variables 183
   quiz 178
   rsh 155
   sash 155
   tcsh 155
      exporting variables 183
      kill signals 220
      setting variables 183
   types of 154–156
   zsh 155
-size option (find) 261
-sl option (xterm) 332
slocate command 47–49
software compatibility 11
sort command 273–276
sorting output 273–276
Space Travel program 2
Stallman, Richard 10
standard error files, redirecting 165
standard input files, redirecting 162, 167
standard output files, redirecting 163, 167
stat command 77
SunOS 4
swap space, formatting 355, 367
system administration, command reference summary 393
system attributes, identifying 351
system files, command reference summary 394
system resources, setting limits on 240
System Utilities menu option 325
System V 4

T

-T option (xterm) 332
tail command 277–278
talk command
  blocking messages 28
  sending messages 27
Tanenbaum, Andrew S 6
tapes, command reference summary 391–393393
tcsh shell
  definition 155
  exporting variables 183
  kill signals 220
  setting variables 183
technical support
  Internet sites 39
  user groups 40
tee command 171
terminal environment shell variables 179, 181
text editors
  command reference summary 389, 398–402
  ed 143
  Emacs 143
  ex 143
  exercises 144–151
  quiz 151
  view 143
  vim 127
Thompson, Ken 1
time zone, configuring 374
Torvalds, Linus 8
touch command 86
transmitting commands, command reference summary 393
twm manager 320
-type option (find) 261

U

-u option (who command) 21
UI (Unix International) trade association 5
ulimit command 240
ULTRIX 4
umask command 114–115, 117, 240
umount command 81
unalias command 246–247
undoing vi commands 136
UNIX International (UI) trade association 5
UNIX Time-Sharing System 3
UNIX, history of
  AIX 4
antitrust consent decree 3
AT&T/Bell, antitrust consent decree 3
AT&T/Bell, purchase of SUN Microsystems 5
BSD 4
commercialization 4
derivation of name 2
HP-UX 4
IBM versions 4
Kernighan, Brian 2
market share 7
McIlroy, Douglas 1
MINIX, birth of 6
Multics, origin of 1
Novell buys Unix System Laboratories 6
number of current versions 7
open architecture standards 4
OSF (Open Software Foundation), 5
OSF/1 5
Ossanna, Joseph 1
POSIX 6
proliferation of versions 4
Ritchie, Dennis 1
Space Travel program 2
standardization 4
SunOS 4
System V 4
Tanenbaum, Andrew S., 6
Thompson, Ken 1
UI (Unix International) trade association 5
ULTRIX 4
Unix Time-Sharing System 3
X/Open formed 4
X/Open given Unix trademark 6
XENIX 4
unset command 185
unzip command 302
usage facility 49
user accounts
  creating 15
  name format 240
  naming conventions 15
user environment, customizing
  $HOME/.bash_profile file 242–243
  $HOME/.bashrc file 243–244
  /etc/bashrc file 241
  /etc/profile file 238–241
  default shell variables, setting 235–244
  exercises 251–253
  global profile 238–241

INDEX

-user option (find) 261
USER, shell variable 240
useradd command 16
user-defined shell variables 181
users logged-in, getting information on 20–21
utilities 282
    cat 303–305
    cmp 299–300
    comm 298
    diff 294–298
    diff3 298
    egrep command 272–273
    exercises 279–281, 307–310
    fgrep command 272–273
    file 293
    find 287–288
    find command 255–262
    grep 287–288
    grep command 265–268
    gunzip 302
    gzip 301–302
    head command 276–277
    mtools 84
    quiz 311
    sort command 273–276
    tail command 277–278
    whatis command 263–264
    whereis command 264
    which command 265
    xargs 283–288
    zcat 302

V

vi command 129
vi editor
    adding text 131
    Command mode 128
    command reference summary 398–402
    copying text 136
    cursor movement 132
    customizing 140
    deleting text 133
    executing Linux/Unix commands, 138–139
    exiting 130
    features of 128
    Insert mode 128
    invoking features of other editors 142
    Last-line mode 129
    moving text 135
    reexecuting commands 142
    search-and-replace 133–134
    starting 129–130
    text commands 134
    undoing last command 136
video adapter, detecting 380
view editor 143
vim editor 127

W

-W option (xterm) 332
wall command
    blocking messages 28
    sending messages 27
wc command 32
Welcome! dialog box 360–361
whatis command 263–264
whereis command 264
which command 265
who am i command 21
who command 20
    -m option 21
    -u option 21
whoami command 21
wildcards
    ! (exclamation point 159
    * (asterisk 156–158
    ? (question mark) 158
    ? (question mark), 159
    and hidden files 158
window frame 327–328
window managers 319–321
Window Operations menu option 326
write command
    blocking messages 28
    sending messages 25
write permission 118

X

X client features 317
X Display Manager (xdm) program 322–323
X server 318–319
X Window System
    About winmgr menu option 326
    desktop 324
    display components 325
    exercises 338–345
    Exit winmgr menu option 326
    exiting 322
    history of 313–315
    iconified windows 325

icons 328–329
information window 325
input focus 326
location cursors 327
Lock Screen/Screen Saver menu option 326
mouse pointers 326
New shell menu option 325–326
potential monitor damage 313
Programs menu option 325
quiz 346
resizing windows 327–328
root menu 325–326
root window 324
starting automatically 322–324
starting manually 322
System Utilities menu option 325
window frame 327–328
Window Operations menu option 326
XFree86 315
X Window System, networking
AfterStep manager 320
CDE manager 321
client/server environment 316–317
Enlightenment 320
fvwm manager 320
GNOME manager 320
KDE manager 321
mwm 320
olvwm manager 320
restricting remote access 336–337
running clients remotely 333–336
sample network 315–316
twm manager 320
window managers 319–321

X client features 317–318
X server 318–319
X Windows sources, Web site 56
X/Open
  formation of 4
  given Unix trademark 6
xargs command
  combining commands 283–288
  combining with grep and find 287–288
xcalc 317
xclock 317
xdm (X Display Manager) program 322–323
XENIX 4
XFree86 315, 319
xhost command 336–337
-xrm option (xterm) 332
xterm 317
xterm windows
  becoming the root user 333
  closing 330
  copying text 329
  creating 329
  customizing 331
  definition 325
  options 331
  restricting remote access 336–337
  running clients remotely 333–336
  scrollbars, creating 330

Z

zcat command 302
zip command 302
zombies 220
zsh shell 155

GEARHEAD PRESS

Gearhead Press is committed to delivering technical information to IT professionals who challenge themselves to learn new technologies and advance their skills. To provide you with quality learning tools, we've taken the unprecedented step to publish only authors who are professional technical trainers.

The Expertise of a Professional Trainer in Every Book

Professional technical trainers are subject-matter experts, skilled developers and network engineers, and effective communicators. As authors, technical trainers will develop books that reflect a combination of skill, knowledge, and years of classroom experience that is highly valued and sought after by corporations and professionals worldwide.

Three Series to Meet Your Needs

We currently offer three series to help you grasp new topics, acquire functional or network administration skills, and develop integrated solutions to real-world business challenges. Each series offers a distinctive editorial approach and learning style.

- ***In the Trenches:*** A fast-paced series of books, written by authors who have been "in the trenches" as IT professionals themselves, that will introduce you to a new technology, help you become proficient, and serve as long-lasting references.
- ***Virtual Workshop Gold:*** A full-color series of books, each with a unique blend of information, examples, exercises, and review questions for self-paced, hands-on learning and reference.
- ***Point to Point:*** A series that invites you to join a project and implement a technology in a real-world environment, contending with problems such as legacy systems, planning, product integration, implementation, system maintenance, and more.

Gearhead Press books are available at bookstores, online retailers, or at www.gearheadpress.com

THE GEARHEAD GROUP

Gearhead Press • Gearhead Curriculum • Gearhead Training • Gearhead Online

UPCOMING BOOKS FROM GEARHEAD PRESS

In the Trenches: Customizing and Upgrading Linux by Linda McKinnon and Al McKinnon is a version-independent reference that examines key issues of the proper planning, installation, and customization of Red Hat Linux as it guides network administrators and engineers with a working knowledge of UNIX through the critical steps.

$49.95 (U.S.)
ISBN 1-930713-01-0
Available October 2000

In the Trenches: Windows 2000 Automated Deployment by Ted Malone and Rolly Perreaux is a blueprint for administrators who want to save time and money installing and upgrading software by using the new automated-deployment tools included in Windows 2000 Professional.

$49.95 (U.S.)
ISBN 1-930713-06-1
Available January 2001

Virtual Workshop Gold: Web Application Programming with PHP by Matt Bridges uses a unique blend of reference information, exercises, and online resources to teach programmers in a Windows or Linux environment how to develop real-world, data-driven Web applications using PHP 4.0.

$59.95 (U.S.)
ISBN 1-930713-07-X
Available February 2001

Virtual Workshop Gold: Windows 2000 Programming
by Donis Marshall contains experience-based insights, examples and exercises to instruct developers in system-level, API programming using Microsoft's Platform Software Development Kit (SDK), showing Visual Basic, MFC and J++ programmers how to build faster and more robust Windows applications.

$59.95 (U.S.)
ISBN 1-930713-05-3
Available March 2001

Point to Point: Migrating to Microsoft Exchange 2000
by Stan Reimer invites readers to join the IT team at North American Airlines — a model company with multiple Windows NT 4.0 domains and several Exchange Servers spread across multiple sites — as they embark on the migration path from Exchange 4.0 or 5.x to Exchange 2000.

$49.95 (U.S.)
ISBN: 1-930713-08-8
Available March 2001

Visit us at www.gearheadpress.com for detailed descriptions, tables of contents, author bios, and sample chapters, plus access to online resources!

Gearhead Press

Delivering technical information to IT professionals

Gearhead Press is a division of the Gearhead Group

GEARHEAD TRAINING

Gearhead Training travels to Fortune 100 and other companies worldwide, educating corporate IT developers and network engineers about leading-edge technologies and products. We work with companies to meet their technology and business goals by helping their IT staffs:

- Update their technical skills
- Be productive by using products and technologies more effectively
- Learn new tools and technologies

Gearhead trainers are certified IT professionals who have honed their expertise "in the trenches," first as practitioners and then as trainers.

As leaders in the IT community, Gearhead trainers:

- Earn multiple certifications from leading vendors, including Microsoft, Novell, Compaq, IBM, and SUN Microsystems, as well as various Linux certifications.
- Convey technical information succinctly, anticipate students' problems, and respond to questions by drawing upon real-world anecdotes and examples.
- Write white papers, author books, give presentations at conferences, and contribute articles to leading trade and industry journals.

Choose from our catalog or develop a custom course

Each Gearhead Training course has been carefully developed and fine-tuned to ensure that our clients and students achieve their training goals. In addition, we develop customized courses with curriculum based on the specific technologies and products an IT team is using (or planning to use), its current processes, and its overall strengths and weaknesses. Whether you choose a course from our catalog or customize one, we guarantee a productive training experience for all.

Contact us today for information about current course offerings, or to explore customized training solutions.

Gearhead Training
A division of the Gearhead Group
www.gearheadtraining.com

GO ONLINE
WITH GEARHEAD PRESS

Gearhead Press supplements each book it publishes with a valuable collection of technical information and resources. When you purchase a Gearhead Press book, you can gain free, 24/7 access to its numerous resources. Simply log on to our Web site, www.gearheadpress.com, and enter the code 002B7C4.

Go online and take advantage of:

- Online Help Desk (Q&A) to obtain answers to pressing questions and expert advice
- White Papers to gather information on vendors' technologies and products
- Tech Notes to help you make maximum use of technologies and products
- Updates on new functionality and features, workarounds, patches, and more
- Example Code to use as a guide, or to modify to meet your needs
- Chat Sessions where you can interact with Gearhead Press authors, editors and other IT experts
- Supplemental Exercises, which you can practice to develop new skills faster
- Professional Networking Opportunities, including links to user groups, associations, trade journals, and more
- Gearhead Press News for information on new books, series, and resources available to address your needs

**Bookmark this Web site and visit it frequently.
We're continually posting new information and we welcome your comments.**

Gearhead Press
Delivering technical information to IT professionals
www.gearheadpress.com

LICENSE AGREEMENT

This book includes a copy of the Publisher's Edition of Red Hat Linux from Red Hat, Inc., which you may use in accordance with the license agreement accompanying the software. The Official Red Hat Linux, which you may purchase from Red Hat, includes the complete Official Red Hat Linux distribution, Red Hat's documentation, and may include technical support for Official Red Hat Linux. You also may purchase technical support from Red Hat. You may purchase Official Red Hat Linux and technical support from Red Hat through the company's web site (www.redhat.com) or its toll-free number **1-888-REDHAT1.**